FOCUS ON FINANCE

Everything You Need to Know About Financial Management

FOCUS ON FINANCE

Everything You Need to Know About Financial Management

Ivan K. Cohen
Richmond American University, UK

World Scientific

NEW JERSEY • LONDON • SINGAPORE • BEIJING • SHANGHAI • HONG KONG • TAIPEI • CHENNAI • TOKYO

Published by

World Scientific Publishing Co. Pte. Ltd.
5 Toh Tuck Link, Singapore 596224
USA office: 27 Warren Street, Suite 401-402, Hackensack, NJ 07601
UK office: 57 Shelton Street, Covent Garden, London WC2H 9HE

Library of Congress Cataloging-in-Publication Data
Names: Cohen, Ivan K. author
Title: Focus on finance : everything you need to know about financial management / Ivan Cohen, Richmond American University, UK.
Description: Singapore ; Hackensack, NJ : World Scientific Publishing Co. Pte. Ltd., [2026] | Includes bibliographical references and index.
Identifiers: LCCN 2025054716 | ISBN 9789819825905 hardcover | ISBN 9789819828913 paperback | ISBN 9789819825912 ebook | ISBN 9789819825929 ebook other
Subjects: LCSH: Finance | Business enterprises--Finance | Corporations--Finance | LCGFT: Textbooks
Classification: LCC HG173 .C653 2026
LC record available at https://lccn.loc.gov/2025054716

British Library Cataloguing-in-Publication Data
A catalogue record for this book is available from the British Library.

For any available supplementary material, please visit
https://www.worldscientific.com/worldscibooks/10.1142/14664#t=suppl

Desk Editors: Murali Appadurai/Nicole Ong

Typeset by Stallion Press
Email: enquiries@stallionpress.com

This fully-revised and updated edition of *Focus on Finance* is dedicated first and foremost to my family: my wife, the ever-patient **Jeanine**, our son, **Dave**, our daughter, **Maya**, and her husband, **James** (and their dog, Toby). Second, it is important to acknowledge the profound impact of a small number of colleagues (and thus friends) with whom discussions over the years have had a major influence: this includes the late Professor Nick Wilkinson (Richmond American University in London), the late Professor Joseph Sulock (University of North Carolina at Asheville), and Professor K. Alec Chrystal (City University, London). More recently I have been inspired by many wide-ranging conversations with Nicholas Baigent. Finally, this book is dedicated to my many former students who have gone on to successful careers in finance or other branches of business.

Original (2005) dedication

This book is dedicated to those who came before, and to those who follow on.

Firstly, this book is dedicated to the memory of my late father, Issy (Israel) Cohen *z"l*, and my beloved mother, Irene Cohen. Together they brought me up to be a *mensch*, and their love and support has enabled me to live a fulfilling life without giving up on fun.

Secondly, this book is dedicated to my two children, David Jonathan (Yoni) and Maya Isabella, whose energy and vitality keep me going even as they run me ragged! The link between the two groups is my incredible and beautiful wife, Jeanine, whose love continues to be a constant source of strength.

Preface

This revised and updated volume has been a long time in gestation. For many years I had hoped to produce a second edition, but my proposal received a positive response only recently. I would like to thank Ms. Nicole Ong Shi Min for her patience and kindness during the writing of this book and also to Murali Appadurai for insightful and eagle-eyed editing. Thanks are also due to Amirah Emily Bowes-Gardner (Bank of America, and a former student), and to my brothers, Steven, Alan and Neil, for reading through elements of the draft and helping improve it. Any errors remaining are not due to any of them but remain fully and completely my own.

It is my sincerest hope that this book will prove to be a useful addition to the library of many students, primarily undergraduate but also postgrads for whom the basics of finance would be helpful. The first edition, and the original handouts on which that was based has seen many generations through their various degrees and often into successful careers in business, both in finance and otherwise.

Preface to original (2005) edition

This book began its journey to fruition many years ago when I was a Lecturer at the Management School at Imperial College. At that time I was approached by Tony Moore and asked to contribute a textbook in Finance to the Imperial College Press. Early progress was swift, but soon slowed down due to the interference of "life's rich tapestry" as appears to often be the case. Having started the book as a single man with no major attachments (notwithstanding a passion for Tottenham Hotspur F.C.!), this book enters publication with the author a married man with two young children.

In writing this book I have been led by my own comments on texts from my student days, as well as by those of my own groups of students on the many contemporary texts in this area. One consequence is that I have tried to keep this book relatively short, to the point, and maintain a good flowing narrative. Too often, undergraduate textbooks drown the reader in a sea of numerous examples, so that the flow of the material gets lost and it becomes difficult to "see the wood for the trees". I have deliberately opted for a short, focused text, rather than the more encyclopædic variety that inhabits and weighs down too many student bookshelves. I have also tried to maintain a sense of high quality, readable English that treats the reader as an equal. I hope that I will be regarded as successful in these areas. As always, any errors, both of omission and commission, remain my own responsibility.

Ivan K. Cohen

About the Author

Raised in Hackney, east London, Ivan is Emeritus Professor in Finance and Economics at Richmond American University in London (www.richmond.ac.uk) where he worked for 23 years teaching a variety of courses in Finance and in Economics. His research has included work on UK pension funds, macroeconomics, football finance, and more recently the impact of digital technology on healthcare and higher education.

During the 1980s Ivan spent his career working in the United States of America. While there he regularly undertook media interviews (particularly television), including on CNN to discuss the Wall Street Crash of 1929. He also earned his USSF soccer coaching license. and was regarded as a pioneer of the girls' and women's game in western North Carolina.

Ivan holds a B.A. (Honours) and M.A. in Economics from the University of Essex, as well as a Ph.D. in Economics from the University of Sheffield. Prior to joining Richmond he worked at The University of North Carolina, Trinity College (Hartford, Connecticut USA), Imperial College, London, and The University of Notre Dame (London).

Contents

List of Figures

List of Tables

Chapter 1

Introduction to Finance

1.1 What is Finance?

The purpose of this book is to introduce and familiarise the reader with the financial management of the business enterprise. This means learning the **language** of finance, the **environment** in which finance takes place, as well as some key **methods** of financial analysis. Several finance theories are discussed in the knowledge that understanding them will enable making better financial decisions. Because some theories have not yet found a consensus among financial economists we consider several views where relevant.

While my aim is to make finance 'user friendly', there is some technical material that cannot be avoided. However, mathematical material has been kept to a discreet minimum, and even the most 'mathematics-phobic' should understand more than the gist of the argument!

For many people 'finance' and 'money' are equivalent, the words used interchangeably. This obscures the wide range of real insights that finance has to offer. While money enhances trade, finance is about decision-making concerning the use of both money and credit. As will become clear, finance is both an art and a science. All economic decision-making, including finance, involves a comparison of benefits against costs. In economics, cost refers to **opportunity cost:** *the cost of the next best alternative foregone.* Cost is not simply what has been paid for a given commodity, but what else *might* have been purchased instead. While both benefits and costs can be

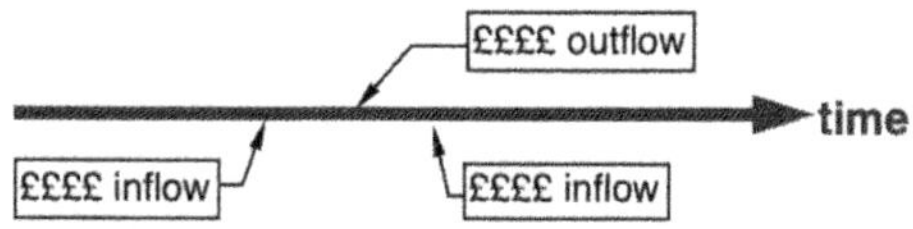

Figure 1.1. Cash flow (flow of funds) timeline

Table 1.1. Cash flow (flow of funds) timeline

Time period	0	1	2	3	4
Cash inflows			£ 3,000	£ 5,000	£ 6,000
Cash outflows	(£ 10,000)	(£ 1,000)	(£ 500)	(£ 500)	(£ 500)
Net cash flow	(£ 10,000)	(£ 1,000)	£ 2,500	£ 4,500	£ 5,500

measured in monetary terms in many cases, this is not always possible, although finance experts are constantly seeking methods to estimate or 'proxy' non-monetary valuations. Costs and benefits for which no market valuation is available are known as **externalities**. Their measurement (valuation) is especially important for investments being undertaken in the public sector or those likely to have a significant social or environmental impact (which might be positive or negative).

It is important to think of finance as an economic phenomenon that occurs **in time**. For any economic agent—an individual, a business, or government—the timing of inflows of funds and outflows of funds will not automatically balance. Almost everyone who has been a student or on a low income has experienced the problem of bills needing to be paid when the student loan or income for the current period has run out. Finance might be thought of as the art of bringing fund inflows and outflows into some kind of balance. Thus, finance can be considered visually (Figure 1.1), occurring along a timeline.

Flows of funds can also be illustrated using a spreadsheet (Table 1.1).

1.1.1 *The stuff of finance*

Finance is about making decisions. **Personal finance** deals with individual and family financial decisions: where to bank, where to save, what type of insurance or pension scheme meets a person's or family requirements, and so on. This book focuses on **corporate finance**: financial decision-making by companies. The same principles apply equally to the not-for-profit firm. Other, specialised sub-areas of finance include investment management, wealth management, and financial markets and institutions.

The aim of financial theory is to provide financial decision-makers with better tools—*better tools make for better decisions*—although occasionally it can appear abstract or very technical. Finance can also help decision-makers better understand the environment within which they operate. A good financial manager needs both to understand the markets and institutions with which they are dealing, as well as the ongoing and often relentless driving forces which bring about changes to the financial system.

As the world of business has evolved over time, so has the subject matter of finance. Before the twentieth century finance was largely about the study of banking, and the relationship of a firm to its bank. The start of the 20th century saw the beginning of a secular growth of other, non-bank financial intermediaries (NBFIs) as well as an ever-expanding financial system—both financial markets and institutions—bringing a change in perspective. For the first half of the 20th century finance remained a largely descriptive, institutional subject, more the precinct of legal minds than economists. However, by the 1950s things had begun to change, and finance as we know it today was beginning to take shape.

With the work of Joel Dean [1951] real investment appraisal (**capital budgeting**: Chapter 6) began to develop, and with it the use of mathematical techniques for financial analysis and decision-making. It is with the seminal work of Harry Markowitz [1952, 1959] on financial investment appraisal (**portfolio theory:** Chapter 7), the subject matter of finance took flight, becoming both more technical and more insightful. This trend has continued ever since and is likely to continue, especially given the vogue for establishing models for the pricing of derivatives and other more arcane and complex financial instruments. Individuals involved in constructing such models are often referred to as 'rocket scientists' because they often come from a strongly numerate background in physics, for example. However, it is worth noting that it is often several years before developments in finance theory are taken up by practitioners: there are still areas of finance theory yet to be exploited in practice.

1.1.2 *Finance versus Accounting*

'Accounting' and 'finance' are often (incorrectly) used synonymously. Although there is a strong connection, there is a distinct difference between the two. In smaller firms, the 'finance' and 'accounting' functions might be undertaken by the same person or team of people. It is possible to argue that 'finance' is performed by the **treasury** function, and 'accounting' by the **control** function (Figure 1.3). Strong anecdotal evidence suggests that accountants tend to overemphasise the closeness between accounting and finance, while financial economists tend to emphasise the distinction. In the United Kingdom the appointments columns for financial positions are largely advertisements for qualified accountants. Larger companies operate a clear division of labour within the finance function.

Primarily, accounting is responsible for financial record-keeping: the provision of information by which sound financial decisions can be made. Accounting provides both a stewardship and accountability function. Accounting records the firm's financial activities and audits them to ensure that the best possible (legitimate) use is made of the firm's resources. These records are produced as financial reports—the 'accounts'. According to the International Accounting Standards Board (IASB) the object of financial reporting is:

> "to provide financial information about the reporting entity that is useful to existing and potential investors, lenders and other creditors in making decisions relating to providing resources to the entity.[2] Those decisions involve decisions about:
>
> (a) buying, selling or holding equity and debt instruments;
> (b) providing or settling loans and other forms of credit; or
> (c) exercising rights to vote on, or otherwise influence, management's actions that affect the use of the entity's economic resources." (IFRS March 2018, Section 1.2)

Financial reports are the primary source by which shareholders (the principals) can check on the actions of management (their agents). They also allow debt-holders, other stakeholders and analysts, to gain insight into what the firm has been doing. The accounts are the basis on which a company is subject to taxation.

Finance is about making financial decisions. To make sound decisions financial managers require the best possible information—financial and other—both accurate and timely. Finance may be seen as a decision-making structure built on the foundations of sound accounting. However imperfect, the past is the only true guide to the future. Nonetheless, because the type of information contained within financial reports is primarily for reporting purposes, it is not necessarily the same kind of information that financial managers require for making decisions. Financial reports for public consumption are usually referred to as **financial accounts** while reports used internally for decision making are referred to as **managerial accounts**.

Financial accounts are usually prepared on an accrual basis, because valuation calculations require cash flows (see Chapters 3 and 6 in particular). Earnings per share and cashflow per share are not the same, as the former includes monies which have yet to flow into or out of the firm. In fact, it is possible to find a company which appears profitable but is suffering from negative cash flows.

While financial accounts are signed off by auditors as being a "true and fair view" there may be some elements which are estimated or subjectively assessed. This can lead to issues of 'window dressing' or 'creative accounting'. By adopting certain accounting policies companies may try to give the impression that their business is in better shape than it is, partly to maintain investor confidence; sometimes they try to make the firm appear worse off to avoid paying taxes! Profits—the 'bottom line'—are calculated based on a series of assumptions, such as those laid down by the International Accounting Standards Board (IASB) the standard-setting body of the International Financial Reporting Standards (IFRS) Foundation. Nonetheless, there remains some inconsistency: some cynics still argue that corporate accounts are a work of fiction. However, providing a company adopts a time-consistent policy for accounting it is possible to compare its year-on-year performance, although comparison with other firms (who may have different accounting policies) may be more spurious, especially when cross-border.

1.2 The firm

1.2.1 *What is a firm?*

A firm may be defined as "a partnership for the undertaking of business" or even "the business itself". It is not uncommon for words such as 'firm', 'business', 'company', 'organisation' and even 'concern' to be used interchangeably. 'Enterprise' is also used, but usually to imply an ambitious firm, perhaps with a more cavalier attitude towards risk. A more rigorous definition is helpful: we can define a firm either on a legal basis or on a functional or economic basis.

A firm can be viewed as a set of legal relationships between its various components (**stakeholders**). Usually expressed in contractual form, these relationships may be either explicit or implicitly via custom. Thus, a firm will have an internal contractual relationship with its shareholders, another contractual relationship with its employees, whether they are in a management role or labour. A firm also has a relationship with its customers and suppliers, usually defined by the contractual terms of the sales invoice. Firms have contractual agreements with those who fund them by way of loans, embodied in the loan agreement. A firm also has a contractual relationship with the state: implicitly through abiding by the rule of law and more explicitly if the firm is a **corporation** (see Section 1.3.3). A multinational enterprise (MNE) will have relationships with several governments, in those countries in which the MNE operates.

The firm may be seen in terms of its functions: a 'black box' where inputs or resources are converted into outputs for sale (Figure 1.2).

Economists refer to inputs as 'factors of production'. The main factors are **land** (including extractive and natural resources), **labour** (of all kinds, including entrepreneurial), and **capital** (meaning *real capital*, or productive equipment, rather than *financial capital*). Capital should include *human capital*, which encompasses human knowledge and experience, and the wisdom to employ that knowledge ('technology' in its broadest context). Figure 1.2 is the diagram equivalent of the economist's production function, which says that the level of output of a firm, q, is a function of the level of its inputs:

$$q = f(g, l, k) \tag{1.1}$$

Figure 1.2. The firm as a 'black box'

where g = land, l = labour, and k = capital. The level of output, q, is the firm's sales volume, with anything unsold going into inventory. q depends upon demand for the firm's products. The labour input, l, is the hours worked by labour and management, the amount of which is partly dependent upon wages (the level of remuneration).[1] Given that labour is a significant stakeholder in the firm, the welfare (utility) of labour is significantly dependent upon the well-being of the firm. Additionally, labour remuneration may sometimes consist of a 'share option' component, giving labour a shareholder stake in the firm.

The purchase of land and capital is funded from a mix of debt funding (e.g. loans from banks, bondholders, etc; see Chapter 4) and equity funding (from shareholders; see Chapter 5). The value of the firm is the sum of its debt and equity funding:

$$V = B + S \tag{1.2}$$

where V = the value of the firm, B = the value of debt, and S = the value of equity. The immediate implication would appear to be that the value of the firm is independent of the *mix* of debt-to-equity funding. This issue is examined in Chapter 9.

1.2.2 *The objective of the firm*

Any organisation, including a business, should be operated in the best interests of those who own it. Microeconomics teaches that a business tries to maximise its *profits* (subject to the costs imposed by the production function). This is a simplified 'single period' view of the firm's objective. Does the pursuit of **profit maximisation** increase the well-being (welfare or utility) of the business' owners, the shareholders? While different shareholders may have different preferences, management seeking to increase the value of shareholder wealth should act to increase the overall welfare of shareholders *in toto*. The true objective for the firm should be the maximisation of shareholder wealth. This would mean maximising the value of the

[1]This is a hangover from the early industrial era. With the move from factory-based manufacturing to a service and information economy, some component for 'effort' and human capital would need to be included.

firm as measured by the price of each share. However, management should seek to maximise shareholder wealth by operating the company efficiently, effectively and profitably. Shareholder wealth is the by-product of a successful business.

1.2.2.1 *Profit maximisation versus wealth maximisation*

Value maximisation—maximisation of the value of the firm, or the maximisation of shareholder wealth—is a broader objective than profit maximisation: *value maximisation encompasses profit maximisation.* For single-period analysis, the two methods are equivalent. For multi-period analysis value maximisation is preferable. Partly this is because profits are short run: they are measured on an annual or semi-annual basis. While the accrual of profits enhances the value of the firm, the maximisation of current profits may involve undertaking activities that might jeopardise future profits. One example might be a firm improving its current profits by reducing maintenance spending on its capital equipment. This would probably shorten the useful length of the equipment's lifetime, requiring a significant increase in future expenditure on capital; a case of "penny wise, pound foolish". To maximise value the firm must consider the long-run stream of future profits (more accurately, cashflows).

Additionally, profit maximisation fails to account for **risk**. Consider two possible investment projects: a firm operating under the goal of pure profit maximisation would undertake the project offering the highest expected future profits, even it that project meant having to take levels of risk that might be considered unacceptable. The lower-risk alternative might offer a more robust, if smaller, level of profits, more acceptable to shareholders. As we shall see (Chapter 8), value explicitly incorporates risk, so value maximisation takes account of risk in a way that profit maximisation does not.

Thus, value maximisation offers a more robust basis for decision-making than profit maximisation. It better describes the true objective of the firm and provides a logical basis for optimal decision-making based on rigorous analytical procedures. Nonetheless, this is not enough. Value maximisation is unlikely to inspire the energy or enthusiasm of managers, employees or other stakeholders. Directors need to provide a corporate vision, a strategy, and the tactics which will serve to unite the various stakeholders in pursuit of value maximisation. [Jensen 2010]

1.3 Business structure

In this section we consider the various forms of business structure which exist in the United Kingdom. Similar forms exist in other countries, sometimes with variant names and slight differences in detail.

1.3.1 *Sole proprietorship*

Once known as the 'one-man firm' the sole proprietorship (or **sole trader**) means that the firm *is* a single individual, with no legal distinction between the firm and the owner. The person is often referred to as 'self-employed'. Such a firm has **unlimited liability**: the assets of the owner can be called upon to meet the obligations of the firm. Because the firm is not a separate legal entity, it is not subject to corporate taxation. However, the owner is subject to personal income taxes on the firm's earnings, and the personal assets of the owner could be used to pay off the firm's debts.

Because it has unlimited liability the sole proprietorship is unlikely to be able to attract sizeable amounts of external funding. In part, this is due to the limited resources a sole proprietor has by way of collateral. If, as is often the case, a sole proprietorship grows its owner will eventually seek to incorporate. However, because the existence of the firm depends on the identity of its owner, the lifespan of the sole proprietorship depends on the lifespan of the owner.

Because under a sole proprietorship the owner is the firm (legally they are considered identical) there is a natural tendency to think of the firm as having no other employees. This is not necessarily the case.

1.3.2 *Partnership*

A partnership consists of two or more individuals associating for the purpose of conducting business. A partnership agreement may be verbal or a more formal, contractual basis. Partnership profits are taxed as personal income, usually on a *pro rata* basis. Not all partners need contribute financial resources; some partners may be included because of the skills they bring to the venture. It is on this basis that some forms of accountants and lawyers in the United Kingdom establish partnerships. Partners in these professions often work their way up through the ranks and may be rewarded ultimately by being made a partner in the company.

Under a partnership agreement the partners share *pro rata* in the profits of the company and are "jointly and severally liable" to make good any losses. They are personally liable for any debts the firm incurs. The death or withdrawal of a partner, or a new partner coming into the business, results in the cessation of the existing partnership and the creation of a new one. For a partnership to work well the partnership agreement must be established to avoid potential conflicts. Terms and conditions for distribution of assets upon dissolution may be included in the agreement. It has become common practice for each partner to carry life assurance, with the other partners named as beneficiaries.

Some partners might be included in a partnership agreement with limited liability. With a **limited partnership (LP)** there must be some general partners with unlimited liability.

The limited partnership has been expanded to **limited liability partnerships** (LLPs) in which *all* partners have limited liability. In the United Kingdom these were initially proposed by government in February 1997 and came into being on 6 April 2001. An LLP is a separate legal entity from the partners, but disclosure requirements are similar to those of a corporation, with financial information filed equivalent to that of limited companies, including annual accounts.

1.3.3 *Limited companies*

A limited company (or **corporation**) is a separate legal entity from its owners and managers. It is an 'artificially created legal person'. The owners of the corporation—the **shareholders**—hold shares according to the proportion of the company they own. In the event of the company having to liquidate, any individual owner's liability is limited to their stake in the company as measured by the value of their shares. Personal assets may not be taken to pay off the company's debts; *the company's liabilities are limited to the assets of the company itself.*[2]

The benefit of limited liability is that all profits accrue to the shareholders. Any firm with limited liability is subject to *corporate* taxation. Shares in corporations are usually transferable from one individual to another.

Because a corporation does not depend on who are its shareholders, its lifespan can far exceed that of those shareholders: its lifespan is indefinite. At each corporation's Annual General Meeting, the shareholders elect a Board of Directors (who might also be shareholders) to run the company on their behalf. As a company grows its management may become increasingly divorced from its ownership: the directors may choose to employ others ('managers') to administer the day-to-day affairs of the company. For England and Wales, the Companies Act 2006 outlined seven key duties of a company director:

(1) Company's constitution: follow the company's constitution and its articles of association. These provide a set of rules and regulations for managing and controlling the internal affairs of the company and prescribe the power and duties of the directors and officers and the rights of the shareholders.
(2) Promote the success of the company: i.e. act in the company's best interests to promote its success.
(3) Independent judgement: Directors must not allow other people to control their powers as a director. They can accept advice but must use their own independent judgement to make final decisions.
(4) Exercise reasonable care, skill and diligence.
(5) Avoid conflicts of interest.
(6) Third party benefits: directors must not accept benefits from a third party that are offered because they are a director. This could cause a conflict of interest.
(7) Interests in a transaction: a director must tell the other directors and members if you might personally benefit from a transaction the company makes.
[www.gov.uk/guidance/being-a-company-director#general-duties-of-a-company-director]

[2]The exception being in the case of fraud by a director/officer of the company.

Forming a limited company in England and Wales is straightforward:

- Digital filing via Companies House involving a fee of £ 50.[3] If the company name is not on The Register and the proposed directors are not barred from being directors, incorporation will be completed "within 24 hours".
  [www.gov.uk/government/organisations/companies-house]
- Through a company formation agency. This is a little more expensive but offers the advantage of dealing with professionals who do this on a frequent and regular basis.
- People already in business—perhaps as a sole proprietor—sometimes incorporate using their accountants or lawyers as the formation agent. This is more costly: often the lawyer or accountant will employ a company formation agency to do the work and add a margin to the bill they send their client.

Part of the registration process involves identifying any "person with significant control" (PSC), i.e. someone who owns or controls your company. Also known as 'beneficial owners', these are individuals who own more than 25% of shares in the company, have more than 25% of voting rights in the company, and have the right to appoint or remove the majority of the board of directors.

A certificate of incorporation with the company registration number is issued by Companies House. The Memorandum and Articles of Association sets out the rights and obligations of the company. These form a contract between the corporation and the state. A great deal of company information held at Companies House is freely available.

Partnerships and limited companies are both required to register with HMRC (UK tax authority). There are financial penalties for late filing of company accounts or annual returns with Companies House.

Companies House (England and Wales) recognises four types of company:

Private Company Limited by Shares: has a share capital with limited liability: the liability of each member is limited to that amount. A private company cannot offer its shares for sale to the

---

[3]Information accurate as of 1st December 2024.

public—they are not freely transferable. Shareholders may transfer (sell) their shares to a third party, but only with the express permission of the corporation. Private limited companies are required to use the phrase "**Limited**" or "**Ltd**" after the company name in all of their documentation. In the United States "Inc." or "Incorporated" is used.

Private Company Limited by Guarantee: does not have a share capital. Its members are guarantors rather than shareholders. The members' liability is limited to the amount they agree to contribute to the company's assets if it is wound up.

Private Unlimited Company: may or may not have a share capital but there is no limit to the members' liability.

Public Limited Company (plc): has a share capital with the liability of each member limited to the amount unpaid on their shares. Shares can be sold to the public and may be quoted on the stock exchange.

Public limited companies are required to use "**plc**" after the company name in all of their documentation. Note the distinction between **public limited companies** (plcs) and **listed companies**: a listed company must be a plc, but not all plcs are listed on the London Stock Exchange. For a plc to become listed it must meet a number of requirements:

- Minimum capital requirement, which currently stands at £ 30 million.
- At least 25 per cent of its shares must be in public hands.
- Sufficient working capital for the group's requirements for at least 12 months from the date on which the prospectus relating to the listing is published.
- A company applying for a Premium listing of shares in London needs to have a trading record of at least three years, including a three-year revenue earning record covering at least 75% of the company's business. There may be some exceptions for specialised companies.

Similar arrangements for formation of a corporation exist in most countries. In the USA, where each state has its own laws, many businesses prefer to incorporate in Nevada or Delaware, where the regulatory burden is considered less onerous. Table 1.2 provides a comparison of the main forms of business structure.

Table 1.2. Business structures compared

	Sole trader	Partnership	LLP	Corporation
Ease of setup	***	**	*	*
Ease of operation	***	**	*	*
Tax efficiency	*	*	**	***
Personal protection	*	*	***	***
Scalability	*	**	***	***

More stars ⇒ greater ease

1.4 The finance function

The **finance function** is that part of the firm concerned with the firm's financial matters. It may also be referred to as the finance department, or the firm's financial managers.

Because the objective of the firm is to maximise the value of the firm (thereby maximising shareholder wealth), it follows that *the main function of financial management is to plan for, acquire, and utilise funds in such a way that shareholder wealth is maximised.* To fulfil this role, the financial manager must have a keen knowledge and sound understanding of both the firm and the financial system. This can be summarised as in Figure 1.3:

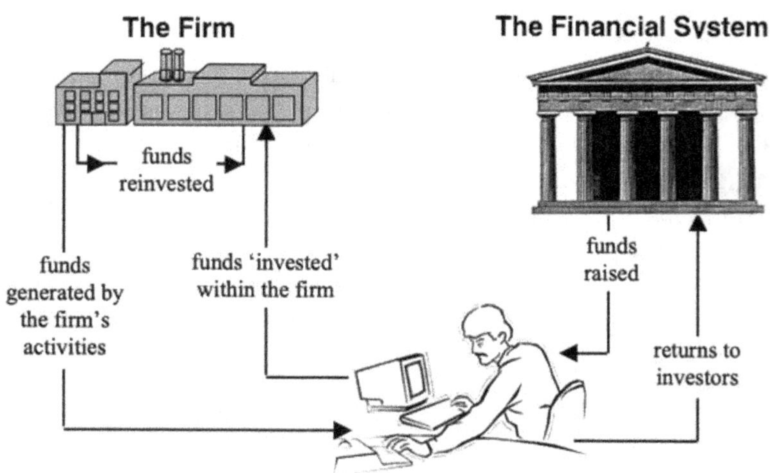

Figure 1.3. The Financial Manager

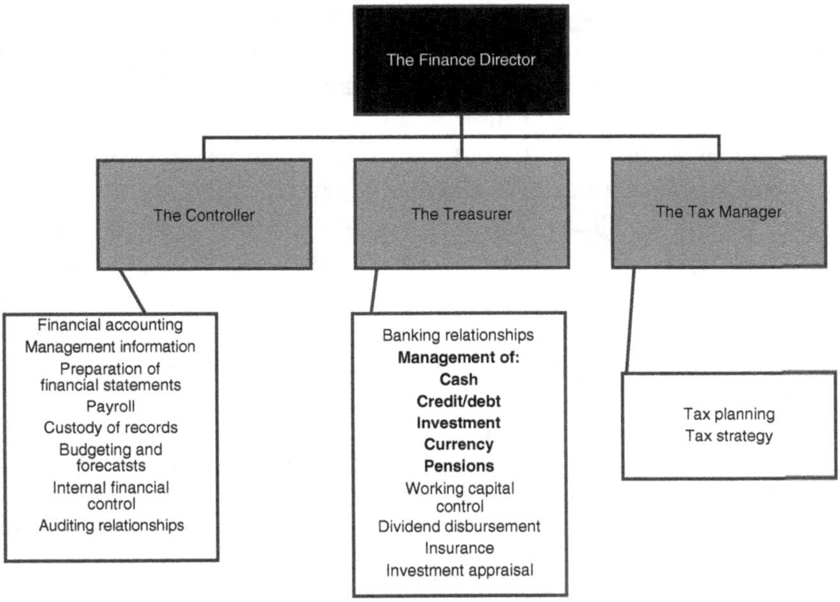

Figure 1.4. Key aspects of the finance function

In larger firms the functions of the Financial Manager (Financial Director or CFO—Chief Financial Officer) are often divided into (at least) two major areas of responsibility:

- **Treasurer:** Responsible for the acquisition and custody of funds.
- **Controller:** Responsible for accounting, reporting and control.

The Control function is sometimes sub-divided to include a separate function with responsibility for taxation issues, which are particularly significant for firms operating across national boundaries. This division can be understood diagrammatically (Figure 1.4).

1.5 Principals and agents

Like contemporary small family-run businesses, in the early days of the industrial revolution firms were usually managed by those who owned it. A modern corporation tends to be large and complex, with a division between those who own the business (shareholders) and those who manage it (the Board of Directors). It is the task of management—the **agents**—to administer the business on behalf of its owners—the **principals**: an **agency relationship**. Consequently, there may be a conflict of interest between those who own the firm and those who manage it. There can be a tendency for managers to make decisions that might be in their own self-interest but not in the interest of shareholders nor consistent with the risks bondholders accepted when they purchased their stake in the company. These conflicts give rise to additional costs: **agency costs**. While such costs are not easily measured in monetary terms, they represent opportunities foregone. For example, while management might consider a corporate jet useful, it might not be in the shareholders' interest. One way of minimising these costs is to turn agents into principals. This can occur by making the directors of a company shareholders (a primary objective of the use of employee share options).

There are four key forms of agency cost:

- Costs to minimise the incentives for management to act contrary to the interests of shareholders
- Costs of monitoring the actions of management
- Bonding costs to protect shareholders from managerial dishonesty
- Opportunity costs of lost profits due to complex organisational structures, which limit managerial decision-making flexibility

There may also be a conflict of interest between the firm's managers and its labour force. Thus, the firm's operations could give rise to a three-way conflict of interest.

Further conflicts of interest can arise from the firm's sources of financing. Investors can provide funds to a firm via debt or equity. Bondholders—a shorthand term for *all* providers of debt to the firm—are likely to be affected differently than shareholders by the firm's decisions. The key conflict relates to the risk appetite of these groups. Because shareholders wish to see their wealth maximised *ceteris paribus*, they would prefer management to leverage their returns via prudent risk-taking. However, bondholders are primarily interested in the company doing enough to ensure that they receive their payments of interest (and repayment of principal in the longer run), which may involve a lower risk strategy. It may also be that conflicts of interest occur within a group of shareholders, or within a group of bondholders.

There is a large body of literature considering issues relating to conflicts of interest between a business's **stakeholders**. Building on the earlier approach of Berle and Means [1932], the seminal work of Jensen and Meckling [1976] distinguished between **maximising** and **satisficing** behaviour: the former indicating behaviour with the objective of maximising the value of the firm (or shareholder wealth), the latter indicating behaviour whereby management does 'just enough' to keep shareholders satisfied.

1.5.1 *Maximisation vs satisficing*

Economic theory assumes that individuals are rational maximisers. The objective is for individuals to act to maximise their well-being subject to the constraints imposed by limited wealth or income. Economists use the concept of **utility** as a measure of an individual's well-being or welfare, but it is largely a subjective measure: the individual determines what is in their self-interest. However, this does not mean that individuals act in a purely selfish manner; there is a vast difference between acting in one's own interest and acting selfishly. It might be an individual's self-interest to donate funds to charity or consider how their actions impinge on others above their own immediate requirements. Self-interest includes the notion that most individuals prefer less risk to more, *ceteris paribus* (other things being equal); i.e. individuals are **risk-averse**. Self-interest also implies that an individual prefers to receive a given sum of money now rather than in the future, *ceteris paribus*.

Maximising involves optimisation of a given objective: striving for the best possible outcome. Alternatively, satisficing behaviour involves a willingness to settle for less than the best possible outcome. Jensen and Meckling [1976] established that a manager with fractional ownership (including zero ownership) might be inclined to adopt satisficing behaviour, rather than seeking to maximise the wealth of all shareholders. This imposes an agency cost on the shareholders. The increasing use of perquisites (perks) is sometimes cited as a symptom of satisficing behaviour. Shareholders should structure the remuneration of directors to ensure maximising rather than satisficing behaviour.

1.5.2 *Management goals*

In a corporation managers are employed to act on behalf of the shareholders. However, managers might substitute their own goals in place of the objectives of the shareholders: to see their own wealth maximised. As well as perks, managers may seek to pay themselves large salaries and other forms of remuneration—e.g. pensions, share options—regardless of the performance of the company. For some years strong shareholder concern about directors' remuneration has been reported, an issue referred to in the press as 'fat cats' pay'. In the United Kingdom, this issue can lead to 'shareholder revolts' at company AGMs. In some cases, these are brought about by larger, institutional investors, while in other cases groups of individual shareholders have been moved to actively voice their concerns.

Managers may also have an agenda of 'empire building', trying to enhance their own reputation through the pursuit of 'status goals' such as the numbers of staff or the size of budget for which they are responsible. Because these goals focus only on part of the firm's operations, they may be inconsistent with shareholder wealth maximisation.

Finally, because managers depend on their position for their livelihood, they might be prone take a satisficing, more risk-averse view of the company's activities than would suit shareholders. Unlike management, shareholders have the option of diversifying away some of their risk by holding a portfolio of shares in different companies (see Chapter Seven). Corporate governance remains an issue which continues to test the minds and imaginations of both regulators and the regulated, although the solution never seems to get closer.

1.5.3 *Shareholders' goals*

The primary aim of *any* shareholder is to promote their individual well-being, usually in terms of their wealth. For shareholders this increased wealth can be through income from dividends, and/or capital gains through increases in the price of the shares. Capital gains may be **realised** (when the shares are sold) or **unrealised**, i.e. 'paper increases' in shareholder wealth. Capital gains can also be negative, i.e. capital losses.

Depending upon individual preferences, some shareholders will prefer to maximise their wealth through capital gains, while others may be more interested in the stream of dividend payments. Institutional investors, such as pension funds and insurance companies, are a prime example of the latter, using the regular dividends they receive to meet their outgoings, such as pension payments. Investors who seek to make capital gains in the short-term from newly issued shares are known as 'stags'.

Whether investors are interested in capital gains or dividends, these can only arise from a company being successful (profitable) in the longer-run: the interests of shareholders can be met only if the company is successfully adding value. This requires the investor to take a view on what the future holds for the company and is considered speculative activity. It therefore requires a lower degree of risk-aversion by the investor than if they were to hold bonds, for example.

1.5.4 *Bondholders' goals*

Although 'debtholder' might be more appropriate and accurate, **bondholder** is the traditional term for any entity which has lent funds to a business, regardless of whether bonds (marketable or otherwise) have been issued. Thus, a bank which has extended a loan to a firm comes under this classification.

By nature, bondholders are more risk averse than shareholders. Bondholders have opted for a certain return by way of regular interest payments on the funds they have lent to the business. Shareholders have opted for the greater uncertainty of dividends and/or possible capital gains. It follows that bondholders will typically prefer the firm to undertake less risky investments than would be preferred by shareholders.

1.5.5 *Other stakeholders' goals*

In addition to those who have a capital stake in the company—holders of debt or equity—there is a broader group of stakeholders whose activities directly affect the successful running of the firm. The goals of these stakeholders may conflict with those of shareholders, in whose interest the firm is supposed to be run. There are also stakeholders with a more tenuous connection to the company, yet still have an interest in its well-being. These other stakeholders include:

- **Customers:** without whom a business has no *raison d'être*. There is a direct connection between a company that can offer customers the products they desire over time, and one that successfully achieves value maximisation.
- **Workers:** those employed by a business to undertake the work. History is full of examples of conflicts between the workforce and the management of a company. It should be noted that management are also part of a company's workforce.
- **Suppliers:** successful operation of a business requires stability from its suppliers, in terms of price and quality of product, ability to deliver, and the supplier's continued existence. Suppliers include those who provide raw materials (to a manufacturer, for example), distributors, and those who provide indispensable services to the firm, including the company's accountants, any legal services required, and those who offer peripheral services such as local caterers offering lunch facilities.
- **The local community:** firms operate within their local community, and should abide by local culture and customs, and pay taxation. Local infrastructure (e.g. transportation) is important to enable the labour force to be able to get to and from work, and for the firm to be able to take delivery of raw materials and deliver its products to the customer.
- **Government:** the (national) government provides infrastructure and the laws within which businesses operate. Firms must operate within national laws of contract and other legal property rights, as well as comply with laws on taxation.
- **Society 'at large':** society places pressures on the way in which firms operate, through changing acceptable public standards (e.g. the environment, sustainability, ethics, etc), via pressure groups. These play an ever-increasing role in societal norms and standards.

1.5.6 *In summary*

It is a given that managers might not operate in the best interests of shareholders. But shareholders are not powerless. There are many ways shareholders can incentivise management compliance with their goals:

- **Contracts:** judicial arrangements for management's compensation and remuneration can be written into their contracts. Performance-related measures, such as share options, are often put in place.
- **Directors:** because shareholders elect the board of directors, they can be terminated if they are dissatisfied with their performance. Experience suggests that this is more likely in theory than in practice.
- **Takeovers:** if a firm is considered sound except for its management, it will be liable to be considered for a takeover bid. In the event of a takeover, existing management would be sacked and replaced. Fear of takeover provides an incentive for managers to pursue actions which will positively impact the share price, thereby maximising shareholder wealth.
- **Labour market competition:** There is a labour market for management, much as there is for other forms of labour. Poor managers can be replaced by better managers. Firms willing to pay the most can attract the best management. The existence of a *global* market for top management is one argument put forward (in the United Kingdom) to justify large executive compensation packages. However, there is evidence to suggest a degree of segmentation of national markets for executives. While the argument for executive market competition seems to hold for a very large economy like the United States, the evidence for the United Kingdom is more questionable.

1.6 Sample questions (discussion)

(1) Suzi is a well-known local artist who wishes to become a full-time professional and sell her paintings. She has no real work experience since leaving art college and little understanding how to develop a business that captures the value of her artistic creations. What corporate structure would you recommend to Suzi? Explain fully, including the various advantages and disadvantages.

(2) You have decided to apply for the role as CFO of your company, a position that is currently vacant. For the application you are required to write a memo to the CEO covering (a) what your company's primary financial objective(s) should be and (b) your opinion on the alternative approaches to measuring the company's success in meeting these objectives. Be sure to justify your point of view (citing and refuting other views where relevant) or you won't get the job!

(3) Do you agree with using warrants (employee share options) to ensure alignment of managerial and shareholder objectives? Use information from reputable websites and other sources to support your argument.

Chapter 2

The Financial Environment

2.1 Introduction

Anyone considering a venture into finance, for practical or academic reasons, needs to have a sound knowledge of the financial environment. The finance function (financial manager) of the firm needs to be knowledgeable about the workings and state of the financial system, because it is from this sector that funds are raised, and to which funds need to be repaid. Also, the financial system is subject to periodic changes to its format and structure due to the forces of innovation and regulation. Because the financial sector is a crucial component of the wider macroeconomy this is where we begin.

2.2 Finance and macroeconomics

Although all too infrequently noted there is a strong relationship between macroeconomics and finance. This is clearly seen in the **Circular Flow of Income** diagram (Figure 2.1) which is standard in most macroeconomics texts:

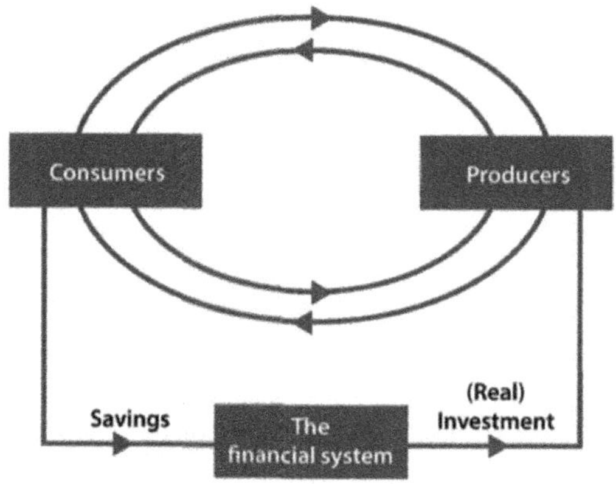

Figure 2.1. The (Basic) Circular Flow of Income

This shows the role of the financial system in channeling funds from savers to productive investments. Savers are 'surplus units' (they have more current income available than they immediately require), while investors are 'deficit units' (they have less current income available than they immediately require). Because the financial system is a conduit channeling funds from surplus units to deficit units, it:

- provides an increased incentive for saving to take place, and
- encourages and facilitates real investment. The higher the level of real investment then the higher the level of economic activity (measured by GDP: Gross Domestic Product) *ceteris paribus*.

2.3 The financial system: markets and institutions

The financial system is one of the least understood aspects of the economy. The amounts of money discussed are often so large they resemble international telephone numbers; the periodic crises and scandals that occur do little to reassure people of the integrity of those who work within the financial system. But the financial system is a crucial component of the modern macroeconomy, one with which everyone comes into almost daily contact.

Some of the mystery about the financial system is because it operates on both a retail and a wholesale basis, although most people are only exposed to the retail side: the high street banks, building societies, and, less frequently, insurance companies and pension funds. Only a small proportion of people have direct experience of the retail side of trading in company shares or bonds. In terms of volume of transactions, the retail side is significantly smaller.

Any mystery is easily dispersed with the knowledge that the role of the financial system is to transfer funds from surplus units (savers) to deficit units (borrowers). This is true for any country and throughout all periods of history. Although governments now play a significant role, historically, most fund-raising has been by firms, enabling the purchase of capital equipment, often on a large scale. Capital equipment is an engine of economic growth both directly—because workers need to be employed in its manufacture—and indirectly—it enables firms to produce their products more efficiently and profitably. Without the financial system, firms would have to fund their capital purchases from their own reserves, making investment less likely to occur.

At the heart of the financial system is money. It is the financial core enabling us to perform our daily transactions. It provides a medium by which transactions can be postponed: something can be sold now for money, and that money retained for a future transaction. This is not the case with a barter transaction, where both sides occur simultaneously. Around this monetary core are three pillars which comprise the financial system:

- **The financial institutions:** banks and building societies, insurance companies and pension funds, and the various investment companies, private equity, venture capital trusts, etc.
- **The financial markets:** the stock exchange, where both shares and debt instruments are issued (the 'primary market') and then traded (the 'secondary market'), the foreign exchange markets, and the derivatives markets.
- **The regulators:** in most countries, financial markets and institutions are subject to constraints on their activities imposed by the regulatory regime. This consists of self-regulatory organisations, or regulatory agencies set up by the government, or some combination of both.

Both financial institutions and financial markets serve as conduits for channelling funds from savers to investors. Ordinarily we see the retail aspects of the institutions, but direct experience of the markets is more limited. The same is true for firms: larger firms are likely to have greater, direct experience of all aspects of the financial system than smaller firms. For example, it is unlikely that the owner of a small fruit stall in a street market will try to raise funds via a share flotation on the stock exchange! However, almost all firms of every size will have an overdraft facility (i.e. line of credit) with their bank.

As well as the usual laws pertaining to property rights and contracts, financial systems are subject to regulation. Regulation has several primary objectives:

(1) to ensure the soundness and stability of the financial system and thereby maintain confidence in it. This deals with issues of systemic risk, the risk of failure of the entire system.
(2) to ensure consumer protection. This deals with both information asymmetry and the agency problem.
(3) to prevent any build-up of monopoly power.

Regulatory bodies can be external to the system—such as a government agency—or internal, such as a self-regulatory organisation. In most countries the banking system is regulated by the central bank which is often also responsible for the conduct of monetary policy. In some countries the central bank operates directly as an agency of government, while in higher-income economies the central bank operates independently of government, although central bankers may be appointed by government.[1]

The legislation which established current financial regulation in the United Kingdom is the Financial Services Act 2012. Coming into force in April 2013, this established the Financial Conduct Authority (FCA) which regulates financial firms providing services to consumers and maintains the integrity of UK financial markets. This includes conduct at both the wholesale and retail level. Independent of government, the FCA operates alongside the Prudential Regulation Authority (for banks, building societies, and credit unions) and

[1]Following the 1997 election of the Labour government the Bank of England was granted 'operational independence'. The Bank of England no longer operated monetary policy as a branch of central government but independently within inflation guidelines established by the government via legislation.

the Financial Policy Committee (a committee of the Bank of England) to establish regulations for the financial sector.

2.3.1 *Financial markets*

The many kinds of financial market are typically based on the type of financial asset being traded. The financial manager needs to be familiar with both the panoply of markets and the language of those markets. One key distinction is between the **debt** markets and the **equity** market. In the former, securities which represent corporate or government debt obligations ('bonds') are traded; in the latter, equity securities such as ordinary shares ('common stock' in the USA) are traded. These are discussed in detail in Chapters Four and Five respectively.

Another distinction is between money markets and capital markets. This is based on the time to maturity of the assets traded: **money markets** trade financial instruments with a maturity of less than one year. **Capital markets** trade instruments with a maturity of more than one year. Because equity has a (potentially) infinite lifespan, the money markets are exclusively debt markets by definition, whereas the capital markets include both debt (medium-term and long-term) markets and equity markets.

Financial markets also distinguish between primary markets and secondary markets. **Primary markets** are those in which securities are traded for the first time, such as when a company's shares are first 'floated'. **Secondary markets** refer to those in which previously issued securities are traded. Thus, it is only in the primary markets that firms raise funds; secondary markets provide for liquidity by allowing the transfer of ownership of securities.

There are also markets for **derivative securities**. These are securities which have no intrinsic value: they derive their value from some underlying asset: either a financial asset (such as ordinary shares, or interest rates) or a real asset or commodity (such as gold, silver, oil, etc). The underlying assets are said to trade in a 'cash market'. The largest and oldest derivatives market is the Chicago Mercantile Exchange (CME Group), which merged with the Chicago Board of Trade in 2007. In the UK derivatives are traded in several markets, including the London Stock Exchange Group (LSEG), the Baltic Exchange, the London Metal Exchange (LME), and ICE Futures Europe. This latter was formed after a series of takeovers which included the original LIFFE (London International Financial Futures Exchange; founded 1982).

The primary purpose for which derivatives were designed is the hedging (i.e. offsetting) of risk (see Chapter 5). However, some derivatives are leveraged instruments, i.e. a relatively small payment offers a disproportionately large exposure to price movements in the cash markets. This payment is known as a **margin** in the futures market, and a **premium** for options transactions. Designed for hedging, leverage allows for speculation. It is because of speculative activity that went severely awry that derivatives have become well-known. Derivatives fall into three basic categories: futures, options, and swaps:

- **Futures** are standardised forward contracts. In their simplest form one counterparty is paying an agreed price now for the future delivery of a commodity, which has a standardised quality, a standardised quantity, and a standardised delivery date. Futures contracts may be 'financial' or 'commodity'. **Financial futures** include interest rate futures, exchange rate futures, and stock index futures. **Commodity futures** include both 'soft' commodities such as foodstuffs (including e.g. orange juice futures, pork belly futures, etc), and 'hard' commodities (metals, oil, etc). Futures markets operate through a central clearing house, which guarantees the trade to both counterparties.
- **Options** are derivatives which offer the right (but not the obligation) to buy or sell the underlying asset at a guaranteed price on or before the expiration date. An option to buy is a **call option**; an option to sell is a **put option**. The price paid for an option is the 'option premium', usually a small fraction of the market price of the underlying asset. The price paid to exercise the option (that is, to buy or sell the underlying asset) is called the **strike price** or **exercise price**. Options come in two basic 'flavours': **American options** allow the option to be exercised any time up to and including the date of expiration; **European options** can only be exercised on the expiration date. The largest single category of options is equity options, which are standardised, hence easily tradable in formal markets. However, less standardised, over-the-counter (OTC) options are feasible, if not always marketable.

- **Swaps** are an exchange of payments (cash flows). Because these are unstandardised there is no formal market in which they can be traded. They are considered over-the-counter (OTC) transactions.

2.3.2 *Efficient markets*

Efficiency means getting the most out for the least in. In a sense, efficiency is effective laziness. The output of any market is the quantity of products traded; the input is the cost of swiftly transferring the product from suppliers to purchasers. Thus, a market can be said to be efficient if the largest possible quantity of products is traded quickly at the lowest possible cost. For a financial market, the product is funds or financial capital.

Price in a market adjusts to reflect the activities of buyers and sellers. In an efficient market price will adjust swiftly to fully reflect the information available to buyers and sellers on which they base their activities. Any profits which can be made due to existing information will already have been realised, i.e. profitable opportunities will be 'arbitraged' out. In an efficient market it is not possible to earn returns superior to the market consistently, except by chance.

One implication is that if a market is efficient then all information is said to be already discounted (i.e. reflected in the price), and no excess (risk-adjusted) returns can be made except as the result of actions based on new information. Key here is the nature of the information used to make decisions by market participants. Intuitively, it makes sense for information about (listed) companies to be considered relevant. Equally, investors ought to be concerned with key macroeconomic indicators, such as inflation and GDP, as well as government policy designed to influence the economy. It would make less sense to consider (e.g.) the weather as a factor influencing capital market returns. Nonetheless, the notion that the economy is affected by weather, which is in turn due to sunspot activity, has a long legacy dating back to William Stanley Jevons (1835–1882). More recent studies have begun to link economic activity with the threats of disease (AIDS, SARS, COVID-19) or terrorism. More fanciful notions include the positing of relations between overall market returns and key national sporting events (how the England national soccer team performs, or the results of the Super Bowl in American football), as well as the 'hemline' theory, which argued that stock market returns are related to the length of women's skirts!

Based on the unpublished work of Harry Roberts [1967] economists posit three levels of efficiency for capital markets, based on the nature of the information:

Weak-form efficiency

The lowest degree of market efficiency: current security prices fully reflect *historical* information on prices or, their inverse, rates of return. If a market is characterised by weak-form efficiency no investor can earn excess (above market) returns using a strategy based on historical information. The implication is that past prices (returns) are a poor indicator of future prices (returns). Past trends or cycles do not act to predict future trends or cycles. There is a large body of empirical literature that offers evidence to suggest that capital markets in the developed world are at least weak-form efficient.

Semi-strong-form efficiency

A market is semi-strong-form efficient if current security prices fully reflect *all publicly available* knowledge: in addition to historical data, public announcements—changes in macroeconomic policy, corporate policy changes that affect the firm's cash flows, takeover announcements—will be swiftly incorporated into the price (return) on securities. It is not possible to earn excess returns using publicly available information: it will already have been discounted (included in the price). There is strong empirical evidence that this form of market efficiency exists in capital markets with high volume and liquidity, such as those in the UK, the USA, Japan, Canada, and much of western Europe.

Strong-form efficiency

Strong-form efficiency means that current security prices fully reflect *all* available information, whether publicly available or not. With strong-form efficiency it is impossible to make excess returns by 'insider dealing' (i.e. trading on private information). The existence of insider trading regulations, and the high profile of insider dealing court cases strongly suggest that strong-form efficiency probably does not exist.

The relationship between the degree of efficiency of a financial market and the information available can be depicted graphically (Figure 2.2):

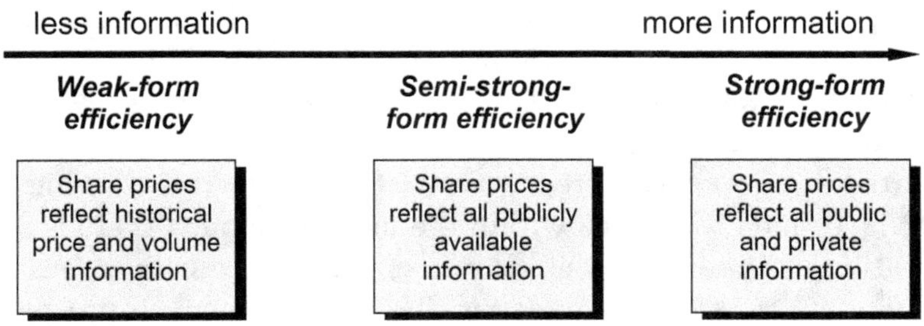

Figure 2.2. Degrees of market efficiency

One implication is that if markets are efficient then no trend in prices will be discernible. This is because prices adjust swiftly to reflect new information, which becomes known randomly. Prices in an efficient market will follow a 'random walk'. The notion of a random walk has its origins in empirical work: in a paper presented to the Royal Statistical Society the statistician Maurice Kendall [1953] examined the behaviour of share and commodity prices to try and find cyclical patterns and was surprised when he could not find any. This should have come as little surprise as his results had been anticipated in the doctoral work of Louis Bachelier [1900]. In addition, the random nature of commodity prices had been noted during the 1930s by Holbrook Working, a food economist [1934]. From a corporate perspective, the key implication focuses on the objective of the firm: value maximisation. If capital markets are efficient, then share prices will be an unbiased estimate of the value of the firm. In recent years the existence of efficient markets has been called into question by studies in behavioural economics.

2.4 Finance and Investment

Investment occurs when funds are paid out now in the expectation of increased future cash flows. Investment is embodied in time. **Real investment** is when funds are used to acquire capital equipment (usually by a firm), with which it expects to increase its value by enhancing its future profit stream. **Financial investment** occurs when the funds are supplied to a corporation in the expectation of future dividends (equity investment) or future interest payments (loans), as well as a possible capital gain on the security. From a macroeconomic viewpoint financial investment is an act of saving, (see Figure 2.1: the Circular Flow of Income). The financial system converts acts of financial investment into acts of real investment, i.e. the financial system channels the funding which allows real investment to take place.

In the same way as there is a separation between the savings and (real) investment decisions within the macroeconomy, there is also a separation of the investment and financing decisions by a business. In Chapter 6 we examine in detail the process by which prospective (real) investments are assessed, primarily by way of their contribution to the firm's objective of maximising value. It is important to recognise that there are two distinct stages to this process. First, any investment must be judged on its contribution to adding value to the business. Second, the investment needs to be judged depending on how it is to be financed. In Chapters 8 and 9 we shall come across the (theoretical) proposition that how investments are financed is irrelevant to the investment decision. It is conceivable for an investment to be unprofitable *per se* yet become profitable due to financing considerations. In this case, the business would be better off ignoring the investment project, and profit by buying and selling financial claims (borrowing and lending) as it is this which is adding value. Theoretical underpinnings for this separation are to be found in Hirshleifer [1958] which built upon the earlier work of Fisher [1930].

2.5 Accounting for finance

To make sound financial decisions a financial manager must be able to read and interpret the financial records of the company. Equally, investors may wish to examine the financial records of companies in which they are considering investing. However, the financial records of a company are historical. While imperfect, they offer the only guide to a company's future. Such 'matters of history' for all United Kingdom companies with limited liability can be obtained from the records at Companies House (www.gov.uk/government/organisatio ns/companies-house).

The financial records of a company are contained in its accounts or financial statements. These come in three basic forms, which firms trading as limited companies in the United Kingdom are required to publish:

- the balance sheet
- the income statement (or profit and loss statement), and
- the cash flow statement

These are presented to shareholders, prospective shareholders and other interested parties in the form of an Annual Report and Accounts. The Annual Report also contains a statement from the Chairman of the Board of Directors a listing of the directors, and a note from the company's auditors verifying that the accounts are a "true and fair view of the state of affairs of the company", "free from material misstatement". For smaller firms Annual Reports are often little more than a basic attempt to meet legal requirements. Larger firms, especially those with stock exchange listings, often produce glossy brochures that go beyond the legal requirements, appearing to be more the product of the company's marketing department than its accounting department. The required financial statements normally present little more than an overview, supplemented by more detailed "notes to the accounts". Obviously, firms in different industries are likely to have different items appearing in their financial statements. This makes it difficult on occasion to compare and contrast firms. It is also the case that firms within the same industry may have different accounting policies, again making it difficult to compare them via their financial statements. However, the application of International Financial Reporting Standards, required or permitted in 160 countries, aims to improve comparability, accountability and transparency for firms. [www.ifrs.org/use-around-the-world/use-of-ifrs-standards-by-jurisdiction/]

The balance sheet

The balance sheet represents a snapshot picture of the firm's financial position *at a given point in time*. It is divided into two columns, with the firm's assets in one, and the claims on its assets (liabilities plus net worth) in the other. In the USA, the columns are depicted in terms of decreasing liquidity, with more liquid assets towards the top. **Current assets** are those expected to be converted to cash within a year. Less liquid assets—**fixed assets**, such as plant and equipment—are not expected to be converted to cash within a year. Similarly for claims on assets: **current liabilities** are those which

Balance sheets as at 31st May current year			
		Current year **£ '000**	*Previous year* *£ '000*
Fixed assets	Note		
Intangible assets	11	**15,816**	*10,901*
Tangible assets	12	**34,025**	*24,249*
Investments	13	**-**	*-*
		49,841	*35,150*
Current assets			
Properties for resale		**-**	*225*
Stocks		**188**	*263*
Debtors	14	**2,312**	*1,884*
		2,500	*2,372*
Creditors:			
Amounts falling due within one year	15	**(15,077)**	*(11,243)*
Net current liabilities		**(12,577)**	*(8,871)*
Total assets less current liabilities		**37,264**	*26,279*
Creditors:			
Amounts falling due after more than one year	16	**(9,949)**	*(3,393)*
Net assets		**27,315**	*22,886*
Capital and reserves:			
Called up share capital	18	**4,005**	*4,005*
Share premium account	19	**1,192**	*1,192*
Revaluation reserve	19	**2,916**	*2,969*
Profit and loss account	19	**19,202**	*14,720*
Equity shareholders' funds		**27,315**	*22,886*

The financial statements were approved by the Board of Directors on 20th September current year

Signed on behalf of the Board

xxxxx
yyyyy } Directors

Figure 2.3. UK balance sheet

must be met within a year. One example of a UK company balance sheet is presented in Figure 2.3. Note that typically figures are presented for both the current year and the previous year.

The income statement

Known in the UK as a **Profit and Loss account** (or 'P & L'), the income statement shows the results of events which have impacted a firm *over a given period of time*. As with the balance sheet, both current date and the previous year are stated. If a balance sheet is analogous to a photograph, an income statement is a video. Everything in this account stems from the revenues the company generates from its sales, i.e. **turnover**. Because profits are the difference between

Consolidated profit and loss account Year ended 31st May current year					
	Note		Current year £ '000		*Previous year* *£ '000*
Turnover continuing operations	2		**25,083**		*22,326*
Cost of sales and distribution costs			**2,776**		*3,089*
Player and match expenses			**11,839**		*12,197*
Administrative expenses			**4486**		*5,903*
			19,101		*21,189*
Operating profit on continuing operations	5		**5982**		*1,137*
Net interest payable	4		**(629)**		*(252)*
Profit on ordinary activities before taxation			**5,353**		*885*
Taxation charge on profit on ordinary activities	6		**(443)**		*(288)*
			4,910		**597**
Profit on ordinary activities after taxation					
Dividends—declared	7	**(481)**		*(160)*	
—less waived		-		*85*	
			(481)		*(75)*
Retained profit for the financial year	9		**4,429**		*522*
Earnings per share	10		**30.7p**		*3.7p*
Statement of total recognised gains and losses					
			Current year **£ '000**		*Previous year* *£ '000*
Profit for the financial year			**4,910**		*597*
Unrealised deficit on revaluation of freehold land and buildings			-		*(164)*
Total recognised gains and losses relating to the financial year			**4,910**		*433*
Movements on reserves are shown in note xy to the financial statements					
The notes on pages xx to zz form part of these financial statements					

Figure 2.4. UK profit and loss (income) statement

a firm's revenues and its costs, the costs of production, distribution, and any financing costs are deducted from turnover to derive profits. Figure 2.4 shows the profit and loss account for the same firm whose balance sheet considered previously:

The cash flow statement

Accrual accounting means that for any given accounting period funds paid out by way of expenses and those received for goods sold may not relate to the same items. For example, a company may purchase raw materials to use in its production process yet not pay for them for some months due to trade credit conditions. Also, firms sell goods or services but might not receive payment for some time due to credit arrangements. Therefore, the profit and loss account may not accurately reflect the actual flow of cash into and out of a company's coffers. Additionally, there may be non-cash items (such as depreciation) in a firm's other financial statements, which are book-entry items for which there is no commensurate flow of cash, hence the need for a cash flow statement which shows the actual sources and uses of cash during a given accounting period. Figure 2.5 shows the cash flow statement for the company already considered:

Consolidated cash flow statement Year ended 31st May current year					
	Note	**Current year £ '000**		*Previous year £ '000*	
Cash inflow from operating activities	21				
Returns on investments and servicing of finance					
Interest received		14		*29*	
Interest paid		(521)		*(221)*	
Interest element of hire purchase and finance lease payments		(11)		*(25)*	
Dividend paid		(75)		*(321)*	
Net cash outflow from returns on investments and servicing of finance			(593)		*(538)*
Tax paid					
Advance corporation tax		(19)		*(93)*	
Corporation tax		(215)		*(55)*	
			(234)		(148)
Investing activities					
Payments to acquire players' registrations		(8,409)		*(4,676)*	
Receipts from sales of players' registrations		4,035		*3,430*	
		(4,374)		*(1,246)*	
Payments to acquire tangible fixed assets		(8,432)		*(3,396)*	
Receipts from sales of tangible fixed assets		76		*64*	
Receipts from sales properties for resale		225		-	
		(8,131)		(3,332)	
Net cash flow from investing activities			(12,505)		*(4,578)*
Net cash flow before financing			(4,732)		*(1,053)*
Financing					
Net increase in obligations under hire purchase and lease contracts	23	1,606		*38*	
Bank loand drawn down	23	2,400		*2,600*	
Bank loan repayments	23	(750)		-	
Other loans drawn down	23	1,800		-	
Other loans repaid	23	(1,550)		-	
			3,506		*2,638*
(Decrease)/increase in cash and cash equivalents			(1,226)		*1,585*
The notes on pages xx to zz form part of these financial statements					

Figure 2.5. UK cash flow statement

2.6 Taxation and inflation

A significant amount of a business's resources is devoted to dealing with taxation. Some would argue that not only does business have to pay taxes, but they are also required to devote too much of their time and energies to dealing with the bureaucracy imposed by the tax authorities. Tax significantly affects a firm's decisions, especially its financial decisions. This can be all the more onerous because the tax system can often change annually. In the UK the Chancellor of the Exchequer announces changes to the tax system in the annual Budget speech to Parliament. This has traditionally taken place in March.

In principle, governments often prefer changes in taxation to be neutral, i.e. taxation itself should not be a major determinant in economic decision-making by individuals and business. The reality is that taxation tends not to be neutral, instead 'distorting' economic activity as individuals and businesses make decisions based on minimising their tax liability. To make sound financial decisions stakeholders in a firm need to remain well-informed about taxation. This is especially the case for the finance manager and those who invest in a firm. For small firms, the accountant is often the primary source of taxation information. So, what taxes must the firm take account of in its decision-making?

Taxes can be either direct or indirect; direct taxes are levied on incomes, whilst indirect take the form of a sales tax or value-added tax. In modern economies income taxes (including corporate income tax) are typically *progressive*: those better able to pay (considered as those with higher incomes) pay tax at a higher rate. Indirect taxes are *regressive*: people are taxed at the same rate regardless of their ability to pay. In what follows only the most basic features are covered; full details are much more complex, an indication as to why the services of accountants are so highly regarded and in high demand.

2.6.1 *Personal taxation*

In the UK individual incomes above a minimum level are subject to personal income tax. This threshold for an individual taxpayer (the 'personal allowance') was £ 12,570 in 2024–2025. Tax rates for income above this amount are shown in Table 2.1:

Table 2.1. Personal tax rates UK 2024–2025

Band	Taxable Income	Tax Rate
Personal allowance	Up to £ 12,570	0%
Basic rate	£ 12,571–£ 50,270	20%
Higher rate	£ 50,271–£ 125,140	40%
Additional rate	Over £ 125,140	45%

A different level of allowance exists for married couples and those older than 75. Full details are at www.gov.uk/income-tax-rates.

Taxable income may differ from an individual's actual income because some expenditures are allowable against tax. For example, payments into an occupational pension scheme are deducted from income before income tax is levied. Other deductions in the United Kingdom include charitable donations out of payroll. In the United States, items such as medical payments, some educational expenses and charitable donations are tax-deductible.

Some economies also like to distinguish between earned and unearned (or investment) income for taxation purposes. However, currently in the United Kingdom these sources of income are taxed equivalently. In the past, the top rate of personal income tax in the UK has been as high as 90%! In theory, both tax rates and allowances are adjusted to account for the rate of inflation. The reality is somewhat more *ad hoc*.

In addition to personal income tax there is also a payroll tax in many countries. In the UK this consists of National Insurance Contributions (NIC), paid by both the employer and employee. The calculations of NICs are more complex than for personal income tax (www.gov.uk/national-insurance/how-much-you-pay). NICs theoretically provide funding for the state pension, the National Health Service (NHS) and other welfare benefits. In truth, these monies have never been ring-fenced and have rarely provided enough money for the services they are meant to fund.

2.6.2 *Capital gains tax*

Investment income such as interest or dividend payments is subject to personal income tax. However, financial investments (e.g. shares and bonds) may also realise a capital gain when sold. A capital gain occurs when the sale price of an asset is above its purchase price. Capital gains realised through the sale of real assets (e.g. property) or securities and above a given threshold (the 'Annual Exempt Amount', currently £ 3,000) depend on whether the taxpayer pays the basic rate or higher rate of Income Tax, and whether the capital gain is on 'residential property', 'carried interest', or 'other chargeable assets'. Full details are at www.gov.uk/capital-gains-tax/rates.

2.6.3 *Corporate taxation*

Corporations are liable for taxation on their earnings in a similar manner to individuals on their incomes. As with income tax, corporation tax is levied on a graduated basis with some income tax-deductible. This latter includes (e.g.) capital allowances, but not entertainment expenses. The main rate of corporation tax on company profits in the UK is 25%. A lower rate of 19% exists for smaller companies, defined as companies with taxable profits below £ 50,000. More detail is at www.gov.uk/corporation-tax-rates.

2.6.4 *Inflation*

Inflation is confusing. If your favourite product has increased in price, there is a natural tendency to blame 'inflation'. While this *might* be the case it could also be increased demand which has caused its price to increase. To make sound economic and financial decisions we must distinguish clearly between an individual price increase and inflation.

Inflation is *a sustained increase in the general level of prices.* The general level of prices is a weighted average of the prices of all goods and services. In the United Kingdom this is usually proxied using the Retail Price Index (RPI) or the more internationally acceptable Consumer Price Index (CPI). It is entirely feasible for this average to be rising while the price of your favourite product is falling, or even vice versa. For there to be inflation the increase in the general level must be *sustained.* That means the general level of prices must be rising over a lengthy period, such as a year or more.

Before the Second World War (1939–1945) inflation and economic growth tended to move together over the course of the business cycle: when the economy was in recession the price level would also be in decline, i.e. **deflation**. The post-1945 era has been characterised by almost continuous inflation, especially in Western countries. Economic growth and inflation often coincide: as the pace of growth increases the rate of inflation also increases. In a recession there is typically **disinflation**: a reduction in the rate of inflation.

An increase in the price level is equivalent to a reduction in the value of a unit of currency: with inflation a pound (£) will buy you less today than it did a year ago; there has been a reduction in its purchasing power. Consequently, if a firm is making greater profits this year than the previous year, it becomes crucial to understand whether this is due to better performance by the company or simply the result of inflation. It may be that a company with higher profits *due to inflation* will find itself in a higher tax bracket. Although in some years tax thresholds have moved in line with the rate of inflation to offset such effects. One method of dealing with the impact of inflation is to distinguish between real and nominal values:

Nominal value is the value of a commodity (its price) in terms of the currency unit (e.g. pounds) today. Nominal values can be misleading as they do not account for inflation. Most company accounts are prepared on the (implicit) assumption that prices are stable. To remedy this nominal values can be converted into real values to account for the rate of inflation.

Real values are prices measured in terms of the value of the currency at a given point in time. Real values are calculated based on what the pound would buy in a given **base year**, e.g. 2000. While there have been attempts to prepare company accounts using real values no agreement has been reached as to the best way of achieving a consistent method of allowing for the distortions caused by inflation.

Despite inflation, financial calculations are usually performed in terms of nominal values. However, conversion to real values brings its own set of methodological issues, often raising more questions than were trying to be answered in the first place. While nominal values can be converted into real values by use of a proxy for the general price level, which index is used is a matter of choice but remains subject to criticism. CPI and RPI will give different real values.

The need for consistency is crucial. Making financial calculations for decision-making requires the use of either real values throughout or nominal values throughout. Like oil and water, real and nominal values do not mix well together. Which is why most people in finance continue to use nominal values.

It is important to note that a given rate of inflation does not affect all prices to the same degree. It is entirely possible for a business to find its product prices going up at a faster rate than its costs, with inflation positively impacting its profits. It is also possible for the reverse to occur. Inflation is confusing.

2.7 Sample questions (discussion)

(1) Some commentators regard the financial sector as little more than a casino for enriching the "already rich". Using the material in this Chapter explain fully whether you agree or disagree with this view.
(2) Select a stock market of your choice. Does the price data tend to move with news (the flow of information)? What degree of efficiency, if any, does this suggest?
(3) Select a country of your choice. How do UK rates of taxation compare with those of that country? Looking at basic macroeconomic data (GDP, inflation, unemployment, for example) is there any correlation?

Chapter 3

Value: Finance Foundations

The foundation of finance is value. A large part of the finance literature deals with defining and refining techniques for calculating value: i.e. valuation techniques. As seen, the objective of the firm is to maximise its value, so valuation techniques are an important part of the finance specialist's toolkit. The most important economic decisions are those which involve investment in real assets, whether by individuals or by companies, as the impact is long-lasting. The key to making such decisions lies in deciding whether a particular asset will add value.

3.1 Introduction

The concept of value has bedevilled philosophers since the dawn of time. There is a natural human instinct to value things subjectively; what one individual regards as a bargain another might consider exploitation. For economists value is reflected in the price of a commodity, determined by the interaction of supply and demand. This measure of value is objective and reconciles the conflicting subjective values of all 'players'—buyers and sellers—in the market.

The value of a commodity is not static: values change over time with changes in supply and demand conditions. Were this not the case, the value of a commodity today would be the same as its value in the future. But for that unique commodity known as *money* there is even more.

Imagine being given the choice of receiving (e.g.) either £ 100 today or £ 100 a year from now. Most people would opt for now. ("A bird in the hand...") Consequently, a given sum of money must be considered worth more if received today than if it were to be received in the future. Some of this is due to **uncertainty**; at its most extreme the receiver will not be sure that they will live to collect the money! It is one reason why people tend to prefer 'jam today' over 'jam tomorrow'. This is true even in the presence of deflation (negative inflation), when money's purchasing power increases over time.

The difference in the value of money at different points in time is reflected in the rate of interest, which is the market's determination of **the time value of money**. A given sum of money today—the **principal**—is equivalent in value to that amount plus what it might earn in interest payments. To understand value, we must begin by understanding interest. Interest can be earned on loans in two ways: **simple interest**, and **compound interest**.

3.2 The time value of money I: Simple interest

When the principal alone earns interest over the life of a transaction, the interest earned is referred to as **simple interest**. If:

P = the principal
r = the rate of interest (*per annum*, unless otherwise stated)
and T = the time period for which the principal is invested, then the interest due, I, is given by:

$$I = P * r * T \tag{3.1}$$

Example 3.1: Consider a sum of £ 1,000 invested at 8% for 60 days. The interest due will be:

$$I = P * r * T$$

$$I = £\,1{,}000 * \tfrac{8}{100} * \tfrac{60}{365} = £\,13.15$$

At the end of the period the investor would have both principal (£ 1,000) and interest (£ 13.15), giving a total of £ 1,013.15.

Because interest is usually stated on an annual (*per annum*) basis, we measure the time of the investment in annual terms (60/365). If interest was quoted semi-annually the time of the investment would be a number of six-monthly periods. This **dimensional consistency** is crucial. In more general terms it follows that:

$$FV = P + I \tag{3.2}$$

$$\textit{future value} = \textit{principal} + \textit{interest}$$

Going further, because:

$$FV = P + I$$

$$\text{and} \quad I = P * r * T, \ \text{then}$$

$$FV = P(1 + rT) \tag{3.3}$$

Example 3.2: What is the future value of £ 700 invested at 10% for 2 years?

$$FV = P(1 + rT)$$

$$FV = 700(1 + [0.1 * 2])$$

$$FV = £\,840$$

It is also possible to calculate **the rate of return** or **yield** on a simple interest loan. If:

$FV =$ the final sum received
$P =$ the principal invested
$T =$ the time period for which the principal is invested.

Then the rate of return (in %) earned over time T is given by:

$$\frac{FV - P}{P} * 100 \tag{3.4}$$

Because some simple interest loans may be for periods of less than one year, it is convenient to be able to calculate the rate of return on an *annualised* basis:

$$\frac{FV - P}{P} * 100 * \frac{365}{T} \tag{3.5}$$

Example 3.3: Consider a simple interest loan of £ 1,000 for 60 days. The principal, $P = £\ 1{,}000$, and $T = 60$ days.

If the loan has a future value, FV, of £ 1,013.15, then the rate of return is:

$$\frac{1{,}013.15 - 1{,}000}{1{,}000} * 100 = 1.315\%$$

and the annualised rate of return is $1.315 * \frac{365}{60} = 8\%$, as expected.

3.3 Simple interest: Applications

Perhaps surprisingly, there are several occasions in reality when simple interest is the norm.

3.3.1 *Term loans*

For both the individual and business the first source of (short-term) funding is often the overdraft facility at the bank. For smaller enterprises it may be the only source. The major pitfall of relying on overdraft facilities is that they may be removed 'on demand'. Although some businesses may resort to the use of credit cards, a better (cheaper) alternative is funding via term loans. These emerged in the USA during the 1970s, particularly for larger companies. Term loans are for an agreed sum (the **principal**) lent for a fixed term, involving both interest payments and a fee.

Interest on term loans is usually on a floating rate basis plus a margin. In Britain there are two key floating base rates:

- **Bank Rate** or **Base Rate** is the rate of interest the Bank of England charges to banks and other lenders. It therefore is an appropriate and convenient 'anchor' rate of interest for the rates charged by banks when they lend money. This applies particularly to mortgages, personal loans and overdrafts. It is the headline rate of interest reported as an instrument of monetary policy. As such it changes infrequently. Further details including as far back as 1694 can be found at www.bankofengland.co.uk/monetary-policy/the-interest-rate-bank-rate.

- Before June 2023 **LIBOR** (the London InterBank Offer Rate) was the key floating base rate for term loans and a globally-accepted benchmark for inter-bank short-term loans and USD-denominated derivatives. Originally established in 1986, LIBOR was calculated and published daily by the Intercontinental Exchange (ICE). However, following scandals surrounding its possible validity due to potential manipulation it was phased out. Many of the issues with LIBOR became apparent following the financial crisis of 2007–2008. Although it took years to agree on a replacement, LIBOR was ultimately replaced by the Secured Overnight Financing Rate (**SOFR**). This new benchmark for USD-denominated is considered superior to LIBOR, being based on observable transactions data whereas LIBOR was based on than estimated future borrowing rates. SOFR data can be found at www.newyorkfed.org/markets/reference-rates/sofr.

In both cases the margin charged should reflect the borrower's creditworthiness and the size of the transaction, both aspects of the risk involved. This is not always the case in practice. The margin will usually also include an additional amount to cover administrative fees.

Interest on term loans is typically calculated using simple interest. For LIBOR-related (or SOFR) transactions repayments may be based on quarterly or six-monthly intervals. Interest payable on such a loan would be:

$$Principal * [LIBOR + margin] * \left[\frac{loan\ period\ (days)}{365}\right] \tag{3.6}$$

3.3.2 *Discount claims*

Financial claims in the money market usually trade at a **discount**. They may offer zero interest; the only source of gain for the purchaser is the discount. The discount is the difference between the maturity value and the purchase price. Instruments traded on a discount basis include (e.g.) Bills of Exchange, Treasury Bills, UK local authority bills, Bankers' Acceptances, and commercial paper (especially in the USA). They are usually quoted on a *per annum* discount rate basis.

Example 3.4: Suppose there is a discount of 8% on a £ 100,000 bill for 91 days. Then the discount is:

$$£\,100{,}000 * \frac{08}{100} * \frac{91}{365} = £\,1{,}994.52$$

The purchaser would pay (£ 100,000 − £ 1,994.52) = £ 98,005.48 and receive £ 100,000 on maturity. The rate of return earned (i.e. the true yield) would be:

$$\frac{maturity\ value - purchase\ price}{purchase\ price} * \frac{365}{t} * 100$$

$$\frac{£\,100{,}000 - £\,98{,}005.48}{£\,98{,}005.48} * \frac{365}{91} * 100 = 8.16\%$$

Note that the true yield will *always* be higher than the discount rate.

For very large companies (turnover above £ 54 million) with a very strong credit rating and well-known (e.g. via a stock exchange listing), one alternative source of funds is through the issuance of **commercial paper (CP)**. Commercial paper is directly-issued short-term debt in the form of unsecured promissory notes, with a maturity between seven days and one year. CP is sold on a discount basis. These criteria are much the same as for the issuance of medium-term notes, which have a maturity between one year and five years.

Companies which issue CP or medium-term notes go directly to lenders via financial markets, thereby avoiding borrowing from financial intermediaries such as banks, a process referred to as 'disintermediation'.

Typically, a company will have an agreement with a syndicate of banks permitting it to issue CP at short notice and for varying amounts (a minimum of £ 100,000 is required) and for varying maturities (91 days or less is common in the UK; somewhat longer is the norm in the USA). In turn, the banks may keep the CP or, more likely, sell it on to investors. The funding cost to the company is lower than an overdraft, but the process is less flexible. The return to the investor is higher than that on government-issued bills, but with an associated corporate credit risk.

3.3.3 *Yield-quoted instruments*

Possibly the most well-known instrument quoted on a yield basis is the **Certificate of Deposit** (CD). These became popular in the USA during the deregulatory period of the 1980s and are a form of **time deposit** with a bank. A CD is essentially a receipt for a deposit made with an issuing bank, with a given principal, nominal rate of interest, date of issue, and maturity date. CDs are usually bearer instruments, and negotiable without endorsement.

The return offered on a CD is usually higher than on a similar government-issued bond, even though the risks are not perceived as greater due to the existence of the underlying deposit. There exists a fairly efficient secondary market for prime bank CDs, which is often used by companies as a haven for short-term surplus funds by way of an alternative to using 'traditional' bank deposits. Made by bankers and brokers in London, the active secondary market helps maintain liquidity, increasing the attraction of these claims.

The value of a (sterling) CD on maturity is:

$$Value = principal * \left(1 + \left\{r * \left(\frac{life\ in\ days}{365}\right)\right\}\right) \tag{3.7}$$

where r is the nominal interest rate. On the secondary market the value of the CD would be:

$$Value = principal * \left(\frac{1 + \left\{r * \left(\frac{life\ in\ days}{365}\right)\right\}}{1 + \left\{yield * \left(\frac{remaining\ days}{365}\right)\right\}}\right) \tag{3.8}$$

Note that the 'day count' differs from country to country: a year is counted as 365 days under UK financial market conventions; United States' dollar CDs are based on a 360-day year.

Example 3.5: Consider a 90-day CD with a nominal principal of \$50,000, issued at a nominal rate of interest of 8%. If the CD was bought at issue, held for 60 days, and then sold on a yield of 9%, the proceeds would be:

$$Price = \$50,000 * \left(\frac{1 + \left\{8\% * \left(\frac{90}{365}\right)\right\}}{1 + \left\{9\% * \left(\frac{30}{365}\right)\right\}} \right) = \$50{,}620.35$$

and the annualised rate of return would be $\frac{620.35*360*100}{50{,}000*60} = 7.44\%$

3.4 The time value of money II: Compound interest

3.4.1 *The mechanics of compound interest*

Albert Einstein is reputed to have said that "compound interest is the eighth wonder of the world". Unlike simple interest, compound interest works on the premise that interest payments are reinvested and earn the same rate of interest as the principal. Thus, compound interest means that both principal and interest earn interest. The use of compound interest can be traced far back into antiquity, even as long ago as c.1800 BC in Babylon. The best way to understand compound interest is by example.

Example 3.6:
P = the principal = £ 1,000
r = the rate of interest (*per annum*) = 10%
T = the number of time periods for which the principal is invested = 3 years.

The interest, I, due at the end of year 1, is given by:

$$I = P_1 * r * T$$

At the end of year 1 this gives a total of:

$$P_1 + I = £\,1{,}000 + £\,100 = £\,1{,}100$$

The investor now has P_2 = £ 1,100 as principal available for investment in year 2.

At the end of year 2 the interest earned will be:

$$I = P_2 * r * T$$

At the end of year 2 this gives a total of:

$$P_2 + I = £\,1{,}100 + £\,110 = £\,1{,}210$$

By the end of year 3 the wealth will have accumulated to:

$$P_3 + I = £\,1{,}210 + £\,121 = £\,1{,}331$$

Thus, interest earned over the three-year period is £ 331, which is £ 31 more than would have been earned via simple interest.

In general terms the following is true:

end year 1: $P(1 + r)$

end year 2: $P(1 + r)(1 + r) = P(1 + r)2$

end year 3: $P(1 + r)(1 + r)(1 + r) = P(1 + r)3$

Extrapolating gives:

$$FV_T = P(1 + r)^T \tag{3.9}$$

If interest is paid several times a year (say n times) then for dimensional consistency this formula must be adjusted accordingly:

$$FV_T = P(1 + r/n)^{T*n} \tag{3.10}$$

Example 3.7: Consider £ 1,000 invested for 8½ years at 17% *per annum*, compounded quarterly. Applying formula (3.x) gives:

$$FV_{8.5} = £\,1{,}000(1 + 0.17/4)^{8.5*4}$$

$$FV_{8.5} = £\,1{,}000(4.11705) = £\,4{,}117.05$$

The true or effective yield *per annum* is:

$$\frac{FV - P}{P} * 100 \tag{3.11a}$$

$$= \frac{P(1 + r/n)^{T*n} - P}{P} * 1001 \tag{3.11b}$$

$$= (1 + r/n)^n - 1 \tag{3.11c}$$

which, over T years gives a total yield of $= (1 + r/n)^{T*n} - 1$.

Practitioners in the markets find that some special cases of these formulas are more common than others. For example, it is useful to be able to switch easily between annual yields and semi-annual yields. If r_A = annual compound yield, and r_S = semi-annual compound yield, then:

$$(1 + r_A/100) = (1 + r_S/100)^2 \tag{3.12}$$

A simple example might be:

Semi-annual %	8.00	10.00	12.00	14.00	16.00
Annual %	8.16	10.25	12.36	14.49	16.64

A more general rule for conversion of different compounding periods would be $(1 + r_x/x)^x = (1 + r_z/z)^z$ where x and z refer to the number of time periods in which compounding occurs per year.

3.4.2 *Comparing simple and compound interest*

Although mechanically simple there is a power to compounding, S. Branch Walker of Stamford, Connecticut wrote to *Life* magazine illustrating this power by applying compound interest to a well-known tale from north American history:

> Sirs:
>
> The Indian who sold Manhattan for $24.00 was a sharp salesman. If he had put his $24 away at 6% compounded semiannually, it would now be $9.5 billion and could buy most of the now-improved land back.
>
> [*Life*, August 31, 1959]

It is relatively simple to calculate, either manually or with the use of a spreadsheet, how much \$9.5 billion in 1959 would be worth today if compounded semi-annually at 6%. The power of compounding can be illustrated using a simple example:

Example 3.8: Consider a principal, P, of £ 1,000. Suppose the rate of interest is 8% *per annum*. What will be the future value annually for the next ten years under both simple interest and compound interest?

Begin by constructing a table of values:

Year	1	2	3	4	5	6	7	8	9	10
Simple interest	1,080	1,160	1,240	1,320	1,400	1,480	1,560	1,640	1,720	1,800
Compound interest	1,080	1,166	1,260	1,360	1,469	1,587	1,714	1,851	1,999	2,159

Plotting this on a graph (Figure 3.1) clearly shows the power of compound interest:

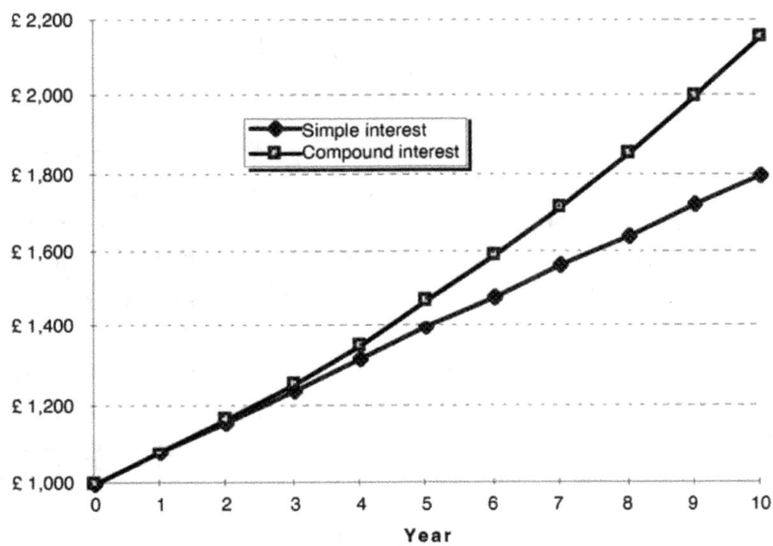

Figure 3.1. Simple and compound interest

Some simple deductions worth noting include:

(1) For relatively short periods of time there is little difference between the future value based on simple interest and that on

compound interest. This is probably why short-term debt tends to be on a simple interest basis, while medium- and long-term debt is on a compound interest basis.

(2) The longer the passage of time the more lucrative is compound interest *vis-à-vis* simple interest. With a higher rate of interest this difference becomes even more pronounced.

3.4.3 *Annuities*

Following examination of the future value of a single sum of money which earned interest, we now consider an **annuity**. This is an asset paying a fixed amount of money each year. The term (obviously) derives from payments originally being annual. An annuity can be more broadly defines as *a finite series of cash flows of a constant sum*. This applies equally to whether or not the payments are being received or if they are being paid. The future value of an annuity is calculated using the following formula:

$$FV = CF\left[\frac{(1+r)^t - 1}{r}\right] \tag{3.13}$$

where $CF =$ the amount of the periodic payment (cashflow), $r =$ the rate of interest, and $T =$ the lifespan of the annuity. Recall that T and r must be dimensionally consistent, so that if T is measured in years, then r represents the annual rate of interest; if T is measured in months, then r represents the monthly rate of interest; and so on.

Example 3.9: You are currently saving €100 each month. How much will you have saved in five years' time, with a savings account earning a rate of interest of 5 per cent *per annum*? Applying formula (3.13):

$$FV = €100\left[\frac{(1+0.05/12)^{5*12} - 1}{0.05/12}\right] = €6{,}800.61$$

This applies to an *ordinary annuity*, when the cash flows are paid (or received) at the *end* of each time period. An **annuity due** is an annuity when the cash flows are paid (or received) at the *beginning* of each time period. The future value of an annuity due is simply the future value of an ordinary annuity compounded for an additional time period. For an annuity due over T periods:

$$FV_T^{due} = FV_T^{ordinary}(1+r) \tag{3.14}$$

3.5 Net present value and internal rate of return

3.5.1 *Net present value*

Compounding calculates what a sum of money today will be worth at some time in the future. It is a process of looking forward along a timeline. **Discounting** is a reversal of that process, looking backwards along a timeline. Discounting allows us to calculate present value: what a sum of money to be received in the future is worth today. Figure 3.2 shows this diagrammatically:

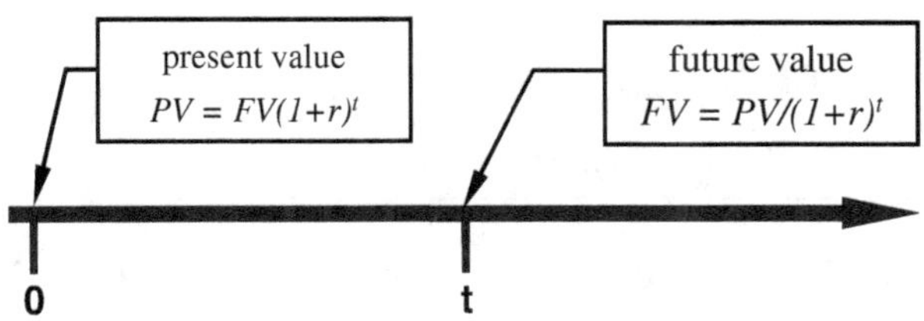

Figure 3.2. Value timeline

Compounding gives $FV = PV(1+r)^t$. Inverting the compounding formula gives:

$$PV = \frac{FV}{(1+r)^t} \tag{3.15}$$

This shows that an amount of money, FV, to be received T periods from now, is equivalent to PV today, if the rate of interest is r. The rate of interest is a measure of the cost of acquiring funds—i.e. the 'cost of capital'—known in this context as the **discount rate**. It is apparent from the formula that there will be an inverse relationship between the discount rate and present value: higher discount rates will lead to lower present values, and *vice versa*.

Ceteris paribus, a rational investor should be indifferent between receiving PV today or FV in the future. Equation 3.13 can be rewritten as:

$$PV = FV\left[\frac{1}{(1+r)^t}\right] \tag{3.15a}$$

where $\left[\frac{1}{(1+r)^t}\right]$ is the **discount factor** or **present value interest factor**, PVIF. In the days before spreadsheets and hand-held calculators were ubiquitous, textbooks used to print tables of discount factors in Appendices as an aid to calculation.

Example 3.10: Find the present value (PV) of £ 2,000 due in 6 years if interest rates are 10% per annum, compounded semi-annually. Using equation 3.15:

$$PV = \frac{FV}{(1+r)^t}$$

$$PV = \frac{£\,2{,}000}{(1+0.1/2)^{6*2}} = \frac{£\,2{,}000}{1.79586} = £\,1{,}113.67$$

Example 3.10 shows calculation of present value for a single future cashflow. The same is true of the next example, a slightly more complex form:

Example 3.11: If current interest rates are 10% per annum, what is the PV of a debt of £ 2,500 due in 8 years, with interest being compounded at 6% quarterly?

(i) Calculate what the debt will be worth when it is due, i.e. its FV

$$FV = P(1+r)^t = £\,2{,}500(1+0.06/4)^{8*4}$$
$$= £\,2{,}500(1.015)^{32} = £\,4{,}025.81$$

(ii) Calculate the PV of the debt from i)

$$PV = \frac{FV}{(1+r)^t} = \frac{£\,4{,}025.81}{(1+0.1)^8} = £\,1{,}787.07$$

The next degree of complexity is the present value of a **stream of cashflows**, i.e. cashflows occurring over a number of years (or periods) in the future. Present value provides a common denominator by which future sums of money in different times can be summed. The present value of each of the individual future cashflows are calculated and then added. If C_t represents the cashflow during year t from an investment that lasts for T years, then the present value of that investment will be:

$$PV = -C_0 + PV(C_1) + PV(C_2) + PV(C_3) + \cdots + PV(C_T) \tag{3.16a}$$

$$PV = -C_0 + \frac{C_1}{(1+r)} + \frac{C_2}{(1+r)^2} + \frac{C_3}{(1+r)^3} + \cdots + \frac{C_T}{(1+r)^T} \tag{3.16b}$$

$$PV = -C_0 + \sum_{t=1}^{T} \frac{C_t}{(1+r)^t} \tag{3.16c}$$

Note that the initial cashflow is negative: 'traditional' investments have a negative cashflow (payment) in the first period leading to positive net cashflows in successive periods. The use of *net* cashflows in each period means that instead of 'Present Value' (PV), **Net Present Value** (NPV) is used. Ignoring the sign of the first-period cashflow:

$$PV = \sum_{t=0}^{T} \frac{C_t}{(1+r)^t} \tag{3.17}$$

The 'rule' for making decisions is that investments offering a positive Net Present Value are worth undertaking, because they will add value to the business by the exact amount of the NPV.

> **Example 3.12:** You have the opportunity to invest £ 9,000 which over the next five years will return £ 1,000, £ 2,000, £ 3,000, £ 5,000, and £ 4,000 respectively. If the discount rate (i.e. the prevailing rate of interest) is 12% is this a worthwhile investment?

First, set up the NPV equation, e.g. (3.b):

$$NPV = -£\,9{,}000 + \frac{£\,1{,}000}{(1+0.12)} + \frac{£\,2{,}000}{(1+0.12)^2} + \frac{£\,3{,}000}{(1+0.12)^3} + \frac{£\,5{,}000}{(1+0.12)^4} + \frac{£\,4{,}000}{(1+0.12)^5}$$

$$NPV = -£\,9{,}000 + £\,892.86 + £\,1{,}594.39 + £\,2{,}135.34 + £\,3{,}177.59 + £\,2{,}269.71$$

$$NPV = -£\,9{,}000 + £\,10{,}069.88 = £\,1{,}069.88$$

Because NPV is positive this investment will add value and is therefore worthwhile.

3.5.2 *'Special' cashflow streams*

Present value calculates what a stream of future cashflows is worth today. However, different investment projects offer different cashflow profiles, in terms of both amounts and of timing. While many investments offer cashflows with uneven payments in terms of amount, some financial investments have a time-profile which offers a more even stream of payments.

3.5.2.1 *Perpetuities*

Loans usually have a finite lifespan—'who wants to lend forever?'—at the end of which the principal is repaid. However, some loans are perpetual loans, or **perpetuities**, with no repayment of principal. A perpetuity is an annuity with an infinite lifespan, i.e. a stream of (equal) cashflows which never terminate. It is amazing to find that there are perpetual loans in existence, because the implication is that the lender is never repaid the amount lent. The most well-known of all perpetuities in existence are British government undated bonds, commonly known as **Consols**. Originally issued in 1751 by the British government, the aim was to use the proceeds to redeem bonds from other, smaller issues which had been used to finance the war, thereby consolidating the government's debt. Hence, 'Consols'.

Consider an infinite series of cashflows, with a view to finding its present value. Formula (3.16a) is extended to:

$$PV = PV(C_1) + PV(C_2) + PV(C_3) + \cdots + PV(C_\infty)$$

However, because a Consol is a form of annuity, the coupon payments are the same in each time period: $C_1 = C_2 = C_3 = \cdots = C_\infty = C$. Thus:

$$PV = \frac{\mathrm{C}}{(1+r)} + \frac{\mathrm{C}}{(1+r)^2} + \frac{\mathrm{C}}{(1+r)^3} + \cdots + \frac{\mathrm{C}}{(1+r)^\infty} \quad (3.18a)$$

$$PV = \sum_{t=1}^{\infty} \frac{C_t}{(1+r)^t} \quad (3.18b)$$

which simplifies to:

$$PV = C/r \quad (3.18c)$$

Example 3.13: You have been offered the chance to purchase a British government Consol paying an annual coupon of £ 1,000. If the prevailing rate of interest (the discount rate) is 7%, what is the most you would be willing to pay for this Consol?

Using equation 3.18c:

$$PV = C/r = \text{£}\,1{,}000/0.07 = \text{£}\,14{,}285.72$$

The most you should be willing to pay for this Consol is its present value, £ 14,285.72.

If market conditions priced a Consol lower than its present value, then it would be considered 'underpriced', hence a bargain. Such a discrepancy would be noticed by a large number of people, who would try to buy the Consol, increasing demand for it, thus driving up its price towards its present value!

Similarly, if market price were above the present value, then the Consol would be considered 'overpriced', and holders of Consols would likely try to sell their holdings. This would increase the supply, driving down the price of the Consol towards its present value.

Whenever players in a market find an opportunity to make a gain from a pricing discrepancy like these, their actions form a process of **arbitrage**, which eliminates the original profitable opportunity by bringing the market back to equilibrium. Ultimately, arbitrage ensures that prices of market-traded assets are 'true', in the sense that they match their present value.

There is also the possibility of a perpetuity whose payments (coupons) are growing at a constant rate, g. The present value of such a perpetuity can be calculated using a variant of the above, known as Gordon's growth model:

$$PV = \frac{C}{r - g} \tag{3.19}$$

This model is discussed fully in Chapter 5, where its application to equity can be seen fully.

3.5.2.2 *Annuities*

An annuity is a contract providing a series of fixed payments for a given period of time. Thus, an annuity offers the holder a fixed income on a regular basis for a given number of years. Because of this, annuities are often purchased out of the proceeds of an individual's pension fund at the time of retirement: to provide the individual with their pensionable income through their retirement.

Typically, an annuity pays at the end of each period and is known as an **ordinary annuity** or a **deferred payment annuity**. Some, however, pay out at the beginning of each period. These are known as an **annuity due**. In what follows assume annuities to be ordinary annuities, unless explicitly stated otherwise.

The formula for calculating the present value of an annuity is a variation on the standard present value formula. If the regular annuity payment is A for T periods, and the discount rate is r, then the present value of the annuity $PV(A_{r,T})$ is:

$$PV(A_r, T) = \sum_{t=1}^{T} \frac{A}{(1+r)^t} = A\left[\sum_{t=1}^{T} \frac{1}{(1+r)^t}\right] \tag{3.20}$$

The term in square brackets is the **present value interest factor for an annuity** (PVIFA) and can be adjusted to:

$$PV(A_r, T) = A\left[\sum_{t=1}^{T} \frac{1}{(1+r)^t}\right] = \frac{1 - \frac{1}{(1+r)^T}}{r} \qquad (3.21a)$$

which simplifies to $$PV(A_r, T) = \frac{1}{r} - \frac{r}{r(1+r)^T} \qquad (3.21b)$$

One way to view the present value formula for an annuity is to regard it as equivalent to the difference between the present values on two Consols. An annuity over T years is equivalent to the present value of a Consol with its first payment at the end of the current year (e.g. year 0) minus the present value of a Consol whose first payment is at the end of year T:

$$PV(A_r, T) = \frac{A}{r} - \frac{A}{r}\left[\frac{1}{(1+r)^T}\right] \qquad (3.22)$$

Example 3.14: How much should you pay for a five-year annuity offering annual payments of £ 1,000, if the discount rate is 8%?

Using equation (3.21a) $PV(A_r, T) = A\left[\sum_{t=1}^{T} \frac{1}{(1+r)^t}\right]$

$$PV(8\%, 5) = £\,1{,}000\left[\sum_{t=1}^{5} \frac{1}{(1+0.08)^t}\right]$$

$$PV(A_{8\%,5}) = £\,1{,}000[3.99271] = £\,3{,}992.71$$

The most you should be willing to pay for this annuity is £ 3,992.71. As with the case of perpetuities, any discrepancy between its price in the market and its present value will be eliminated by arbitrage.

3.5.3 *The Internal Rate of Return (IRR)*

The present value technique offers a useful means for valuation. By adjusting future cashflows to a common denominator, present value, provides a basis for comparison of cashflows with very different profiles. Present value calculation also allows us to model the value of an asset and compare the outcome with what is on offer in the market. In short, present value is a very useful tool which allows appraisal of potential investments. But there are alternatives.

One alternative for appraising investment is the Internal Rate of Return (*IRR*). This is particularly useful when the discount rate is difficult to determine. The *IRR*, also labelled by the Greek letter rho (ρ), is best defined as *that discount rate which makes the present value of an investment equal to zero.*

The main advantage of *IRR* is that it gives a single number summarising the merits of an investment. The number is intrinsic to the investment: it depends solely on matters internal to the investment, its cashflows. It does not depend on anything external to the investment. Mathematically, *IRR* derives from the same formula as present value. The difference is that the discount rate is now the unknown, and *NPV* is set to zero. Thus, if C_t represents the net cashflow from the investment during period t:

$$NPV \equiv 0 = -C_0 + \frac{C_1}{(1+\rho)} + \frac{C_2}{(1+\rho)^2} + \frac{C_3}{(1+\rho)^3} + \cdots + \frac{C_T}{(1+\rho)^T} \tag{3.23a}$$

$$NPV \equiv 0 = \sum_{t=0}^{T} \frac{C_t}{(1+\rho)^t} \tag{3.23b}$$

There are a number of possible methods to solve this and find the value of ρ. However, they all boil down to various forms of 'trial and error'.

IRR 'by hand'

A traditional method, employed extensively in the time before spreadsheets were ubiquitous. The steps are:

1. Arbitrarily select a value for ρ, e.g. 10%. Calculate *NPV*.
2a. If $NPV > 0$, then *IRR* must be a larger value. Select a larger value for ρ and recalculate *NPV*. Go to 2a or 2b as appropriate.
2b. If $NPV < 0$, then *IRR* is below the value for ρ originally selected. Select a lower value and recalculate *NPV*. Go to 2a or 2b as appropriate.

Ultimately this iterative process should focus in on finding ρ. But it is time-consuming and, in an era of spreadsheets, unnecessary. It is worth noting that it is this same process which the spreadsheet performs 'under the hood'.

Example 3.15: You have the opportunity to invest in a project with the following cashflow profile:

C_0	C_1	C_2	C_3
−£ 1,000	£ 500	£ 400	£ 300

Begin by substituting the cashflows into equation (3.23a)

$$NPV \equiv 0 = -C_0 + \frac{C_1}{(1+\rho)} + \frac{C_2}{(1+\rho)^2} + \frac{C_3}{(1+\rho)^3}$$

to obtain:

$$NPV = -£\,1{,}000 + \frac{£\,500}{(1+\rho)} + \frac{£\,400}{(1+\rho)^2} + \frac{£\,300}{(1+\rho)^3}$$

Following step 1, select a trial value for ρ of 10% and calculate:

$$NPV = -£\,1{,}000 + \frac{£\,500}{(1+0.1)} + \frac{£\,400}{(1+0.1)^2} + \frac{£\,300}{(1+0.1)^3}$$

$$NPV = -£\,1{,}000 + £\,454.55 + £\,330.58 + £\,225.39$$

$$NPV = -£\,1{,}000 + £\,1{,}019.72 = £\,19.72$$

A positive NPV requires a higher value for ρ to obtain $NPV = 0$. However, the NPV is not greatly above zero, so try 12%:

$$NPV = -£\,1{,}000 + \frac{£\,500}{(1+0.12)} + \frac{£\,400}{(1+0.12)^2} + \frac{£\,300}{(1+0.12)^3}$$

$$NPV = -£\,1{,}000 + £\,446.43 + £\,318.88 + £\,213.53 = -£\,978.84$$

A negative NPV, so the value of ρ which will give $NPV = 0$ must lie between the two values we have used. Continued trial-and-error of values for ρ between 10% and 12% ultimately yields the solution (10.65%), but is costly in terms of time, effort and convenience. One alternative is to plot a graph and interpolate as shown in Figure 3.3:

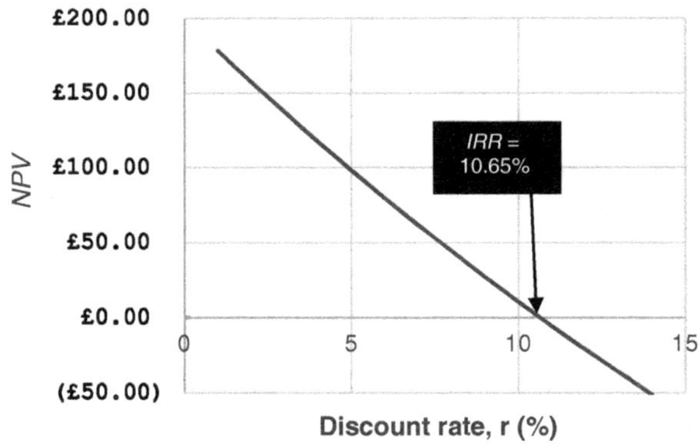

Figure 3.3. *NPV* vs discount rate

IRR 'by spreadsheet'

Today, the best alternative is to make use of a spreadsheet application, such as Microsoft Excel, Numbers (by Apple), or Google Sheets. The spreadsheet works via a series of iterations beginning with your trial 'guess' as to the value of ρ. The format of the formula entered is

$$=NPV(\text{guess, values})$$

where **guess** is the starting value for ρ, and **values** refers to the cashflows under consideration. If you do not enter a value for 'guess' the software automatically uses a default value of 10%.

While this method has much to commend it, there drawbacks to its use in many circumstances. These are not considered here as the focus is on the *mechanics* of valuation methods. Chapter 6 examines the application of both *IRR* and present value techniques to capital budgeting and weighs up the relative merits of each method for that purpose.

3.6 Sample questions

(1) You require an annual return on your financial investments of 8% per annum. What would you be prepared to pay for an annuity that offered you £ 1,000 every six months for the next two years?

(2) As Chief Financial Officer for a medium-sized business you are negotiating with a provider of mobile telephone services. They have offered you a wide array of (bewildering!) tariffs from which you can choose. If the prevailing rate of interest is 8%, which of the following will you recommend to your Board of Directors:

(a) A single payment of £ 120,000 now.
(b) £ 200,000 payable at the end of 5 years.
(c) £ 12,500 a year forever.
(d) £ 20,000 for each of the next 10 years.
(e) £ 7,500 next year, increasing thereafter by 5% a year forever.

(3) What is each of the following investments worth today assuming an annual discount rate of 7%?

(a) A 3-year maturity "B" rated corporate bond with 4% annual interest payments and a principal value of £ 1,000
(b) 50 shares in a company whose senior debt is rated "BBB". The stock pays dividends today of £ 0.75 and has expected dividend growth this year and forever of 3%.
(c) A level pay mortgage on a small retail shop with a maturity of 5 years and quarterly payments of £ 55.
(d) A £ 900 one-year term loan for a start-up company (with interest payable at the end of one year) and priced at 12-month LIBOR with a margin of 150 basis points where 12-month LIBOR is 3.5%.
(e) A British government Consol paying £ 60 annually.

Which investment is the least risky? Explain fully.

(4) Peter Piper expects to retire in 10 years and would like to accumulate £ 100,000 in his pension fund. If the annual interest rate is 6% (Annual Percentage Rate), how much should Peter put into his pension fund each month in order to achieve his goal? (Assume that Peter will deposit the same amount each month.)

(5) You have won the lottery, and can choose any one of the following prizes:

(a) £ 100,000 now
(b) £ 180,000 at the end of 5 years
(c) £ 12,000 every year forever

If the interest rate is 12%, which prize is the most valuable? Which would you pick?

(6) You are considering a number of possible long-term savings accounts at local banking institutions. You decide that you will place £ 1,000 of your hard-earned savings in this account. What will its value be in 12 years if it grows by 8% each year, compounded quarterly? What if it were compounded monthly?

(7) You are interested in accumulating £ 50,000 in 20 years to help finance your (early!) retirement. How much money would you need to save each month in an account offering 8%?

(8) You decide to pay into your bank account £ 1,000 every year for the next 10 years, starting today (total of 10 annual payments of £ 1,000). Five years after the last payment, you decide to withdraw £ 1,000 every year for 10 years. If the annual interest rate is 5%, how much money do you have left on your bank account right after the last withdrawal?

Chapter 4

Sources of Finance I: Debt

4.1 What is debt?

Throughout human history debt has had a bad name. It has been impugned by luminaries from William Shakespeare to Charles Dickens, as well as in many religious texts. Yet today almost everyone has some debt, as does business, and almost all governments.

Debt is an obligation or liability to pay—usually money—to someone else. The obligation arises because a loan has been taken, and the lender must be paid back on or before a given date, usually with **interest**: a series of payments in addition to repaying the amount lent. But the language can be confusing: someone who has borrowed money is said to be 'in debt' (not considered good) or alternatively they can be said to have 'acquired credit' (considered more positively). Put simply, debt requires the payment of interest and repayment of **principal** (the amount borrowed). However, there are also forms of debt where either one of these characteristics is hidden or non-existent. Thus, a zero-coupon bond does not require the payment of interest.

A contract of debt is a legal form of IOU. It includes details of the borrower, the amount borrowed, and the terms of the loan with regard to frequency of repayments, amount of interest, transferability, security, and any penalties upon default. Yet a wide range of different forms of debt exist. The following considers some of the main forms. For convenience, the final section of this chapter provides notes on the characteristics of the major forms of debt.

Bank-originated debt

Bank-originated debt is usually short- or medium-term. For an individual the first type of debt experienced is the bank overdraft facility or debt via the use of credit cards. Additionally, individuals who go into Higher Education will often borrow via the system of Student Loans.

Bank debt is also available to corporate borrowers, who may also acquire debt in other ways. In Chapter Three we considered the **term loan**, a loan for a fixed term, for an agreed sum (principal), involving both interest payments and a fee. Term loans typically incur interest on a floating rate basis plus a margin. And, while an overdraft might be secured on all the assets of a company, security for a term loan is normally restricted to specific assets or the project being financed. One possible alternative to providing security on its own assets is for the company to obtain a guarantee from a third party, such as the parent company if the borrower is a subsidiary.

Trade financing

Trade financing refers to 'invoice discounting' or 'receivables financing', both forms of **factoring** where a company sells the debts it is owed to a specialised factoring agent at a discount, e.g. 80%. The business receives money immediately, but less than the full amount of the value of the debts it has sold. This is not the same as **trade credit**, where a business pays for commodities some time after it has received them. If trade financing occurs transnationally it is referred to as 'forfaiting'.

Asset financing

The raising of funds using the company's existing assets. This includes 'sale and buy-back' or 'sale and lease-back' schemes, or the acquisition of funds for the purchase of a specific asset, including the leasing of assets as well as hire-purchase agreements.

Sale and buy-back is an arrangement by which a company sells an asset, such as land, buildings or equipment, agreeing to repurchase the asset at a specified future date for a given price. Such an arrangement is common in financial markets where it is typically referred to as a 'repurchase agreement' or 'repo'. Sale and lease-back' is an arrangement by which a firm sells an asset to another firm (typically a financial institution) and simultaneously agrees to lease it back, usually for its own long-term use.

4.2 Issuers of debt

Debt is issued by those who wishing to borrow funds, sometimes directly from lenders, and sometimes indirectly via issuing bonds in the financial markets. Debt issuers consist of two main elements: corporations and government. Corporations can be from any sector of the economy, including banks and other financial institutions. Government operates in most countries at a range of levels. In the UK bonds are issued by central government, government agencies and municipalities. It is also possible for overseas governments and corporations to issue bonds in the UK domestic financial markets.

The largest bond market in the world is in the USA. Valued at more than $51 trillion, of which US federal government bonds comprise the largest issue, about 50%. This amounts to almost 40% of the global bond markets. The federal government paid more than $534 billion in interest in 2022. The UK bond market is the fifth largest, with some $4.3 trillion outstanding, comprising 3% of global bond markets. [World Economic Forum, April 2023]

Bonds

In the UK bonds used to be known as 'loan stock'. A **bond** is a debt contract issued by a company or the government in exchange for the funds being borrowed. Each bond stipulates the terms of the loan: time to maturity, interest payments, and principal repayment. The fixed face value of the bond is the redemption value of the bond, and reflects the amount of principal, referred to as **par** value.

While bonds usually carry a fixed rate of interest, there are also bonds paying variable rates of interest. Because they have historically paid a fixed rate of interest they are still referred to as 'fixed income' in the financial markets. The interest payment is called the **coupon**, which is stated as a percentage of par. This is not usually the same as the yield of the bond, which varies with market conditions. In UK domestic markets, semi-annual interest payments are common on a 365-day basis. Some bonds carry little or no interest payments but are offered for sale at a substantial discount. With 'deep discount' or 'zero coupon' bonds the incentive to purchase is the prospect of a capital gain. The former offer a coupon lower than prevailing market rates while the latter pays no coupon at all.

As with all financial instruments, the yield on offer must adequately reflect the risk involved. Bonds issued by a higher risk corporation must offer the investor a higher rate of return by way of compensation. In a financial system where markets are efficient this is ensured via arbitrage. If a bond considered to be relatively high risk did not offer enough yield to match investors' expected rates of return, it would fail to find enough buyers: its price in the market would fall and its yield rise in consequence. Similarly, in the event of a bond offering a rate of return exceeding the investors' expectations: demand would increase, increasing the bond price, and its yield would decline.

Bonds are also 'segmented' in terms of their time to maturity. While the term **bonds** in its broadest sense refers to all debt instruments, more narrowly it refers to long-term bonds: those with a maturity of more than ten years. Bonds of intermediate maturity (between one and ten years) are known as **notes**, while **bills** are short-term bonds with a maturity of up to one year.

Corporate risk reflects the creditworthiness of the corporate borrower. An industry of credit rating agencies (CRAs) developed to independently rate bond issues, particularly in the United States, where the most well-known are S&P Global (Standard & Poor), Moody's, and Fitch Ratings. Known as "The Big Three" these companies dominate the market. S&P Global's ratings run from AAA down to D, while Moody's system runs from Aaa to C. Table 4.1 illustrates:

Table 4.1. Bond rating categories

S&P	Moody's	Fitch	
AAA	Aaa	AAA	Very high quality *Ability to repay interest and principal is very strong*
AA	Aa	AA	
A	A	A	High quality *Slightly more susceptible to changes in economic conditions than higher ratings*
BBB	Baa	BBB	
BB	Ba	BB	Speculative *High risk exposure to adverse conditions*
B	B	B	
CCC	Caa	CCC	Very poor
CC	Ca	CC	
C	C	C	Reserved for income bonds on which no interest is being paid
D		RD	In default; payment of interest or repayment of principal is in arrears
		D	
+ or −			Modifiers for the above categories, to show relative standing within a category

'Investment grade' bonds are the top four categories of bond ratings: for S&P Global this is BBB and above; for Moody's, Baa and higher.

While some bonds are non-tradable (i.e. not traded in a formal market) there is greater incentive for business to issue tradable bonds, which are more attractive to potential lenders due to increased liquidity. In the UK there are two main forms of short- and medium-term debt securities which companies can issue: **commercial paper** (see Chapter Three) and **medium-term notes (MTNs)**. Usually with a maturity between five and ten years, MTNs can theoretically have almost any maturity. In contrast with conventional bonds MTNs can be offered continuously via brokers rather than a full issuance at one time. There is no obligation for MTNs to be underwritten by the broker (e.g. an investment bank). MTNs are traded over-the-counter (OTC) and can offer either fixed or floating rate interest payments.

In the UK long-term debt consists of:

- **Debentures.** In the UK these are usually secured against company assets. In the USA a debenture is unsecured.
- **Unsecured loan stock.** These may be convertible, i.e. they have an option to convert to ordinary shares. And
- **Preference shares.** Known in the USA as preferred stock, these offer some aspects of equity and some of debt, without strictly being either. (See Chapter Five for detail).

Historically, UK banks have been reluctant to lend long-term, although there has been some amount of senior debt (secured) and mezzanine debt (typically unsecured). Senior debt is repaid by the company before mezzanine debt.

It is possible for loan and bond contracts to incorporate a 'restrictive covenant', which constrains the future activities of management. These restrictions might impact future dividend policy, limit the amount of further borrowing the firm might undertake, or restrict the firm's financial ratios—such as the debt service ratio—to within certain ranges.

Some bonds incorporate 'call provisions'. These are a form of option which, after a given passage of time, enables the company to buy back (i.e. 'call') the bond before its date of maturity, for a predetermined amount known as the 'call price'. The call price is usually at or near its par value. From the firm's perspective, this allows the firm to redeem its debt at an artificially low price if interest rates decline, and bond prices rise to the extent that they are above the call price. However, this is unlikely if the market is efficient.

Bond investors

In both theory and in practice anyone with enough funds can invest in bonds, either when first offered or from the markets via the use of a stockbroker. In the UK the largest sector bond investors are the financial institutions, especially pension funds and insurance companies. Bonds, especially government bonds, are also bought by investment funds, banks and building societies. Individual investors also invest in bonds, both corporate and government bonds, although this is a much smaller proportion of the bond market, both in the UK and elsewhere. Additionally, UK bonds are often purchased by a range of overseas investors.

4.3 Valuing debt

Bonds of finite maturity

The value of a bond traded on a secondary market is determined in the same way the price of any tradable commodity is determined: by the interaction of supply and demand. This gives rise to an equilibrium price for the bond, from which its **yield-to-maturity** (*YTM*) can be calculated. This is simply an application of the formula for finding the Internal Rate of Return (*IRR*):

$$P_B = \left[\sum_{T}^{t=1} \frac{c_t}{(1+k_d)^t}\right] + \left[\frac{M}{(1+k_d)^T}\right] \tag{4.1}$$

Where

P_B is the current price of the bond
c_t is the coupon payment at time t
M is the maturity value of the bond (i.e. the repayment of principal, par), and
k_d is the yield-to-maturity, i.e. the cost of debt capital (hence k_d) to the firm.

For most bonds the coupon payment is constant: $c_t = c_{t+1} = c$. Thus, the bond is an annuity, and the present value of the coupons can be calculated using formula (3.18). This assumes the bond has a finite lifespan at the end of which the bondholder receives M.

This same formula can be used to determine a price for a bond *not* traded in financial markets. The coupon and par will be known, and the yield on a traded bond with similar characteristics can be used as a proxy for k_d. These values can be substituted into formula (4.1) to derive the price of the bond.

Example 4.1: A ten-year bond is paying a coupon of 8 per cent annually on a par of £ 10,000. If the prevailing yield on bonds of similar risk is 6 per cent, the price of the bond will be given by:

$$P_B = \left[\sum_{T}^{t=1} \frac{c_t}{(1+k_d)^t}\right] + \left[\frac{M}{(1+k_d)^T}\right]$$

$$P_B = \left[\sum_{T}^{t=1} \frac{(\pounds\,10{,}000) * (0.08)}{(1+0.06)^t}\right] + \left[\frac{\pounds\,10{,}000}{(1+0.06)^{10}}\right]$$

$$P_B = \left[\sum_{T}^{t=1} \frac{(\pounds\,800)}{(1+0.06)^t}\right] + \left[\frac{\pounds\,10{,}000}{(1+0.06)^{10}}\right]$$

$$P_B = \pounds\,5{,}888.07 + \pounds\,5{,}583.95 = \pounds\,11{,}472.02$$

Because the prevailing yield in the market is below the coupon, the bond is selling at a *premium* ($P_B >$ par).

There is an inverse relationship between bond yields and bond prices: when yields fall, prices rise, and *vice versa*. Note that because the coupon payment is fixed, the prevailing yield adjusts to reflect market conditions.

Bonds of infinite maturity

For bonds of infinite maturity ('perpetuities') formula (4.1) reduces to:

$$P_B = \frac{c}{k_d} \tag{4.2}$$

In Chapter 3 Consols were shown as an example of a perpetuity. These were all ultimately redeemed by the UK government in 2015. The only other example of perpetual debt in the UK was the issue of Permanent Interest-Bearing Shares (PIBS) by building societies in the 1990s. The mutual nature of many building societies means that PIBS are as close as possible to holding equity in building societies. PIBS are fixed interest securities with no redemption date. While there is a (perpetual) stream of regular coupon payments, the investment can only be realised by selling the PIBS on the open market (the London Stock Exchange) and making a capital gain or loss.

However, the market for PIBS is relatively small, and it is not always easy to find a buyer (or seller). Because of this, PIBS need to offer a relatively high yield to make them attractive to investors.

Example 4.2: Going back in time, consider a Consol offering a 4% coupon. 'Current' market yields are at 8.56%. Given that Consols were usually quoted in the *Financial* Times in units of £ 100 nominal value, with the price in pounds and fractions (usually thirty-seconds) of a pound, what price would you be prepared to pay?

$$P_B = \frac{c}{k_d} = \frac{(\pounds\,100) * (0.04)}{0.0856}$$

$$P_B = \frac{c}{k_d} = \frac{\pounds\,4}{0.0856} = \pounds\,46.7289 \approx \pounds\,46.73 \approx \pounds\,46\frac{23}{32}$$

4.4 Not-quite-debt: Hybrids

Debt hybrid securities are those which mainly have the characteristics of debt, but also those of other types of security, e g. equity.

4.4.1 *Convertibles*

A convertible bond has the same characteristics as any other bond, with an added attraction: it offers the holder the opportunity to exchange the bonds for ordinary shares in the same company within a given time frame. The bondholder is usually required to pay a conversion fee.

The value of a convertible bond will *always* be at least equal to the value of a non-convertible bond with otherwise identical characteristics. In most cases, the value of the convertible will exceed that of its non-convertible 'twin' as it is essentially a combination of the non-convertible bond and a call option on the company's ordinary shares. Consequently, the value of the convertible bond should equal the value of its non-convertible twin plus the value of the call option. By way of corollary, this means that the yield on a convertible bond will be *less* than that on its non-convertible twin.

4.4.2 *Warrants*

A warrant is an option issued by a corporation on its own shares. Similar to convertibles in many ways, warrants do not offer the holder the right to exchange bonds for equity but are a self-contained option (written by the company) to purchase the company's equity at a predetermined price (the 'exercise price'). Warrants are usually issued as a complement to bonds. If the warrant is exercised the holder still has their existing bonds intact, in addition to the newly-acquired ordinary shares. Because of the separability, a warrant is typically a cheaper form of finance than an equivalent convertible bond.

4.4.3 *Sukuk* (صكوك)

Also known as "*sharia*-compliant bonds", *sukuk* are a relatively recent addition to the panoply of financial claims. Because *sharia* (Islamic law) does not permit the paying or receiving of interest (*riba*), *sukuk* developed as an alternative to traditional 'western' bonds. *Sukuk* may not be used to finance business activities in prohibited sectors: e.g. gambling, alcohol, pork, unethical activities, etc. *Sukuk* are structured to receive profits from business ventures, rather than interest. This is often achieved by having *sukuk* having partial ownership in property or some other tangible assets. Like bonds, *sukuk* investors receive a stream of payments until the maturity date, when they are paid back their original investment (without guarantee). The ownership aspect of *sukuk* gives some resemblance to equity, but like traditional bonds all regular payments cease when the *sukuk* expires. In some respects, *sukuk* are regarded as similar to preference shares.

In 2014 the UK became the first non-Islamic country to issue *sukuk*. The UK Treasury issued £ 200 million priced at the same level as UK gilts (government bonds): 2.036%. Linked to rental income from UK government property, the *sukuk* issue was 11.5 times oversubscribed.

4.5 Interest rate determination

So far, this chapter has considered the institutional aspects of debt financing and some valuation models. The key to understanding debt fully is to understand what underpins the price of debt: interest.

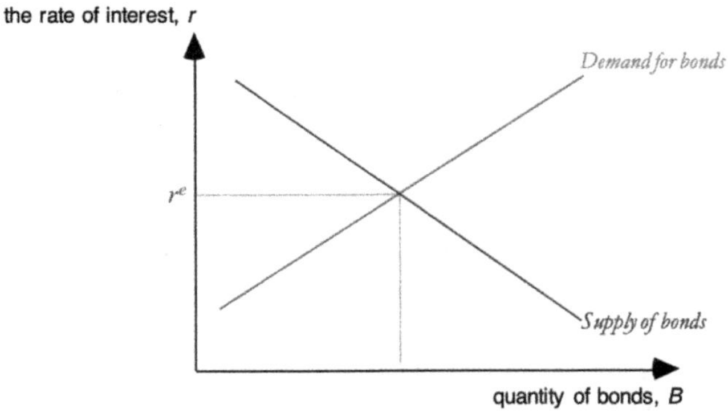

Figure 4.1. Interest rate determination, supply and demand for bonds

All economic exchanges can be categorized according to the timing of the two sides of the trade

- **Spot transaction:** both sides of the transaction occur simultaneously.
- **Credit transaction:** goods or services are supplied now in return for payment in the future.
- **Forward transaction:** current payment is made for goods or services to be supplied in the future.

For a credit or forward transaction to be feasible additional incentive beyond the usual gains from trade is required. This typically takes the form of interest. Interest may be regarded as the price of credit (loanable funds, or debt). Like the price of any other marketable commodity, the rate of interest will normally be determined by the interaction of supply and demand as shown in Figure 4.1.

In one sense, the rate of interest can be considered as rent paid for the (temporary) use of other people's money. This is consistent with a dictionary definition of interest. But there is more to interest than a 'pure rental rate of money'. There is also the need for interest to include some form of compensation for risk. Five risk categories exist:

(1) **Default risk** is the likelihood that the issuer of a security will fail to honour their obligation, either in part or completely. Security issuers with a long history of meeting their obligations punctually are less risky than those issued by less reputable characters.

The amount of default risk may also be influenced (positively) by the time to maturity of a security.

(2) **Purchasing power risk** relates to uncertainty about the purchasing power of the currency. Results from inflation (or deflation). Because interest is usually expressed in nominal terms, a security's real rate of interest will depend upon movements in the general price level. Following Irving Fisher [1930], $R_{real} = R_{nominal} - \Pi$, where R represents the rate of interest (with appropriate subscript) and Π represents the (expected) rate of inflation. Also, the greater the volatility of the rate of inflation the more purchasing power risk is assumed.

(3) **Marketability risk** depends upon the likelihood that a security can be realised (sold) without significant danger of loss. This relates directly to the existence and efficiency of any secondary markets. Silber [1970] argues that this should explicitly include factors such as imperfect knowledge by participants in the secondary market. He also notes that the existence of a small number of traders in the market accounts for the fact that an attempt to sell a large block of the security requires a significant decrease in price (hence greater loss than otherwise). Also known as **reversibility risk**, because it relates to the ability of the investor to reverse their decision.

(4) **Capital value risk** occurs because of uncertainty attached to the security of the principal. The greater the likelihood of the market value of a security fluctuating over time the greater the degree of capital value risk involved. Ryan [1978] says this kind of risk is especially likely if an investor's assets have longer to maturity than their liabilities.

(5) **Income risk**: Clayton and Osborn [1965] argue this occurs because interest income cannot be predicted with certainty beyond the maturity and call dates of a security. Ryan [1978] says this type of risk is most likely when an investor's assets have a shorter maturity horizon than their liabilities.

The key components which make up the nominal rate of interest are:

(i) A 'pure rental rate' of money to compensate the lender for the opportunity cost. Because this component involves no payment for risk it is also referred to as the risk-free rate of interest

(ii) An inflation risk premium to compensate the lender for possible losses of purchasing power
(iii) Other risk premiums to compensate for the other kinds of risk considered above.

Interest might also include a profit margin (for the lender). This margin often appears as the 'spread' between borrowing rates and lending rates, something particularly noticeable at high street banks. The size of the spread depends upon the current degree of competitiveness in the financial markets. The more competition the smaller the spread.

As a final note, central banks, such as the Bank of England, (or the government if the central bank is not independent) focus their policy on an interest rate target as a means of controlling economic activity. This might distort market interest rates in the short-run. In terms of the yield curve (next section) central bank activity operates at the short end of the market.

4.6 The Term Structure of Interest Rates (TSIR)

Economists talk about '*the* rate of interest' despite the existence of a whole spectrum of interest rates. This is not myopic, but a conversational convenience used because interest rates tend to move together. The **Term Structure of Interest Rates** refers to the relationship between the yields on similar securities of differing maturity but otherwise similar risk. The yield curve can be represented graphically as shown in Figure 4.2:

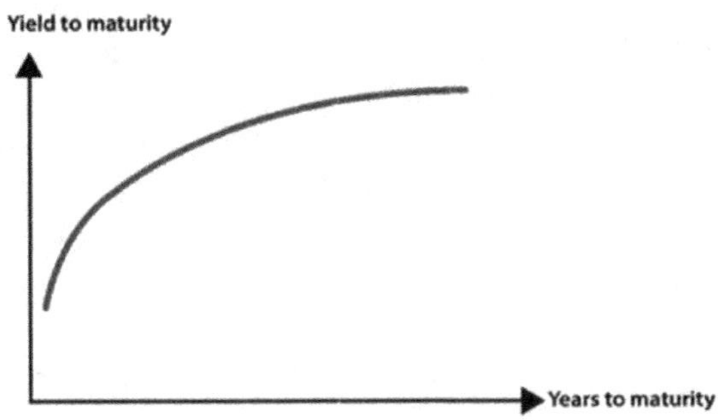

Figure 4.2. The Term Structure of Interest Rates (stylised)

Most commonly experienced is an upward-sloping yield curve. But it is also feasible for a yield curve to be downward-sloping, U-shaped, or even humped (inverted U). Actual yield curves based on data for can be found at the relevant central bank website (e.g. The Bank of England, European Central Bank, Federal Reserve, etc).

A good understanding of the TSIR is crucial when it comes to debt funding by corporates. It helps in deciding whether to borrow long, medium or short by providing both a basis for comparison and a key to understanding how interest rates might change in the future. It is also important because central banks use yield curves to help determine monetary policy. Central banks impact short-term yields by buying or selling short-term bonds as part of their weaponry in the fight to control inflation. There are also those who argue that the slope of the yield curve (the difference between long- and short-term yields) provides a 'leading indicator' in calculating the probability of recession.

There have been a number of competing theories trying to account for the shape and slope of the yield curve. There is also a substantial body of empirical work, yet still there remains little consensus. Despite this, the shape of the yield curve changes in a stable, predictable manner as the economy moves through the various stages of the business cycle. Arguably the most intuitively plausible theory of the yield curve is based on the difference between short- and long-term yields being due entirely to expectations.

4.6.1 *The Expectations Hypothesis*

Originally posited by Nobel Laureate John Hicks [1946], long-term rates of interest are hypothesised as an average of *expected* short-term rates due to *arbitrage*. Expectations play the predominant role in determining interest rates. It has a very intuitive appeal.

The major premise is that bonds of different maturities are close (or, at best, 'perfect') substitutes. For example, suppose investors have a choice between putting their funds into a two-year bond offering a rate of interest of R per annum, or buying a one-year bond for the current year paying r_1 and then placing the proceeds during the second year into a further one-year bond which is expected to be paying r_2. The existence of arbitrage means that:

$$(1+R)^2 = (1+r_1)(1+r_2) \tag{4.3}$$

For equilibrium the yield on a two-year bond and two one-year bonds should be equivalent. To see that this must be the case, consider what happens if the two-year bond offered a greater return than the two one-year bonds:

$$(1+R)^2 > (1+r_1)(1+r_2)$$

Here, there would be no incentive for a rational investor to purchase the two one-year bonds. Investors would place their funds in the higher-yielding two-year bond. This would lead to increased demand for two-year bonds, causing an increase in their price, and consequently a decline in their yield, R. Simultaneously, there would be a decline in demand for the one-year bonds, lowering their prices, and raising their yields, r_1 and r_2. This process—**arbitrage**—will continue until equilibrium is achieved, as shown in equation (4.3).

This can be extrapolated to more time-periods, where the yield on a long-term bond is an average of expected (spot) yields on short-term bonds. Letting ${}_er_t$ represent the (expected) yield on a single-year bond held during year t gives:

$$(1+R)^T = (1+{}_er_1)(1+{}_er_2)(1+{}_er_3)\cdots(1+{}_er_T) \tag{4.4}$$

The Expectations Hypothesis suggests that forward rates of interest should be equal to the expected future (spot) rates. Attempts to validate the Expectations Hypothesis empirically focus on testing forward rates as predictors of future spot rates.

The shape and slope of yield curve implied by the Expectations Hypothesis depends on the interest rate expectations held by market participants:

- If short-term rates of interest are expected to rise, an upward-sloping yield curve (Figure 4.1) should be expected.
- Declining expected short-term rates imply a downward sloping yield curve.
- A period of rising expected short-term rates followed by a decline in expected short-term rates implies a 'humped' yield curve.

Thus, the Expectations Hypothesis offers a plausible explanation for a yield curve of *any* shape. Its primary weakness is that it offers no explanation for *shifts* in the position of the yield curve.

4.6.2 *Liquidity Preference*

The Expectations Hypothesis assumes there will be 'players' (buyers and sellers) in the market who will restore or maintain equilibrium through arbitrage. Hicks [1946] went further by extending his theory of the term structure to include Keynes' [1936] theory of Liquidity Preference. Originally a theory of the demand for money, Hicks' extension treats the term structure as determined jointly by liquidity preference and expectations.

This approach is based on the premise that there is a liquidity risk premium positively associated with a security's time-to-maturity due to risk aversion. The longer a security has before maturity the higher the liquidity premium investors will require to compensate them for the additional risk. Consequently, the actual forward rate must exceed the expected short-rate by a *risk-premium* to compensate for the loss of liquidity. Equilibrium occurs when:

$$\begin{aligned}(1+R)^T &= [1+({}_1r_1+\lambda_1)][1+({}_1r_2+\lambda_2)]\\ &\quad\times[1+({}_1r_3+\lambda_3)]\cdots[1+({}_1r_T+\lambda_T)]\end{aligned} \tag{4.5}$$

Each $({}_1r_t+\lambda_t)$ represents the yield for period t. This consists of ${}_1r_t$, the temporal-risk-free current expected (spot) rate of interest in period t plus $\lambda_1<\lambda_2<\lambda_3<\cdots<\lambda_T$, the monotonically-increasing liquidity risk premiums for the relevant time-periods, 1 through T. It follows that forward rates may not necessarily equal expected future (spot) rates, the difference being the liquidity risk premium. While there have been many attempts to empirically compare the Expectations Hypothesis with Liquidity Preference theory, Kolb argues:

> The conflict between these two theories has yet to be resolved. If there is a liquidity premium, causing forward rates and expected future spot rates to diverge, it is probably quite small. At any rate, both parties agree that forward rates are intimately related to expected future spot rates. [1985: 140]

i.e. the λ_t are very small.

The slope of the yield curve implied by Liquidity Preference depends on the interest rate expectations held by market participants, plus the degree to which they either enhance or offset the increasing liquidity premiums. The monotonically-increasing liquidity premiums make an upward-sloping yield curve more likely than under the Expectations Hypothesis alone. Liquidity Preference offers a plausible explanation for a yield curve of *any* shape, while suggesting that there is a greater likelihood of it being upward sloping. Like the Expectations Hypothesis, the primary weakness of the Liquidity Preference explanation is that it offers no explanation for shifts in the position of the yield curve.

4.6.3 *Hedging pressure/preferred habitat/market segmentation*

One alternative theory of the TSIR is by Jack Culbertson. Based on empirical testing of the Expectations Hypothesis, he concluded:

> ... the explanation of broad movements in the term structure of interest rates must be sought principally in factors other than behavior governed by interest rate expectations. [1957: 502]

Culbertson's view stems from the notion that similar securities of different maturity are *not* good substitutes. Thus, markets for loans of different maturities are 'segmented': what happens in the market for short-term assets has little or no relationship to the market for medium- or long-term assets. Yields on short-term assets can be either higher or lower than yields on assets of longer maturities, depending entirely on the supply and demand conditions independently prevailing in each of those markets.

A key underlying cause of market segmentation is market dominance by large institutional investors, such as life insurance companies and pension funds. The theory of financial intermediation explains that institutions will hedge in the form of **maturity matching** (to reduce risk): if an institution's liabilities are predominantly long-term, the assets they choose to hold will also be long-term. Institutions will find little in maturity switching to commend it. They may be said to have a 'preferred habitat': a maturity range of the market in which they prefer to operate, regarding other maturity ranges as poor substitutes.

In its strongest form this theory argues that investors tend to operate exclusively within a maturity range, regardless of possible arbitrage profits that might be made by maturity switching as suggested by the Expectations Hypothesis. Under this scenario, markets will be segmented strictly with participants at one part of the yield curve not participating elsewhere on the curve.

In a weaker, looser form, although investors might have a preferred habitat there may be circumstances when they could be persuaded to switch to a different maturity range and take advantage of potential arbitrage profits. UK pension funds provide an historic example. Such funds tend to hold small, relatively insignificant fractions (less than 4%) of their portfolio in liquid assets, preferring ordinary shares and long-term bonds. Immediately following the oil crisis of 1973–1974, they dramatically increased their holding of liquid assets to nearly 17% of total holdings. A similar shift occurred during the oil crisis of the very early 1980s.

In an empirical study of the market for government securities, Michaelsen found support for the role of expectations as well as for market segmentation:

> It would appear that most portfolios, and especially those of large institutional holders, have indeterminate rather than fixed liquidation dates, their maturity composition remaining roughly constant over time or changing in response to forces other than the passage of time. [1965: 461]

Malkiel took a more institutional view, which came to represent the hedging pressure approach:

> The bond market is not segmented in any absolute manner. ... we found that most investors substituted broadly among securities over wide ranges of the yield curve in accordance with their expectations ... [yet] strong maturity preferences are present in both sides of the market. A valid version ... asserts simply that many buyers and sellers must be paid differentiated premiums to induce them to move from their preferred maturities.
>
> [1966: 180]

Weaker versions—**preferred habitat** theories—have tried to integrate market segmentation with expectations. This includes the work of Modigliani and Sutch [1967]. According to McCallum these attempts are

> ... characterized by a multiple horizon market and a willingness on the part of investors to acquire non-horizon instruments within a range called a habitat. It is argued that the existence of habitats gives the market a continuity which is not present in the segmentation theory. [1975: 307]

4.6.4 *Clientele effect*

More recent attempts to explain the yield curve, such as the **clientele effect**, have tried to account for institutional factors. This considers the effect of taxation on the yield curve and is an extension of the preferred habitat concept. It depends on the fact that different groups of investors face different tax treatments. This influences their habitat on the yield curve. Especially relevant is the distinction between tax on interest and tax on capital growth, which is likely to impact investor preference for bonds of different maturities.

4.6.5 *Afterthoughts*

Clearly, there is little consensus among economists regarding explaining the TSIR. David Laidler favours a variant of the Expectations Hypothesis:

> The most satisfactory theory of the term structure appears to be one that rests on the proposition that (with suitable adjustment for risk) expected holding-period yields on assets of various maturities tend to be equalized by the market. ... This expected holding-period yield, of course, includes capital gains and losses made over the period. [1985: 91]

But lack of consensus does not imply lack of validity. Empirical evidence suggests that each theory has some validity during specific economic conditions: Liquidity Preference seems to work well when interest rates are expected to remain relatively stable; when interest rates are generally high, and expected to fall, the Expectations Hypothesis seems to be valid; there is mixed evidence on Market Segmentation.

There have been attempts to bring together elements from each of the foregoing into a 'grand unified theory' of the TSIR. These attempts have been very technical and are yet to offer greater insight than the basic theories above. Much of the work has built on that of Cox, Ingersoll and Ross [1981, 1985] recognising that there are many factors which shape the yield curve. Their model attempts to encompass all the elements of earlier theories outlined above.

Finally, it is worth noting that central banks, such as the Bank of England, (or the government if the central bank is not independent) focus policy on an interest rate target as a means of controlling economic activity, especially inflation. This may distort interest rates in the short-run. In terms of the yield curve this means that central bank activity tends to operate on the short end of the market.

4.7 Key sources of debt

These brief note-form pointers refer to the main characteristics of the various forms in which debt exist. It is meant to be illustrative, rather than fully inclusive.

4.7.1 *Short- and medium-term debt*

1. Overdraft facilities

- Borrower can borrow up to an agreed amount at will (very informal)
- Repayable on demand
- Market-related interest (percentage above bank's base lending rate)
- Possible fee
- Security is usually both a fixed (on premises or given assets) and floating charge (on remaining assets)

2. Term loans

- Formal agreement, normally from 2–5 years
- Possible 'grace period', e.g. no principal repayments for 2 years
- Equal periodic payments; some possibility of flexible repayments, so 'bullet' or 'balloon' payments and prepayments possible
- Market-related interest (percentage over base rate)
- Arrangement fee usually involved
- Security on specific assets typical; third-party guarantees possible
- Covenanting on ratio compliance: debt/equity, current ratio

3. Guarantee facilities

- third-party guarantee arranged for a fee by the bank
- used to establish relationship with other lender(s) with access to low-cost financing (usually for specific purposes)

4. Multiple option facilities (MOFs)

- Combination facility: such as term loans and overdraft
- May require third-party guarantees, letters of credit, etc.

5. Syndicated facilities

- where a single borrower deals with many lenders (in syndicate)

6. Asset financing

- Leasing and Hire purchase: allows use of an asset financed by another party
- Sale and Lease-Back/Buy-Back

7. Trade financing

- Factoring: purchase by specialist of trade debts
- Invoice discounting/receivables financing
- Forfaiting: usually on a cross-border transaction

8. Revolving underwriting facility (RUF)

- International source, started in early 1980s
- Issue of short-term paper under a medium-term underwriting commitment
- An institution—e.g. a bank—underwrites fund access at specified rate (normally linked to a base rate)

9. Trade credit

- Deferred payment allowed by trading counterparty (such as a supplier)
- Might include an early payment discount

10. Bills of Exchange

- Primarily used in international transactions
- Roughly equivalent to a post-dated cheque
- "An unconditional order in writing, addressed by one person to another, signed by the person giving it, requiring the person to whom it is addressed to pay on demand, or at a fixed or determinable future time, a sum certain in money to or to the order of a specified person, or to bearer." Bills of Exchange Act 1882, section 3

11. Acceptance credit facilities

- Raising funds by discounting of Bills of Exchange

12. Deferred tax payments
13. Medium-term bank loans

- Available in the UK since 1970s
- Usually 1–5 years
- Repayments: lump-sum/periodic...
- Usually variable interest: 2–5% over base rate
- Arrangement fee
- Security: fixed or floating charge
- Covenant

14. Government-guaranteed loans

- Available in the UK since 1981
- Government guarantees 70% to banker in event of default
- Possibility of moral hazard

15. Merchant bank financing

- Primarily the provision of risk or venture capital
- Loans typically for more than £ 250,000

16. Investors in Industry (3i)

- Parent company of Industrial and Commercial Finance Corporation (ICFC)

- Formed in 1983 to provide finance (through loans and equity capital) for small- and medium-sized enterprises (SMEs)
- Original ownership: 85% by clearing banks, 15% by Bank of England.
- Listed on the London stock exchange

17. Export finance: primary sources

- Overdrafts
- Short-term fixed-interest loans
- Discounted Bills of Exchange
- Acceptance credits
- Export Credits Guarantee Department (ECGD)

18. Debt security issue

- Direct financing: avoids banking sector (lower costs)
- Originally unavailable due to Banking Act 1979, which restricted short-term fund access without Bank of England authority
- Banking Act 1987: allowed for development of sterling commercial paper (CP) market
- Conditions for issuing debt securities:
  (a) net assets of at least £ 25m, and shares or debt traded/listed
  (b) debt securities issues, transferable in minimum amounts of £ 100,000
  (c) maturity: CP 7 days < 1 year; medium-term notes: 1–5 years

4.7.2 *Long-term debt*

1. Bank (and other institutional) loans

- Term loans
- Interest: fixed, floating; around 3–6% margin over base rate
- Arrangement fee: normally around 1%
- Security: property, other tangible assets ('senior debt')
- Sometimes unsecured ('mezzanine debt')

2. Debentures

- Also known as 'loan stock' (in USA debentures refers to unsecured loan stock)

- Usually secured via trust deed, so there is a prior floating charge on the company assets
- Mortgage debenture is a debenture secured on property

3. Unsecured loan stock

- Unsecured, so yield higher than on debentures
- Covenants usual

4. Preference shares

- Considered debt/equity hybrid, with many varieties
- Typically involves some form of ownership
- Periodic payment known as a 'dividend'
- Ranks after debt in claims on the company
- Yield higher than on unsecured debt securities

4.8 Sample questions

(1) A three-year bond is issued paying an annual coupon of 9%. It has a maturity value of £ 100. If the current yield-to-maturity for three-year bonds is 12%, what should be the issue price?

(2) A five-year bond has a $10,000 par value and pays semi-annual coupons of $1,000. The bond's yield-to-maturity is 8%.

   (a) How much would you be prepared to pay for the bond?
   (b) What should the price of the bond be one year from now?
   (c) If all happens as expected, what rate of return would an investor expect if they buy the bond today and sell it in one year?

(3) (a) In October 2010, you purchased a French government bond for €100 (face value) which pays a 1% coupon (nominal interest rate) every year until 2020. Today, in October 2014, similar bonds are issued at a 2% interest rate. What is the value of your bond today?

(4) If the value of the French bond in (3) was €100 today what would be its implicit yield-to-maturity? How would that differ if the French bond was €105 today?

(5) The Very Large MultiNational Corporation is a highly-respected blue-chip conglomerate with an "AAA" credit rating. They are known to have issued 10-year bonds at a par of $1,000, with a coupon of 12 per cent payable semi-annually.

(a) Two years after the bonds were issued the prevailing rate of interest on bonds issued by "AAA"-rated companies fell to 8 per cent. At what price would you expect the bonds to sell at that time?

(b) Suppose that instead of falling to 8 per cent, the prevailing rate of interest had risen to 14 per cent. What would be the expected price of these bonds?

(c) Given the conditions in (a), and assuming they were followed by an 8 per cent rate of interest for the next eight years, what would happen to the price of the Very Large MultiNational Corporation's bonds over time?

Chapter 5

Sources of Finance II: Equity

5.1 What is equity?

Chapter 4 examined debt as one key source of funds for companies. An investor who *lends* to a company receives a return regardless of how well the company is performing. An alternative is to pay for a 'piece of the action'—investing in a company for a share of its ownership and receiving a share of the profits. This is *equity funding*. While the holder of debt has a legal right to be repaid this is not the case for the holder of equity. Equity is considered riskier than debt and would be expected to generate a higher rate of return.

Equity is often equated with 'ordinary shares', although more broadly it implies ownership. The word derives from the root 'equals', implying that any individual share in the company is identically equal to any other share in the company (of the same class). Equity involves part-ownership of the company, according to the number of shares held by the investor. The equity-holder (or shareholder) is a part-owner of the company, entitled to participatory rights. These normally include:

- voting entitlement
- dividend participation
- return of capital in the event of the company's liquidation.

5.1.1 *Types of share capital*

While equity refers to any form of ownership, including in property, there are two main forms in the corporate context: **ordinary shares**, and **preference shares**. **Shares** are often regarded as synonymous with stock exchange activities, but this is only true for companies with a stock exchange listing, i.e. those with a very large capitalisation. The largest number of companies are private limited companies (denoted by the term 'limited' in their title). Listed companies are a subset of public limited companies (denoted by 'plc'). Under the various Companies Acts, all limited liability companies can issue shares (see Chapter One).

5.1.1.1 *Ordinary shares*

These comprise the fundamental equity investment in a company. Every corporation starts life with an issue of ordinary shares, which represents ownership of the company. Shareholders receive a certificate indicating their (part-) ownership. This can be either tangible or digital. The rights and obligations of shareholders are defined within the company's Articles of Association. Ordinary shares ('common stock' in the United States) normally offer one vote per share. It is feasible to have various classes of ordinary shares with different voting rights, but this is not always welcomed by professional investors. Consequently, for many years there has been a general convergence towards a single class of ordinary shares, particularly for listed companies. *This may change.* Under new rules proposed in July 2024 by the UK's Financial Conduct Authority (FCA), companies will be allowed dual class share structures. This is part of a raft of measures which aim to make share listing easier in London, which also includes the ability to make more decisions without a shareholder vote. These measures are aimed at making the London financial markets more competitive with those in New York (in particular).

Because they are part-owners of the company, ordinary shareholders have voting rights in accordance with the Articles and Memorandum of Association. Shareholders vote for a Board of Directors to act as their representatives ('agents') at the company's Annual General Meeting. At the AGM shareholders also (effectively) appoint auditors who, as representatives of the shareholders, are required to check the periodic reports and accounts produced by the Board of Directors for shareholders. The Board is expected to deal with the company's senior management on a regular basis.

As owners of the company shareholders own any profits. Any portion of the profits distributed to shareholders is in the form of a **dividend**. Profits not distributed remain within company coffers as **retained** earnings. Ordinary shareholders do not have an automatic entitlement to a dividend but usually vote on them at the AGM based on the Board's recommendation. Dividends can only be paid out of current or retained earnings. In the event of liquidation, shareholders are paid after all other prior claims have been met from the assets of the business. Shareholders have full rights to the remainder.

5.1.1.2 *Preference shares*

Once a source of long-term finance, preference shares, declined in popularity in the UK following changes to the system of corporation tax in 1966. At that time many companies converted their existing preference shares into debentures.

Legally, preference shares ('preferred stock' in the USA) cannot legally be the only form of equity within a company, although it is possible for them to represent the majority of equity capital. In common with ordinary shares, preference shares pay a dividend, which is not a right, but depends on the recommendation of the Board. Preference shares are usually non-participatory (no vote) and consequently are not always regarded as equity, being seen as closer to debt.

Preference shares have priority over ordinary shares in the payment of dividends, hence they are often paid at a pre-defined rate. This rate may be fixed or adjustable (e.g. based on some floating interest rate). **Participating** preference shares permit the holder to a share in the firm's earnings over and above the pre-defined rate. Preference shares are usually issued as **cumulative** preference shares, whereby any dividend shortfall that occurs is accumulated and must be paid in full before ordinary shareholders can receive any dividend.

In the event of liquidation preference shareholders are paid out to the face value of the preference shares, before ordinary shareholders but after debtholders. Preference shareholders have no further claims on the company. Preference shares are generally redeemable, but only from fresh capital or retained earnings. They may also be 'puttable'—the holders may have the right to insist upon redemption at a predetermined rate on given dates.

Preference shares can also be issued on a **convertible** basis, where they can be converted into ordinary shares at a predetermined rate and on specific dates, but at the option of the preference shareholder.

Preference shares are considered less risky than ordinary shares and consequently have a lower expected return. Convertible preference shares are often issued as **mezzanine finance** to venture capitalists.[1] If the company is doing well the preference shares will be converted into ordinary shares, whereas if the firm performs badly a fixed return is received until such time as there is improvement, or the company is liquidated.

5.1.1.3 *Other points of note*

In addition to the main types of equity there are also equity-related instruments known as **hybrids** which possess characteristics of both debt and equity.

As seen in Chapter 4, **convertible debt** is issued as straight debt with a par value, paying interest, and with a known maturity. However, after a period of time they are *convertible* into ordinary shares at the holder's option at a predetermined rate. Conversion rights are generally protected against dilution (resulting from the issue of more shares).

Conversion rights on corporate bonds acts as an incentive to ensure sufficient investor demand. The conversion option is considered valuable in itself, so convertibles offer a lower coupon (interest payments) than 'pure' debt with similar characteristics. If the company is perceived as successful, then investors may value the conversion rights highly, in which case they may be prepared to accept lower interest payments in the meantime.

In the 1970s **zero-coupon convertibles** were a favoured method of funding for a number of high-flying property and asset-stripping companies. These bonds often possess 'put' and 'call' provisions, giving the company the right to redeem the bonds on given dates if (e.g.) interest rates drop significantly after the date of issue.

---

[1] Mezzanine finance is hybrid financing, combining features of both debt and equity. It typically sits between senior debt and equity in the capital structure.

An equity **warrant** is a long-dated option to purchase a predetermined number of shares at a predetermined price (or prices) at a given time (or range of time) in the future. These are often issued as sweeteners, attached to ordinary bonds to reduce the coupon rate. Typically, option dates are measured in years, although it is feasible to find perpetual warrants. These normally possess call features.

5.2 Raising equity capital

For a small company incorporating (registering for limited liability) at Companies House there must be at least one director, although there is no longer a requirement for a company secretary. Directors are legally responsible for running the company. There must also be at least one shareholder, who could also be a director. The rights and obligations of shareholders are noted in the Articles of Association.

At its initial incorporation the company raises equity capital. Funds are provided by the original shareholders in exchange for ordinary shares. Although a new incorporation can initially issue any number of ordinary shares, each assigned an identical 'nominal' value (or 'par'), smaller limited companies often begin with an authorised share capital of £ 100. This bears no relation to the actual value of the company. The par value of the shares issued is referred to as the 'issued capital'. It is feasible for the shares to be sold for an amount in excess of par. This excess is the 'share premium'. A public limited company (plc) must have authorised capital of at least £ 50,000, with at least 25% of the issued share capital's nominal value plus any premium being paid.

Some companies may decide that issued shares do not need to be paid for in full at the time of issue. Part-payment can be taken on issue, with the remainder being collected at a later date. **Paid-up capital** is the amount actually collected upon issue, the shares being referred to as 'partly paid'. 'Uncalled capital' refers to the unpaid value of the issued shares.

Example 5.1a: A company has authorised share capital of £ 1,000 divided into 1,000 shares at par of £ 1. If the company issues 100 shares partly-paid at 25p each, it will have a paid-up share capital of $(100) * (25\text{p}) = £\,25.00$

Uncalled capital for each share issued is 75p, or $(100) * (75\text{p}) = £\,75.00$ in total.

Example 5.1b: (premiums)
A company allots £ 1 shares at £ 2 per share. The premium per share is £ 1, while the nominal value (par) is £ 1. The company must collect on issue £ 1.25 per share, made up of the £ 1 premium per share, and 25% of the nominal value.

If a company grows and becomes successful it may require additional funding, for expansion, other investment, or even to repay some debt. Initially it might try to raise more capital through debt. Alternatively, a company might try to raise further funds through an additional issue of equity, known as a **rights issue**.

Success occurs when the firm finds investors for its newly-issued shares willing to pay the asking price. Potential holders of the new shares would expect to share in the earnings and dividends of the company in perpetuity with holders of existing shares. The expectation is that funds previously available for distribution to existing shareholders will be reduced, i.e. their pre-existing holding has become 'diluted', and their degree of participation diminished. This is why additional shares are first offered to existing shareholders in proportion to their existing holdings. Shares not taken up by existing shareholders can then be offered to new investors. Known as 'pre-emptive rights', this is a legal requirement when raising additional equity funding in many countries. If a rights issue is successful, the amount raised would be:

$$\text{(number of shares)} * \text{(issue price)} - \text{(expenses)} \tag{5.1}$$

where expenses typically range between 2% and 5%.

Example 5.2: A company has an existing issued equity capital of 1,000,000 shares at a par of 25p. The current share price is 200p. The company wishes to raise £ 375,000, a substantial increase on the company's current market capitalisation of $(200\text{p}) * (1{,}000{,}000) = £\,2{,}000{,}000$.

The company believes that if it offers the new shares near their current market price, it is unlikely to find many subscribers (investors) taking up the offer due to the possible dilution effect. Therefore, it decides to offer them at a discount, at a price of 150p each. Assuming expenses to be zero (for simplicity), this would mean offering (£ 375,000/£ 1.50) = 250,000 shares. Each shareholder would be given the opportunity to buy one new share for each of the four old ones they owned—a 'one-for-four' rights issue.

If a shareholder takes up the rights, then the value of their holding will be:

$$(4 * 200p) + (1 * 150p) = 950p$$

Thus, 950p represents the value of 5 shares, giving an 'ex-rights' price of 190p per share. Theoretically, this should be the price the shares will trade for in the market following the issue.

If an individual shareholder declined to take up their rights, their stake in the company would be diluted. The value of their holding would decline by 10p per share. Hence, if the investor does not wish to take up the rights, they should sell them for 40p per new share, or else they will find their wealth diminished by 10p per share held. The mechanics of this are straightforward: shareholders usually receive an allotment letter for the new shares in proportion to their existing holding; this letter may be sold on to a third party.

This example makes no assumption about any additional earnings the company might be able to make using of the additional capital raised.

After taking advice, it is up to the directors to decide the appropriate ratio in which to issue new shares. Suppose in the example above the directors believed that the current share price was too high, hence a disincentive to potential investors. One possibility would be to offer a 'two-for-one' rights issue. This would imply 500,000 new shares, with a price of 75p each. The ex-rights price would be 158.3p.

If the directors decided the share price was too high but did not wish to raise more capital, then a common solution would be a 'scrip issue'. This means issuing more shares, *giving* them to existing shareholders in proportion to their current holding. A 'two-for-one' scrip issue would mean issuing 500,000 new shares; the ex-scrip price would be $(200p) * (1m/1.5m) = 133p$.

When a company originally incorporates its shares are often 'taken up' (bought) by people already directly involved in its management. As the company grows subsequent rights issues may prove too onerous for original shareholders, so steps must be taken to increase the number of shareholders. One way is via a rights issue, but if existing shareholders elect not to take up their rights, a company might prefer to sell shares via a **private placement**. The shares would then be sold in a concerted fashion to selected financial institutions, for example.

Unlike a private limited company, a public company can sell shares directly to the public. The simplest way to do this would be in an appropriate public environment. Thus, one common way of enlarging the circle of shareholders is to obtain a listing on a stock exchange. A stock exchange, or stock market, provides a marketplace for the shares of the company, so that anybody may purchase or sell them. However, listing is subject to a range of stringent conditions being met:

- The exchange must be provided with information about the company—its history, details about its management, and its profitability—so that prospective buyers may know something about the company.
- A minimum volume of shares must be available for purchase/sale on the exchange. The London International Stock Exchange (LSE) requires at least 25% of the equity capital to be available ("in public hands"). London's Alternative Investment Market, AIM ("market for small and medium size growth companies") has no minimum requirement for shares in public hands. It is unregulated.

If a company grows to the extent that a single exchange does not provide it with a sufficient range of investors, then it may seek to be 'introduced' on another exchange, possibly in another country. Because exchanges have different rules ('listing requirements') which must be satisfied before quotation, it is immensely time-consuming and costly for a company to comply with the information disclosure rules of a number of different stock exchanges. This is particularly true of exchanges in the USA, whose rules are considered to be relatively onerous. For example, in the USA quarterly reporting is the norm, while semi-annual reporting occurs in the UK. Accounting disclosure standards are also much higher in the USA than (e.g.) Germany, which requires little information to be passed to shareholders.

'American Depository Receipts' (ADRs) provide an alternative to a direct listing in the USA. Suppose a UK company deposits sterling-denominated UK-listed shares with a US bank. In turn, the bank sells to US investors dollar-denominated tradeable securities—ADRs—which represent the underlying UK shares. US regulation is such that the ADR has to be registered with the US Securities and Exchange Commission (SEC). The American purchaser of the ADR possesses all the rights and benefits of a UK shareholder, but not the rights and benefits of an owner of a US-listed share. The bank is usually responsible for the handling of aspects of the UK share, such as dividends and rights issues. Because the ADR concept has been quite successful, it has extended to International or Global ADRs, which effectively allow shares to be traded around the world.

5.3 Valuing equity

The prices of company shares listed on a stock market are determined by market forces: supply and demand. If the stock market is efficient then the share price will fully reflect all available information about the company. If a company's shares are not traded on a stock market, or if the market is 'thin' (very few active buyers and sellers) or inefficient, then alternative methods of valuation are required. The key model for valuing shares comes from the application of Present Value.

5.3.1 *Share price valuation I: The basic DVM model*

Monetary benefits to shareholders come in two forms: dividends, and capital gains (or losses). The value of a share will be the capitalised (discounted) value of the expected future income stream. This is the **Dividend Valuation Model** (DVM).

Let P_0 = the current price of a share
P_1 = the expected price of the share at end-period
D_1 = the dividend paid over the next period

The capital gain (loss) *over a single time-period* will be $(P_1 - P_0)$. The expected rate of return to the shareholder, k_e, is:

$$k_e = \frac{(P_1 - P_0) + D_1}{P_0} \tag{5.2}$$

where k_e is the market capitalisation (discount) rate. From the company's perspective, k_e represents the cost of raising funds via equity; i.e. the **cost of equity capital**. This equation can be rewritten as:

$$P_0 = \frac{(D_1 + P_1)}{1 + k_e} \tag{5.3}$$

which expresses today's share price, P_0, as the discounted value of the expected dividend and the future price at the end of the period.

Example 5.3: You are considering investing in listed company, Anderton Enterprises plc. Shares currently sell at £ 10. Based on information in the financial press you fully expect the payment of a dividend of £ 0.75 per share next year. The price of the share is expected to rise to £ 11.00. Your expected rate of return will be:

$$k_e = \frac{(P_1 - P_0) + D_1}{P_0}$$

$$k_e = \frac{(11 - 10) + 0.75}{10} = 17.5\%$$

The reliability of this result depends on the accuracy of the predictions for the future dividend and the future share price. Using the variant in equation (5.3) we can determine the price of the share today.

Example 5.4: Forecasts for Anderton Enterprises plc's dividends and share price next year are £ 0.75 and £ 11.00 respectively. If Anderton Enterprises has a cost of equity capital, k_e, of 13.5% its current share price should be:

$$P_0 = \frac{(D_1 + P_1)}{1 + k_e}$$

$$P_0 = \frac{(0.75 + 11)}{1 + 0.135} = £\,10.13$$

Now, suppose that the prevailing market price for Anderton Enterprises' shares was actually £ 10.50 (higher than £ 10.13). This means that the rate of return was *below* that offered by shares in companies of equivalent risk (there is an inverse relationship between price and rate of return). This would lead to a shift in demand from Anderton Enterprises' shares to companies offering higher expected return. This, in turn, would lead to a decline in Anderton Enterprises' share price, and equivalently an increase in its expected return. The prices of other shares of similar risk would rise, and their expected rates of return would diminish until equilibrium was restored with Anderton Enterprises' share price at £ 10.13. This is another example of the process of **arbitrage** at work. A similar process in the opposite direction would ensue if Anderton Enterprises' share price was less than £ 10.13.

This illustrates how the share valuation model can be used to determine the current price of a share based on forecasts (i.e. expected values) for its dividend and price in the next period (year). This approach can be extended further into the future. Extending equation (5.3) for a second period:

$$P_0 = \frac{(D_1 + P_1)}{1 + k_e} + \frac{(D_2 + P_2)}{(1 + k_e)^2} \tag{5.4}$$

Generalising to T periods:

$$P_0 = \left[\sum_{t=1}^{T} \frac{(D_t)}{(1 + k_e)^T}\right] + \left[\frac{(P_t)}{(1 + k_e)^T}\right] \tag{5.5}$$

This begs the question: what determines the value of P_T? The answer is the discounted stream of future payments received from holding the share *beyond* time T; i.e. the stream of dividends beyond time T. Assuming the company is a perpetual organisation we can extend the equation to an infinite time horizon:

$$P_0 = \left[\sum_{t=1}^{\infty} \frac{(D_t)}{(1 + k_e)^t}\right] \tag{5.6}$$

The dividend valuation model (DVM) offers a robust method for share price valuation in theory. Its usefulness depends on the ability to predict future dividends. For practical purposes the model is often adjusted for a given (simplifying) assumption about future dividends. Of these adjustments the **Gordon growth model** is probably the most-widely known.

5.3.2 *Share price valuation II: The Gordon growth model*

The simplest assumption about future dividends is that they will grow at a predetermined rate. Following Myron Gordon [1959] assume that dividends are expected to grow at a constant rate of $g\%$ per annum:

$$D_t = D_{t-1} * (1+g) \tag{5.7a}$$

$$\text{I.e.} \quad D_t = D_0 * (1+g)^t \tag{5.7b}$$

Substituting into the basic share price (dividend) valuation model (DVM) gives:

$$P_0 = \left[\sum_{t=1}^{\infty} \frac{D_0(1+g)^t}{(1+k_e)^t}\right] \tag{5.8a}$$

$$P_0 = D_0 \left[\sum_{t=1}^{\infty} \frac{(1+g)^t}{(1+k_e)^t}\right] \tag{5.8b}$$

The summation ($\sum$) term reduces to $\frac{(1+g)}{(k_{e-g})}$ giving:

$$P_0 = \frac{D_0\{1+g\}}{(k_{e-g})} \tag{5.9}$$

more commonly written as $P_0 = \frac{D_1}{(k_{e-g})}$, an example of a constantly growing perpetuity. For this formula to make sense then $g < k_e$; i.e. the expected growth rate of dividends must be less than the cost of equity capital (= the required rate of return on equity from the investor's viewpoint). This variant is much easier to use in practical terms than the DVM in equation 5.6. Even if the assumption of constant dividend growth turns out to be incorrect, this model still offers a good first approximation for decision-making purposes.

As with the DVM, rearranging the Gordon growth model can give an expression to calculate the cost of equity capital:

$$k_e = \frac{D_1}{P_0} + g \qquad (5.10)$$

where D_1/P_0 is the **dividend yield**. Clearly, if the expected growth rate of dividends, g, is zero, then the cost of equity capital is equal to the dividend yield.

Example 5.5: Rosenthal plc have a long-established policy of increasing their dividend each year by 5%. The dividend paid this year was £ 0.20 per share. The current share price is £ 1.20. According to the Gordon growth model, the cost of equity capital for Rosenthal plc will be:

$$k_e = \frac{0.21}{1.20} + 0.05 = 22.5\%$$

Gordon's growth model shows the return to shareholders as the sum of the expected return—dividend yield over the next time-period—and the growth rate of dividends. Because next period's dividend is often uncertain in practice the dividend yield can be computed as D_0/P_0, to which an expected annual growth rate can then be applied.

The very simplest variant of the Gordon growth model is when dividends are expected to remain constant at their current level, D. This occurs when the dividend growth rate, g, is zero. In this case the formula reduces to:

$$P_0 = \frac{D}{k_e} \qquad (5.11)$$

This can be recast in cost of capital terms as $k_e = \frac{D}{P_0}$.

While the underlying assumption of the Gordon growth model—a constant growth rate of dividends—appears questionable, the model continues to be used in practice, offering a useful rule-of-thumb measure. Empirically, may not be as questionable as it might seem initially. This is because many companies, especially larger listed companies, try to maintain stable dividend policies, including a stable growth rate of dividends. Partly this is due to the large number of institutional investors (such as pension funds) for whom dividends provide a regular income.

Although the Gordon growth model provides a simpler method of share price valuation than the more general form, difficulties remain. Next year's dividend, D_1, may be uncertain, although it might be possible to estimate it reliably as the current dividend is known with certainty, and the firm's recent dividend payout policy is known from trends or public pronouncements. But there always remains the difficult task of calculating the growth rate of dividends, g. The simplest method is to extrapolate from recent trends. Another alternative is to forecast dividend growth on the company's stated dividend policy. Or use the views of professional analysts which have a track record that suggests their pronouncements are credible.

5.4 Key sources of equity

Raising funds by issuing equity can occur at any time in the life-cycle of a business. When a firm first incorporates it issues its first shares, which raise funds for the company. And the greater the number of shares issued and the higher the share premium the more funds the company raises, *ceteris paribus*. It can be argued that if the founders of a company made more efforts in this direction, they would be less reliant on debt funding in their company's early years. It has been suggested that when first incorporating the founder(s) should try to sell shares in their new venture to almost everyone they know: family, friends, etc.

Once a company is up-and-running it can raise more funds by issuing additional shares via a rights issue (Section 5.2). There is some risk that these additional shares might not be taken up, either by existing shareholders or new investors. There is also the risk of share dilution if they are taken up.

In more recent years newer, more innovative forms of raising funds through equity issue have appeared, under the umbrella term of 'alternative finance'. Possibly the most entrepreneurial of these is **crowdfunding**. This raising of funds occurs by appealing to a large number of people, usually via an internet platform. Possibly the most well-known such platform is Kickstarter (www.kickstarter.com). For the UK there is Crowdfunder (www.crowdfunder.co.uk). In addition to helping businesses raise funds via equity crowdfunding platforms can also be used to raise funds for charitable and other ventures, with no equity offered in exchange.

Another source of equity funding is private equity (PE). A PE company raises funds by offering its own shares to specialised investment funds—e.g. pension funds, insurance companies, sovereign wealth funds and family offices—and not to the general public. PE offers medium- and long-term business finance to help existing companies grow. PE funding is often provided through buyouts and buy ins. PEs will help companies to grow, partly by obtaining a degree of control over management, making operational and other changes to increase profitability and generate better returns. If successful the PE will eventually sell the improved company, adding capital gains to any dividends (and other income) gained during the PE activity.

Venture capital (VC) is a form of private equity (PE) by which financing is provided to startups, early-stage and emerging companies which are expected to have high-growth potential. Funding is provided in return for an equity stake. Because startups (in particular) are highly uncertain investments VCs are assuming high levels of risk. The hope is that by investing in a range of such companies, many will succeed, although some will fail. VC are particularly keen on investing in companies involved with innovative technologies, e.g. IT, 'green' tech, fintech and bio tech, including biopharma.

Angel investors are a form of VC. Often but not always individuals, 'angels' provide capital to business usually for equity or occasionally for convertible debt. Angels have displayed a particular fondness for startups. Support goes beyond funding and may include the provision of advice and management support. Unsurprisingly, angel investors are often retired entrepreneurs or executives, whose interest includes passing on the benefit of their previous experiences.

5.5 Dividends

The share price valuation model shows clearly the importance of dividends to the value of the company as reflected in the price of its shares. Given that the objective of the firm is to maximise its value, and hence the price of its shares, it would be too easy to conclude that a company would have zero value if it has never paid dividends and also seems unlikely to pay them in the future. Alternatively, it is tempting to conclude that a company should distribute *all* of its earnings as dividends to maximise its share price. Yet both views go against the grain of common-sense.

The rationale for these views is seeing dividends as the entire focus of the return on equity. This might be the case for a company whose shares are viewed as 'income stock'. But it fails to consider that shareholders can also make a return via capital gains when they sell their shares. Such a company would be viewed as 'growth stock'. The reality is that a profitable company chooses to retain its earnings because it expects to make a better return on these funds than the individual shareholders might if the funds were distributed as dividends. If investors agree with the firm's view there will be a positive demand for the company's shares, reflected in a growing share price.

One alternative view is that the value of the firm is the discounted value of its future stream of earnings, regardless of whether or not they are retained or distributed as dividends. This gives the following model:

$$P_0 = \sum_{t=1}^{\infty} \frac{EPS_t}{(1+k_e)^t} \tag{5.12}$$

where EPS_t is the earnings-per-share during time t. Because in the complete fullness of time the firm's earnings are eventually distributed to the shareholders, it could be argued that equation (5.12) is identical to equation (5.6) over the firm's lifespan. This model offers a useful tool for valuing the shares of a company which has a zero-dividend payout policy.

The relationship between a company's dividend policy and its earnings (or EPS) can be illustrated via a series of simple illustrative tales:

(1) Cheshunt plc has decided not to undertake any real investment for the foreseeable future. In the short-term, Cheshunt will be able to pay out *all* of its earnings as dividends, as it has no need for the funds itself. If shareholders perceive only the short-term then the price of shares will increase. However, if shareholders are less myopic then because net investment equals real investment less depreciation, Cheshunt will experience negative net investment. This will increasingly lead to problems with its

capital equipment. This will result in increasing costs of maintenance, having a negative impact on profit levels. Lower earnings (profits) ultimately mean lower dividends. Because the stream of dividends will eventually fall to zero, we would expect the price of the share to drop. Eventually dividends will be zero. Competitor firms who have invested in new capital will manifest greater productivity and lower costs of production than Cheshunt plc, ultimately leading to the demise of Cheshunt.

(2) Chigwell plc pays no dividends, preferring to retain earnings to finance internal investment projects. While some of these will add value to the firm, others are likely to be less profitable. If shareholders perceive that a firm is using its retained earnings for projects which yield a lower rate of return than they could achieve if the funds were distributed, they will be tempted to sell off their shareholdings, leading to the ultimate decline in Chigwell plc's share price.

The moral of these tales is straightforward: a company should retain earnings if it can earn a higher rate of return; it should distribute earnings as dividends if shareholders can earn a better rate of return on them.

5.6 A brief introduction to options on equity

Dramatic events in the financial world during the latter decades of the 20th century brought 'derivatives' into public consciousness. This includes the collapse of Barings, and its association with 'rogue trader' Nick Leeson, as well as other spectacularly huge losses due to derivatives' trading, and the role of derivatives in the global financial crisis (GFC) of 2007–2008 have done little to enhance the credibility of the world of finance in the mind of the public. Yet derivatives continue to be a large and growing sector of the financial universe.

There are three major types of derivative: **futures**, **options**, and **swaps**. A derivative is a 'derived security' because its value is derived from the value of some underlying commodity. The primary *raison d'être* for options is for the hedging of risk. In practice, both equity options (also known as stock options) and currency options exist, as well as more exotic variants such as options on futures and interest rate options. Here the focus is on equity options.

There are two types of equity option:

(I) A **call option** gives the holder the right (but not the obligation) to buy the underlying equity (shares) at a predetermined price *on or before* a given date.[2]
(II) A **put option** gives the holder the right (but not the obligation) to sell the underlying shares at a predetermined price on or before a given date (known as the 'expiry date' or 'expiration date').

The price paid for the option itself is known as the **option premium**. The amount paid to exercise the option (i.e. to buy or sell the underlying shares) is called the **exercise price** or **striking price**.

Options can be either 'exchange-traded' or OTC (over-the-counter). The former are standardised and traded on specialised derivatives markets. The latter are highly specialised and lack the standardised qualities to enable them to be traded in a formal market. Trading in stock options first began in 1973 on the Chicago Board Options Exchange. The London Stock Exchange has had some form of option dealing for well over two centuries, although not continuously, and for some time of limited volume. When options are traded in a financial marketplace the option premium is determined by supply and demand. The option premium is usually a small fraction of the price of the underlying share.

There are two sides to every option contract, corresponding to the demand and supply sides of the market. Buying an option is referred to as taking a 'long position', while the 'short position' refers to selling (or 'writing') an option. An investor who writes an option will receive the option premium for it immediately but is subject to the (potential) liabilities of meeting the option's requirements later. Theoretically, anyone who can meet the requirements of fulfilling the option contract if it is exercised can issue ('write') an option. In practice, this is very much the domain of full-time professionals.

It is entirely feasible for a company to issue long-term call options on its own shares, known as 'warrants'. These are often issued as an

[2]This is an 'American' option. A 'European' option gives the holder the right to buy/sell at a predetermined price *on* a given date. European options tend to be less common in practice. The terms have no connection to geographical location.

attachment to a bond to act as a 'sweetener'. It is also possible for a third party, such as a financial institution, to offer either call or put options on a company's shares. These are known as 'covered warrants'.

There are four basic positions an investor can take with respect to options:

- A long position in a call option
- A short position in a call option
- A long position in a put option
- A short position in a put option.

Consider a European call option where X = the exercise price and S = the price of the underlying share. There are three possibilities:

- If $S > X$ the option is said to be 'in the money' and the option is likely to be exercised
- If $S \leq X$ the option is said to be 'out of the money' and will not be exercised
- If $S = X$ the option is said to be 'at the money'

The payoff for the *long position* in this call will be:

$$max.\{S - X, 0\}$$

while for a *short position* the payoff will be:

$$-max.\{S - X, 0\} = min\{X - S, 0\}$$

The value $max.\{S - X, 0\}$ is the **intrinsic value** of a call option. For a put option the intrinsic value will be $max.\{X - S, 0\}$. For an American option, the market value of a call option will exceed its intrinsic value:

$$market\ value = intrinsic\ value + time\ value$$

where *time value* reflects the market's expectation that the price of the option might increase before its expiration date. The time value reflects the 'gamble element' inherent in holding the option to expiration rather than exercising it earlier. On the expiration date there is no time value remaining, so the value of the option is its intrinsic value alone.

As with all derivatives, the primary purpose of options is (or, perhaps, should be) the hedging or management of risk. Consider a (potential) investor in a given company's equity who believes that the price of these shares will rise over the next few months. This investor can either buy the company's shares or buy call options on the company's shares. The first choice requires the investor to pay out the full price for each of the shares purchased. The second only requires the investor to pay out the option premium (a small fraction) of the share price. If the investor's expectations are unfulfilled because the rise in the share price does not come about, then losses under the second alternative will be limited to the option premium alone, whereas under the first alternative they could be much larger. Thus, the use of options has allowed the investor to hedge their risk.

Example 5.6: Joey Kinnear is interested in the equity of Mabbutt plc. He expects the price of these shares will rise from their current market price (S) of 120p. The exercise price of a call option (X) on one share in Mabbutt plc is 100p. The call option has an intrinsic value of 120p − 100p = 20p.

Joey can either purchase 50,000 shares or 'go long' in call options to purchase the same number of shares. But there is always the possibility that the price of shares might go down. By opting for the call options, Joey can limit his risk to the amount he pays out for the call options, exercising the options if the share price rises as expected. If Joey decides to buy the shares directly then his exposure to risk is much greater. The following table shows the payoff from either strategy if the share price actually falls:

	Buy 50,000 shares	**Buy options on 50,000 shares**
Share price drops to:	**Amount of loss**	**Amount of loss**
119p	£ 500	£ 500
115p	£ 2,500	£ 2,500
110p	£ 5,000	£ 5,000
100p	£ 10,000	£ 5,000
60p	£ 25,000	£ 5,000
20p	£ 45,000	£ 5,000
10p	£ 50,000	£ 5,000
0	£ 60,000	£ 5,000

Adopting the strategy of buying options the maximum loss Joey will sustain is £ 5,000, whereas there is a potential loss from buying the shares of £ 60,000. For the option strategy to prove optimal requires the share price to drop by at least the amount of the intrinsic value of the call option.

While this example shows the use of derivatives for hedging risk, they might also be used to generate a 'leverage effect'—magnifying the gains that might be made buying shares directly. Using the price data from the previous example:

Example 5.7: Joey is fully convinced that the share price (S) for Mabbutt plc will rise from its current 120p. He has £ 60,000 available for investment; his choices are either to buy Mabbutt plc shares or to 'go long' in call options on Mabbutt plc shares. Under the first option, Joey can purchase 50,000 shares in Mabbutt plc. Alternatively, he might purchase 300,000 Mabbutt call options at a premium of 20p each.

If Joey's expectations are fulfilled, shares in Mabbutt plc rise to 145p. The intrinsic value of the options will also rise by the same amount. Had Joey bought the shares he will be looking at a capital gain of 25p $*$ 50,000 = £ 12,500. If he had gone long on the call options, however, his gain would be larger at 25p $*$ 300,000 = £ 75,000.

While this seems an almost magical way to make huge gains, the problem with using call options in this speculative manner is that it depends on expectations being fulfilled. If the share price went down rather than up as expected using options would have cost Joey his entire stake, a very costly prospect. This indicates the importance of the *volatility* of the underlying share price as a determinant of the market value of a traded option.

There are six major determinants on the price of a (call) option, most of which can be intuitively divined from the foregoing:

(1) The price of the underlying share (S)
(2) The exercise price of the option (X)
(3) The time the option has to go until expiration ($T - t$)
(4) The volatility of the price of the underlying share

(5) The risk-free rate of interest, r
(6) Any dividends expected before the option expires (these usually affect the underlying share price)

The classic (original) model for pricing (European) call options is Black and Scholes [1973]. The equation appears much more daunting at first sight than it is. Let c be the price of a European call option:

$$c = S \cdot N(d_1) - X \cdot e^{-r(T-t)} \cdot N(d_2) \tag{5.13}$$

where $N(x)$ is the cumulative probability distribution function for a standardised normal variable (i.e. the probability that the variable will have a value less than x). This is little more than a complex variant on the formula for the intrinsic value of a call option $(S - X)$. The complexities introduced are:

- The exercise price (X) is now in present value terms (X is discounted using the risk-free rate as the discount rate). This is because the option is exercised in the future
- Because S and X are both variables assumed to be normally distributed, they are expressed in terms of their underlying probability distributions. This accounts for volatility. Thus:

$$d_1 = \frac{\ln\left(\frac{S}{X}\right) + \left(r + \frac{\sigma^2}{2}\right)(T-t)}{\sigma\sqrt{T-t}} \tag{5.14}$$

$$d_2 = \frac{\ln\left(\frac{S}{X}\right) + \left(r - \frac{\sigma^2}{2}\right)(T-t)}{\sigma\sqrt{T-t}} = d_1 - \sigma\sqrt{T-t} \tag{5.15}$$

Variants on this are used to develop more complicated pricing models used by 'rocket scientists' employed in the world's major financial districts.

5.7 Sample questions

(1) Ordinary shares in Proper Custard plc have a beta coefficient (β) of 2.0, and a required rate of return of 10%. If the risk-free rate is 2% and the market risk-premium is 5%, would you recommend investing in this company's shares?

(2) Shares in Dyspepsia Industries have a beta (β) of 1.5. The company has just paid a dividend of £ 0.80 per share, and dividends are expected to grow at 5% each year. The expected return of the market is 12%, and Treasury bills are yielding 5.5%. The most recent share price for Dyspepsia is £ 61. Calculate its cost of equity using both (i) the DDM method and (ii) the CAPM method; and discuss whether and why the results are different.

(3) Yesterday, the Dull Corporation paid a £ 2 per share dividend. Its dividends are expected to grow steadily at 3% per year.

  (a) How much will each of Dull's dividends be for the next three years?
  (b) If the appropriate discount rate for Dull shares is 5%, what should be the current price of a single Dull share?
  (c) How much should Dull shares be selling two years from now?
  (d) If you buy Dull shares today, and sell them after exactly two years, what rate of return will you realise?

(4) Today is 1st January. The MegaNRG Corporation has developed a product considered to be vastly superior than anything else currently available. MegaNRG justifiably expects a 30% annual growth rate for the next five years. At that time other firms are likely to have developed similar products, so MegaNRG's growth is then expected to diminish to 8% annually (indefinitely). Shareholders' required return on MegaNRG is 12%. The most recent annual dividend (D_0) was £ 1.50 per share, paid yesterday.

  (a) What value of dividends can shareholders expect for each of the next five years?
  (b) What would you expect to be the prevailing share price today?

Chapter 6

Capital Budgeting: (Real) Investment Appraisal

Investment is an immediate outlay of funds (costs) in the expectation of future benefits (revenues). To appraise an investment in a scientific manner costs and benefits must both be measurable in quantifiable terms, i.e., priced in monetary terms. Decision-making is a process of weighing up the costs of the investment against the expected benefits, all in present value (PV) terms. If benefits outweigh costs the investment would be worthwhile. Larger firms typically appraise a *range* of possible investment projects, ranking them according to specified criteria. This chapter examines various techniques for comparing investment costs with (expected) investment benefits.

Financial economists distinguish between two major types of investment: **real investment** and **financial investment**. These closely parallel the two kinds of corporate investment: *capital* investments and *spontaneous* investments.

Capital (real) investment refers to the purchase of (productive) capital equipment by a company in the expectation of increasing its value via an increased stream of future profits. While real investment is traditionally viewed as the purchase of tangible capital equipment, investment in human capital is also recognised. One example is a student paying out now for education or training in the expectation that it will result in better job opportunities, including higher remuneration levels. The rationale behind employee education and training schemes is similar. There is also **social capital**—networks of relationships among people—but both the costs and benefits of 'social' investment tend to be indirect and difficult to quantify.

From a 'pure' finance perspective, capital expenditures are characterised by their irreversibility and the long-term nature of the prospective benefits. While this is most often exemplified by purchases of land, buildings, or capital equipment, permanent additions to working capital (e.g. due to an increase in accounts receivable as a result of permanent changes in the firm's credit policy) may also be included. The trend away from industrialisation towards an 'information society' and towards services means that investment in intellectual property is increasing in both scope and depth. This trend has resulted in an explosion in research and development (R&D), as well as associated areas such as patents and copyrights.

A **financial asset** is a contract which promises the holder the expectation of a stream of future cash flows. The most common forms of financial asset are bonds and shares (equity). **Financial investment** is the purchase of a financial asset in the expectation (hope) of a future income stream via dividends (from equity) or coupons (from bonds) and/or a possible capital gain (in the case of all financial assets). The time horizon of a financial investment depends partly on the preferences of the investor and partly on the characteristics of the financial asset itself. While some financial investment is short-term, much is long-term. However, even when financial investment is long-term it is rarely irreversible, and thus very different to capital (real) investment. For most companies—with the exception of those engaged as financial intermediaries—financial investment is typically short-term, involving the employment of any surplus assets in the purchase of interest-bearing financial instruments which is often more lucrative than holding cash. For the financial economist and the macroeconomist, financial investment is an act of saving!

Changes in current assets due to seasonality or cyclical events are **spontaneous investments**. They occur not as the direct result of the actions of management but due to changing sales levels, for example. Spontaneous investments are typified by short-term benefits and are more normally classified as changes in working capital.

6.1 Investment projects

Companies of all sizes undertake investment projects. Nearly every company will have considered the possibility of (e.g.) buying or perhaps leasing a car. Whether a small firm thinking about the purchase of a personal computer, or a multinational looking at the purchase of a large oil tanker, the same techniques for investment appraisal apply. As a first step it is useful to classify projects according to non-financial criteria.

- **Replacement projects** are when a company updates or upgrades its existing capital equipment. This includes replacement of worn-out or obsolete machinery. In larger companies such decisions might be delegated to the lowest possible level rather than senior management.
- **Expansion projects** are increases to existing capacity. This can take the form of increasing the amount of capital equipment devoted to a particular task. Or it can take the form of newer capital equipment being brought in which can do the same work more productively and/or at lower cost. Such investment may also have elements of replacement.
- **Diversification projects** are a special case of expansion, into new lines of production or where a company invests to expand geographically.
- **Other projects** include all investments which do not fit easily into the previous categories. This might include investments mandated by law, such as those pertaining to environmental controls or health and safety. Mergers and acquisitions might also be included.

It is unusual for a company to consider a single investment project in isolation. A company is more likely to examine and appraise an array of potential investments and then undertake those which meet or exceed some corporate benchmark. Companies also need to recognise the 'dependence status' of the various projects they have under review. Some investments will be *mutually exclusive.* This is when two or more projects offer alternative means of achieving the same goal, requiring only the best alternative to be selected. This is often the case with replacement investment, where there may be several 'machines' available to replace the existing 'machine'. Mutually exclusive investments thus involve an 'accept/reject' decision.

Sometimes a company will find itself considering complementary investments. This is where the ability to succeed in one investment requires the undertaking of a second, complementary, investment. If investments are regarded as complementary, they should be aggregated and appraised together *as if* they were a single investment.

6.2 The crucial importance of cashflows

Techniques for appraising proposed capital investment projects are relatively straightforward in concept. The key issue is estimating the expected cashflows required for those appraisal techniques. Possibly the most important thing to note is that it is *cashflows* and not accounting flows that are relevant. As the simple adage notes:

"profits don't pay bills; cash does."

It is entirely feasible for a company which appears profitable 'on its books' to find itself bankrupt because it does not have enough cash inflows to meet its immediate expenses. This may be partly because there are a number of *non-cash items* which are part of the equation in calculating profits, e.g. depreciation, goodwill. For example, if the only non-cash item in the company's income statement is assumed to be depreciation, then by adding back depreciation the firm's cashflow from operations (*CFO*) can be determined:

$$CFO = net\ income + depreciation \tag{6.1}$$

This 'quick and dirty' method is an over-simplification, which works well enough if depreciation is the only non-cash item on the company's income (profit and loss) statement, as all other items are associated with cash inflows and outflows.[1]

[1]From basic accounting *net income* = *cash inflows* − (*cash expenses* + *depreciation*)

Adding *depreciation* to both sides gives:

$$net\ income + depreciation = cash\ inflows - (cash\ expenses)$$

$$\text{i.e.}\quad net\ income + depreciation = cashflows$$

Greater precision requires inclusion of changes in the company's assets and liabilities. These *balance sheet effects* on cashflows include:

- An increase in assets reduces cash: an increase in *accounts receivable* means less cash will be collected over the accounting period, or cash may have been paid out to purchase fixed assets.
- Asset decreases increase cash, e.g. the sale of *fixed assets.*
- An increase in *accounts payable* means the company is paying out less cash over the accounting period for a given level of supplies. Similarly, an increase in the company's *long-term debt* will lead to an inflow of cash.
- If the company repaid some of its debt during the accounting period, this leads to a decrease in cash.

These changes are summarised in Table 6.1 (below):

Table 6.1. Balance sheet effects on cash

	Asset change	Effect on cash
1	Increase in assets	Reduction
2	Decrease in assets	Increase
3	Increase in liabilities or equity	Increase
4	Decrease in liabilities or equity	Reduction

Consequently, the cashflow formula may be expanded to:

$$CF = net\ income + depreciation - [net\ working\ capital] \tag{6.2}$$

$$CF = net\ income + depreciation - [(change\ in\ assets) + (change\ in\ liabilities\ \&\ equity)] \tag{6.3}$$

This formula is applied to the accounting statements to derive the **statement of cashflows**, which usually includes three broad groups:

- cashflows from operations (CFO)
- cashflows from investing activities
- cashflows from financing activities

For many companies, especially in the industrial and commercial sector, the second group may be limited to cashflows due to interest payments.

The ability to produce a projection of the company's net income begins with a robust projection for future sales. The cashflows necessary for capital budgeting are yet to occur—*expected* cashflows—and therefore must be estimated. The validity of any investment decision depends crucially on the robustness of future cashflow estimates. Cashflows occurring before the decision date are 'sunk costs' and not considered relevant to the capital budgeting decision. The important cashflows are *incremental* cashflows: the difference in cashflows to the company with the project and without the project. This truly measures the cashflows to the company that the new project *per se* will generate. Thus, if a company was considering a new product line that might compete with any of its existing products, then the possible loss of revenue from the existing products (i.e. 'cannibalisation') must be included in the cashflow estimation. Equally, there may be some economies of scale which arise as the result of the new investment. By considering incremental cashflows these issues are all fully addressed.

It is important that cashflows are estimated on a post-tax basis. From a company perspective, taxes are a cost of doing business like any other cost and must be treated accordingly. In countries such as the UK and the USA, tax law is such that depreciation (and other non-cash items) affect the firm's earnings *before* taxation, and consequently the firm's tax bill. Thus, because depreciation can have an indirect impact on the firm's cashflows, these must include any depreciation tax benefits. This same is true of other non-cash items that will indirectly impact the firm's cashflows. The importance of accurate, well-researched cashflow estimates for the capital budgeting decision cannot be overstated, both from the perspective of the company's well-being and for the investment analyst. While no amount of accurate information and research can guarantee the future outcome of an investment project, poor information and research leads to poor decision-making.

6.3 Investment appraisal: Non-DCF techniques

Human nature includes a general reluctance to embrace change: "if it ain't broke, don't fix it". There is a reluctance to recognise when change is required. This is certainly the case with investment appraisal. Historically, the time value of money was not always recognised, and techniques of investment appraisal relied on non-DCF methods. Even after DCF techniques had been 'discovered':

> The businessman's attitude may be also affected by the dominance of the firm's information system by accountants, who in general have not been trained in the techniques [of discounted cashflows] ..., and whose professional attitudes may possibly militate against their acceptance. Bromwich [1976]

Times have long since changed, and discounted cashflows are both common practice and part-and-parcel of the curriculum of the various professional accounting bodies' examinations. Yet, there still remain some firms who cling to older methods, even when they have become superseded by more scientifically valid techniques. So, what are those non-DCF techniques?

6.3.1 *The payback period*

Under this criterion, those investments which recover the principal (i.e. the initial capital outlay) in the shortest period of time are selected. There are two simple methods of calculating the payback period, depending on the nature of the cashflows:

(a) if the cashflows are regular (even), then:

$$\textit{payback period} = \frac{\textit{net investment}}{\textit{annual net chas flows}} \tag{6.4}$$

(b) if the cashflows are irregular (uneven) it is necessary to find the point in time when the cumulative cash inflows just equal the (original) net investment:

$$\textit{payback period} = t - \frac{c}{(d-c)} \tag{6.5}$$

where

$t =$ the last full year in which the cumulative net cash inflows are less than net investment;
$c =$ cumulative cash flow at time t; and
$d =$ cumulative cash flow at time $t+1$.

Example 6.1: The Mullery Corporation is considering two investment projects with the following cashflows for the next six years Project A offers regular cashflows of £ 12,500 each year. Therefore, it has a payback period of (50,000/12,500) = 4 years.

Project B has uneven cashflows, increasing from £ 5,000 to £ 30,000. It's payback period is therefore $4 - \frac{-5,000}{(20,000+5,000)} =$ 4.2 years.

	Project A		Project B	
Year	Net cash flow after tax (£)	Cumulative cash flow (£)	Net cash flow after tax (£)	Cumulative cash flow (£)
0	−50,000	−50,000	−50,000	−50,000
1	12,500	−37,500	5,000	−45,000
2	12,500	−25,000	10,000	−35,000
3	12,500	−12,500	15,000	−20,000
4	12,500	0	15,000	−5,000
5	12,500	12,500	25,000	20,000
6	12,500	25,000	30,000	50,000

Both projects require the same initial outlay (£ 50,000), but Project A recoups the initial outlay quicker and is preferred to Project B. Project A is considered less risky. The payback period would often be compared with a company benchmark. For example, a company's Board of Directors might decide that projects which are likely to take longer than five years to pay back the initial investment will be unacceptable to their shareholders and therefore are too risky.

The main criticism of the payback period criterion as a method of investment appraisal is because it ignores any cashflows occurring after the payback date. It also ignores the time value of money. One possible work round might be to calculate payback period on a present value basis. Despite its shortcomings, in practice it is often used as a risk-filtering device in combination with a discounted cashflow (DCF) technique.

6.3.2 *The finite horizon criterion*

This involves setting a terminal date—a 'finite horizon'—beyond which prospective cashflows are neglected. The rationale behind this approach is that not only is the future uncertain, but the further into the future one looks the greater is that uncertainty. Both this and the payback period criterion depend heavily on an arbitrarily chosen period of time and are, therefore, likely to lead to some rather peculiar and often indefensible conclusions.

6.3.3 *Accounting Rate of Return*

The Accounting Rate of Return (ARR) is based on accounting (accrual) concepts and not cashflows. At its broadest it is defined as:

$$\frac{(\textit{net income})}{(\textit{book value of equity})} \tag{6.6}$$

Note that *net income* can also be referred to as *earnings* or *profits*.

Because ARR is based on figures in published financial statements it is considered a particularly practical measure, especially by users of financial statements, e.g. accountants, information intermediaries, loan officers and government policy advisers. When applied to the capital budgeting decision it is defined as:

$$\text{Accounting Rate of Return, } ARR = \frac{\textit{profit (or earnings)}}{\textit{capital outlay}} \tag{6.7}$$

where *profit* is usually calculated as an annual average, net of accounting depreciation, and *capital outlay* can be the initial capital sum, or an annual average with or without working capital. While projects with higher ARR are preferable, companies may have in mind a target rate they use as a benchmark, only undertaking projects with an ARR above that benchmark. The major criticism of ARR is that it ignores the time value of money.

6.3.4 *Profitability index*

The profitability index (PI) is a cost-benefit ratio which includes the time value of money. It is defined as the ratio of the present value of estimated future cash flows divided by the initial investment, I_0:

$$\text{Profitability index, } PI = \frac{PV(\textit{future cash flows})}{-I_0} \tag{6.8}$$

For an investment to be profitable, and therefore worthy of the firm's consideration, requires a *PI* greater than one.

Many analysts regard the *PI* as rather simplistic. *PI* can also produce rankings which are inconsistent with the present value criterion. However, because *PI* indicates which projects maximise the rate of return for each pound (£) spent on the initial investment it offers a useful decision-making indicator when a firm finds itself in a position of 'capital rationing', i.e. a shortage of funds that forces a company to choose between worthwhile projects. Note that capital rationing can occur due to the company setting a cap on its capital expenditures, as well as due to external constraints (see Section 6.4.3).

6.4 Investment appraisal: Discounted Cashflow (DCF) techniques

6.4.1 *Net Present Value (NPV)*

Net Present Value (*NPV*) is the discounted value of the sum of all net cashflows generated by an investment project minus any initial outlay on the project:

$$NPV = \left[\sum_{t=1}^{T} \frac{CF_t}{(1+k)^t}\right] - I_0 \tag{6.9}$$

where CF_t = net cashflows during period t; k = the appropriate discount rate (or cost of capital); I_0 = initial outlay. The *NPV* rule is:

- If $NPV > 0$ the project is acceptable
- If $NPV < 0$ reject the project

Projects with a positive *NPV* are acceptable and will likely increase the value of the company by the *NPV*. However, because a project is considered acceptable does not necessarily mean that the company should undertake it. The investment should be compared with other possible investment projects in terms of their *NPV*s. A ranking or league-table of investments based on their *NPV*s should be constructed. The projects with the highest *NPV* should be undertaken first. Then the project with the second-highest *NPV*, and so on.

Example 6.2: Blanchflower Creative plc is considering an outlay of £ 50,000 for equipment that will yield a series of increasing cash-flows over a six-year time-horizon, after which the equipment will have no salvage value. The discount rate is 14%

Year	CF	PV factor @ 14%	PV (CF)
1	£ 5,000	0.877	£ 4,385
2	£ 10,000	0.769	£ 7,690
3	£ 15,000	0.675	£ 10,125
4	£ 15,000	0.592	£ 8,880
5	£ 25,000	0.519	£ 12,975
6	£ 30,000	0.456	£ 13,680
			£ 57,735
		less *I*	(£ 50,000)
		NPV	**£ 7,735**

The *NPV* of this project is positive indicating that if the project were undertaken **the value of the firm would increase by £ 7,735**. Thus, the firm should regard this project as acceptable. If this is the only project under consideration, then the firm should definitely undertake it.

Suppose Blanchflower Creative was considering the cashflows above but subject to a higher discount rate, e.g. 20%? This would result in:

Year	CF	PV factor @ 20%	PV (CF)
1	£ 5,000	0.8333	£ 4,167
2	£ 10,000	0.6944	£ 6,994
3	£ 15,000	0.5787	£ 8,681
4	£ 15,000	0.4823	£ 7,234
5	£ 25,000	0.4019	£ 10,047
6	£ 30,000	0.3349	£ 10,047
			£ 47,119
		less *I*	(£ 50,000)
		NPV	**£ (2,881)**

The *NPV* of this project is negative. Were the project undertaken *the value of the firm would decrease by £* 2,881. Blanchflower Creative should regard this project as unacceptable. There is an inverse relationship between a project's discount rate and its *NPV*: when the discount rate is increased the *NPV* decreases: This inverse relationship can be seen clearly graphically in Figure 6.1:

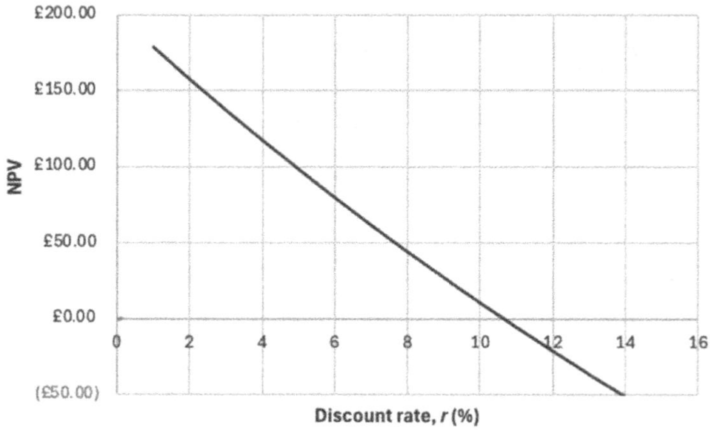

Figure 6.1. *NPV* vs discount rate, r

These examples show a company appraising an independent project: a single investment project in isolation. If the *NPV* is greater than zero, the project is considered worthwhile (i.e. it will add value to the company). However, it is more likely that a company will examine a range of possible independent investments and rank them according to their *NPV*s. The company will undertake the project with the highest *NPV*; if further funding is available, it will then undertake the project with the second-highest *NPV*; and so on until all available funding for investment projects is exhausted (see Section 6.4.3) or remaining projects fail to meet or exceed the firm's benchmark *NPV*.

Companies also appraise investments which are *mutually exclusive*, i.e. one or more projects offering alternative means of achieving a single goal. Here, only the best alternative needs to be selected. A prime example of mutually exclusive projects might be a company considering replacing its current equipment with newer equipment. Although it is easy to compare *NPV*s, it is sometimes simpler to find the *NPV* for the differential cashflows between the two alternatives. We consider the implications of mutually exclusive investments in Section 6.5.

Note that a company is essentially an aggregate portfolio of the investment projects it undertakes. On that basis, and because *NPVs* are additive, a company could be valued as the sum of the *NPVs* of its investment projects.

Invariably problematic is the choice of appropriate discount rate. This ought to reflect how much it will cost the company to obtain the funding necessary to undertake its investment project(s). Companies usually employ their **cost of capital** (a measure of the company's average cost of funds; see Chapter 8), which should also reflect the market's assessment of the risk involved in the project. But even this has its problems, as there may be difficulties in its estimation. The cost of capital, for example, is historically-based and may not reflect the future when the project occurs. Many companies prefer to specify a proprietary 'hurdle rate' cost of capital, which incorporates the company's own estimation of the risk involved, although companies are extraordinarily reluctant to reveal how it has been determined, or even what value it takes! Over the years studies of British companies' cost of capital have found it to be much higher than market estimates would suggest. Given these difficulties, it is easy to understand why an alternative DCF technique for appraising capital investment projects is required.

6.4.2 *Internal Rate of Return (IRR)*

The Internal Rate of Return (ρ) is that discount rate which gives an investment project a Net Present Value of zero:

$$NPV \equiv 0 = \left[\sum_{t=1}^{T} \frac{CF_t}{(1+k)^t}\right] - I_0 \tag{6.10a}$$

Alternatively:

$$\left[\sum_{t=1}^{T} \frac{CF_t}{(1+k)^t}\right] = I_0 \tag{6.10b}$$

The *IRR* may be found 'by hand' using trial-and-error (Chapter 3), which is old-fashioned, or using a modern financial calculator. Most common and highly effective is the use of a spreadsheet

IRR function, such as in (e.g.) Microsoft Excel, where the formula is:

$$=\boldsymbol{IRR}(\textbf{values, guess})$$

where **values** is "an array or a reference to cells that contain numbers for which you want to calculate the internal rate of return" and **guess** is "a number that you guess is close to the result of *IRR*".

If calculating 'by hand':

- If $NPV > 0$ the next guess for the *IRR* must be higher (due to the negative relationship between the discount rate and *NPV*).
- If $NPV < 0$ a lower value guess of *IRR* must be chosen.

The iterative process of plugging in 'guesses' for *IRR* continues until a value is found such that the $NPV = 0$. With a spreadsheet this iterative process is performed 'behind the scenes' by the software. Yet even state-of-the-art software requires a starting guess, usually set by default to 10%.

Once *IRR* (ρ) has been determined it can then be compared to a reference rate, usually the cost of acquiring funds (r). If

- $\rho > r$ the project is acceptable
- $\rho < r$ reject the project

Example 6.3: Trial-and-Error

William Nicholson is planning his own business. He estimates startup costs of £ 70,000 and expects in the first five years to net the following income: £ 12,000, £ 15,000, £ 18,000, £ 21,000, and £ 26,000, respectively. *IRR* (ρ) is the discount rate which gives an investment project a *NPV* of zero

$$\frac{£\,12{,}000}{(1+\rho)} + \frac{£\,15{,}000}{(1+\rho)^2} + \frac{£\,18{,}000}{(1+\rho)^3} + \frac{£\,21{,}000}{(1+\rho)^4} + \frac{£\,26{,}000}{(1+\rho)^5} = £\,70{,}000$$

Substituting $\rho = 0.1 = 10\%$ into the above equation

$$\frac{£\,12{,}000}{(1.1)} + \frac{£\,15{,}000}{(1.1)^2} + \frac{£\,18{,}000}{(1.1)^3} + \frac{£\,21{,}000}{(1.1)^4} + \frac{£\,26{,}000}{(1.1)^5} = £\,70{,}000$$

Calculating the present value interest factors (the denominators):

$$\frac{£\,12{,}000}{(1.1)} + \frac{£\,15{,}000}{(1.21)} + \frac{£\,18{,}000}{(1.331)} + \frac{£\,21{,}000}{(1.4641)} + \frac{£\,26{,}000}{(1.61051)}$$
$$= £\,70{,}000$$

$$NPV = £\,10{,}909.09 + £\,12{,}396.69 + £\,13{,}523.67 + £\,14{,}343.28 + £\,16{,}143.95 - £\,70{,}000$$

Thus $NPV = -£\,2{,}683.31$

Clearly this value of ρ is too high: it gives an $NPV < 0$. *IRR* must be lower than 10%. Try $\rho = 8\%$:

$$\frac{£\,12{,}000}{(1.08)} + \frac{£\,15{,}000}{(1.08)^2} + \frac{£\,18{,}000}{(1.08)^3} + \frac{£\,21{,}000}{(1.08)^4} + \frac{£\,26{,}000}{(1.08)^5} = £\,70{,}000$$

$$NPV = £\,11{,}111.11 + £\,12{,}860.08 + £\,14{,}288.98 + £\,15{,}435.63 + £\,17{,}695.16 - £\,70{,}000$$

Thus $NPV = £\,1{,}390.96$

This value of ρ is too high, as it $NPV > 0$. Thus, *IRR* must be lower than 10% but higher than 8%. Successive approximations will eventually lead to the result that the value of ρ is 8.66%.

Although trial-and-error 'by hand' offers a foolproof method for accurately determining the Internal Rate of Return (*IRR*) of an investment project, it is tedious and time-consuming. One way of circumventing the need for successive iterations is to find two discount rates that correspond to a positive and negative *NPV* respectively, and then by interpolation calculate an approximate value for *IRR*. From example 6.3:

Discount rate	***NPV***
$\rho_1 = 8\%$	$NPV_1 = £\,1,390.96$
$\rho_2 = 10\%$	$NPV_2 = -£\,2,683.31$

It is clear that the *IRR* lies between 8% and 10%. This can be clearly seen on a graph of *NPV* against the discount rate:

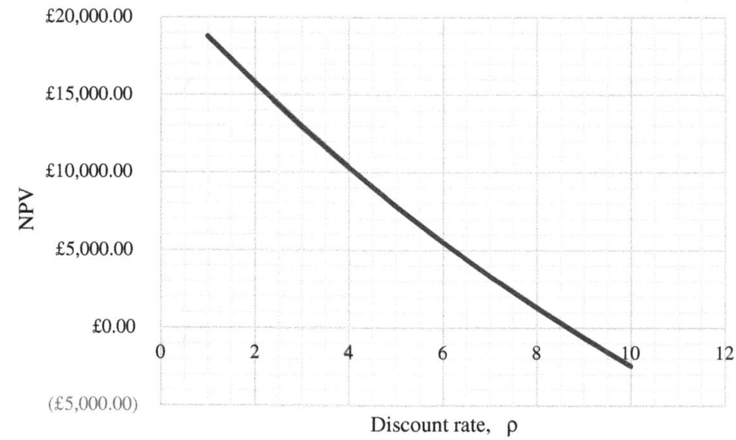

Figure 6.2. *NPV* and ρ

Assume the slope of the graph is (or approximates) a straight line, then the following formula can be used to calculate an approximate value for *IRR*:

$$\rho^* = \frac{\rho_2 NPV_1 - \rho_1 NPV_2}{NPV_1 - NPV_2}$$

Applying this to example 6.3:

$$\rho^* = \frac{0.1 * (1{,}390.96) - 0.08 * (-2{,}683.31)}{(1{,}390.96) - (-2{,}683.31)} = 0.0868$$

i.e. $IRR = 8.68\%$. Figure 6.2 confirms this. But it must be emphasised that this is an approximation—the result assumes a linear relationship between *NPV* and the discount rate (ρ). Although in this example the difference between the actual result and the approximation is quite small, in many cases the difference might prove to be substantial, so any approximated *IRR* should be used with appropriate caution.

Calculation 'by hand' of *IRR* can be tedious. Spreadsheets make light work of such calculations. Applying Excel to Example 6.3, the formula is **=*IRR*(B2:G2,0.1)**.

	A	B	C	D	E	F	G
1	**Year**	**0**	**1**	**2**	**3**	**4**	**5**
2	**Cashflow**	(£70,000)	**£12,000**	**£15,000**	**£18,000**	**£21,000**	**£26,000**
3							
4	**IRR =**	**8.66%**					
5							

Note that some analysts prefer variants of the *IRR* method. For example, with the "dual-rate" approach one rate is used for discounting up to payback, and a different rate thereafter. This requires dividing the project into two parts: first, when the project is a net borrower (net cash outflows, thus riskier); and second, when the project has a cash surplus (net cash inflows, thus less risky).

Once *IRR* had been calculated a decision has to be made as to whether or not the project is feasible. This requires comparison of *IRR* with the cost of acquiring funds (the cost of capital). Section 6.5 compares the two DCF techniques of investment appraisal: *IRR* and *NPV*.

6.4.3 *Capital rationing*

Under the idealistic circumstances posited by economic theory a company would undertake *all* potential projects which satisfy its capital budgeting criterion. Thus, a company using *NPV* for appraising investments would undertake each and every project with a positive *NPV*; a company using *IRR* would undertake each and every project with an *IRR* greater than it's hurdle rate cost of capital. But the real world differs from economic theory, and companies frequently find themselves restricted in the amounts of financing they are willing (or perhaps able) to utilise for capital expenditures. When this happens 'capital rationing' occurs.

With capital rationing a company fails to undertake projects which might help maximise its value. Thus, capital rationing implies that value maximisation is not an objective of the company *per se*. Instead, the company objective is value maximisation subject to the company's capital ceiling, i.e. constrained value maximisation. Financial managers facing capital rationing should maximise the sum of the *NPV*s of the projects selected. This will happen by ranking potential investment projects in terms of their *NPV*, undertaking those at the top (e.g. with the highest *NPV*) then moving down the list to those projects with lower *NPV*s until the capital ceiling is reached.

6.5 Comparison of *NPV* with *IRR*

Given that both the Net Present Value (*NPV*) and Internal Rate of Return (*IRR*) techniques are discounted cashflow (DCF) techniques of investment appraisal, which method offers superior recommendations?

Because firms rely on DCF techniques to make decisions on capital expenditure it is important for the results to be credible. For example, expected values such as the projected cash flows need to be wholly believable by the decision-makers. It should always be possible to justify the projected data with robust, rational argument. Unlike other aspects of a firm's decision-making, the capital expenditure decision is one involving an inflexible long-term commitment. Most capital equipment is highly specialised in its usage, and for most equipment there is rarely (if ever) a well-ordered secondary market. A capital expenditure decision which proves to be ill-fated is not one that can be turned around quickly.

6.5.1 *Number of solutions*

One of the advantages offered by *NPV* is that it gives a unique conclusion, whereas *IRR* may yield multiple solutions. By way of example consider the following three-period cashflow profile:

$$I_0, \quad CF_1, \quad CF_2$$

where I_0 represents the initial outlay to finance the investment, and CF_i are the net cashflows in year i. To find *IRR* solve the equation:

$$\frac{CF_1}{(1+\rho)} + \frac{CF_2}{(1+\rho)^2} - I_0 = 0$$

Using cross-multiplication this can be rewritten as:

$$CF_1(1+\rho) + CF_2 - I_0(1+\rho)^2 = 0$$

which is a quadratic equation in $(1+\rho)$. Quadratic equations have two possible solutions ('roots'), although it is feasible for the two roots to be identical.

For a time-horizon of more than three time-periods, *IRR* calculations result in a polynomial equation:

- a four-period cashflow results in a cubic equation, with three roots;
- a five-year cashflow profile results in a quartic equation, with four roots; and so on.

The formula for *IRR* will always yield a polynomial of degree n, which has $n-1$ roots, where n is the number of time-periods. Under these circumstances the question as to which root is economically meaningful for the purposes of capital budgeting is crucial, as first noted by Lorie and Savage [1955]. Fortunately, in practice most roots turn out to be negative or imaginary, so they can be ignored providing that at least one root turns out to be positive.

Descartes' 'change of sign rule' suggests that there will be as many positive roots as there are changes in sign for the cashflow. Thus, if the net cashflow is always positive after the initial outlay then there will be a single positive root for $(1+\rho)$, thus a unique solution for ρ.

Where the appraisal is of a single independent investment project, and the only decision is either to accept or reject the project, *NPV* and *IRR* calculations yield identical recommendations: when *NPV* is positive, *IRR* (ρ) will exceed the cost of capital, and vice versa. This is a mathematical truism. However, when the firm is ranking a range of possible investment projects or considering mutually exclusive investments, it is entirely feasible that *NPV* and *IRR* appraisals will offer different recommendations. Because *IRR* might give the wrong recommendation most analysts tend to prefer *NPV*.

Example 6.4: Keane Properties is considering two mutually exclusive investment projects with the following cashflows:

	0	1	2	3
Project X	−£ 216,500	£ 102,838	£ 102,838	£ 102,838
Project Y	−£ 108,250	£ 55,424	£ 55,424	£ 55,424

Comparing the results from the two DCF methods yields:

	NPV	*IRR*
Project X	£ 39,242.89	20%
Project Y	£ 29,581.28	25%

NPV recommends Project X be selected: it adds £ 39,242.89 to the value of the company (more than Project Y's £ 29,581.28). This contrasts with the *IRR* recommendation, which recommends Project Y with the superior rate of return: 25% as compared to X's 20%.

Because *NPV* relates directly to the company's objective (value maximisation), its recommendation is intuitively superior. However, when considering why *NPV* and *IRR* offer different recommendations we can establish more clearly the superiority of *NPV*, as well as methods for adapting the *IRR* method so that it also offers correct recommendations.

6.5.2 *Scale and duration*

In example 6.4 there was a difference in the scale of the two projects considered by Keane Properties. Project X required an initial outlay of £ 216,500 while Project Y only required an initial outlay of £ 108,250. This difference in scale means that Project X can be considered the 'economic equivalent' of Project Y *plus* an (theoretical) additional project (Project F) consisting of the differential cashflow between X and Y:

	0	**1**	**2**	**3**
Project X	−£ 216,500	£ 102,838	£ 102,838	£ 102,838
Project Y	−£ 108,250	£ 55,424	£ 55,424	£ 55,424
Project F	*−£ 108,250*	*£ 47,414*	*£ 47,414*	*£ 47,414*

Project F has an *NPV* of £ 9,661.60 and an *IRR* of 15%. Project X can be regarded as the same as undertaking *both* Project Y and Project F: this combination gives a combined *NPV* of (£ 39,242.89 + £ 9,661.60) = £ 29,581.28 (the same as the *NPV* of Project X). However, Project F yields an *IRR* of 15%, which is a weighted average of the *IRR*s from Project F and Project Y. *IRR* offers us an 'average' measure of the investment, with no regard to the size of the investment, whereas *NPV* offers an absolute measure which does take the size of the investment into account.

6.6 Investment appraisal; general guidelines

(1) Use cashflows, not accounting flows.
(2) Use incremental cashflows at the time they occur. The financial impact of a project is measured by the incremental cashflows: i.e. new cashflows less old cashflows.

(3) Use after-tax cashflows, thereby including tax effects.
(4) Accountants frequently separate current expenses from capital expenses. Don't!
(5) Use allocated costs with considerable care as these are often based on subjective judgements.
(6) Do not include sunk costs.
(7) Do not include financing costs, at least in the first instance.
(8) Ensure the discount rate chosen reflects the project risk. Ask

- Should revenues and costs be discounted at the same rate?
- Should the same discount rate be applied for each time period?

(9) Treat inflation consistently (see below).
(10) Examine the sensitivity of the capital budgeting decision to key factors (see below).
(11) Ensure cash inflows in any time-period are adequate to meet cash outflows.
(12) *NPV* measures how much the firm is expected to increase in value in absolute terms; *IRR* is a relative measure with nothing to say about size.
(13) Some problems with *IRR* (ρ):

- Multiple solutions may occur if there are a number of changes of sign in the cashflows;
- Project scale is ignored;
- *IRR* assumes all cashflows are reinvested at *IRR* (ρ) rate;
- *IRR* is not suitable in a situation of capital rationing because it does not account for project scale.

6.6.1 *Real and nominal values*

Economists distinguish between real values and nominal values. Traditionally, prices are denominated in nominal values, which means that goods are priced in terms of the unit of currency at that time. However, the economic experience is one of ongoing inflation (albeit at different rates over time). Thus, the value of the currency—its purchasing power—is depreciating and may therefore give a false sense of value to goods priced in that currency. This is known as 'money illusion'.[2] One economic variable which is immediately impacted by inflation will be the rate of interest. Interest rates typically incorporate an 'inflation premium' to offset the declining purchasing power of money occasioned by inflation. This will further impact the firm's overall cost of capital, and thus its capital budgeting decision. It is crucial, therefore, that capital budgeting values are denominated either entirely in real terms or entirely in nominal terms. Any inconsistency is likely to lead to a downward bias in the investment decision, as the following illustrates:

Example 6.5: Mackay Steelworks is planning investment in a new plant which would yield £ 250,000 per annum over five years. The cost of the plant is £ 1,000,000, and the applicable cost of capital (the discount rate) is 7 per cent. Assuming zero inflation, the *NPV* of this project is:

$$NPV = \left[\sum_{t=1}^{T} \frac{CF_t}{(1+k)^t}\right] - I_0$$

$$NPV = \left[\sum_{t=1}^{5} \frac{£\,250{,}000}{(1+0.07)^t}\right] - £\,1{,}000{,}000 = £\,25{,}049$$

In this example the nominal cost of capital (7%) is also the real cost of capital, resulting in a positive *NPV*. How would this be affected by an inflation rate of 3%, expected to prevail over the five-year life of the project?

The Fisher [1930] equation—often approximated as $i_{nominal} = i_{real}$ + (expected inflation)—shows the relationship between nominal and real rates of interest:

$$(1+k)(1+\pi) = (1+k^*)$$

[2]Many economists argue that 'money illusion' is irrational. However, in reality it may not always be easy to distinguish a rise in the price of a given commodity from a (sustained) rise in the general price level. Only the latter is inflation.

where k^* is the cost of capital in nominal terms, k is the cost of capital in real terms, and π is the expected rate of inflation. The nominal cost of capital is:

$$k^* = [(1 + k)(1 + \pi)] - 1$$
$$k^* = [(1 + 0.07)(1 + 0.03)] - 1 = 10.21\%$$

Recalculating *NPV* in Example 6.5 using this higher (nominal) cost of capital results in a lower *NPV*:

$$NPV = \left[\sum_{t=1}^{5} \frac{\pounds\,250{,}000}{(1 + 0.1021)^t}\right] - \pounds\,1{,}000{,}000 = -\pounds\,57{,}366$$

Thus, a moderate inflation level of 3% leads to a project being rejected which was acceptable when inflation was zero. But this is to ignore the fact that the cashflows are also likely to be affected by inflation. On the assumption that the cashflows grow in line with the rate of inflation, the capital budgeting problem becomes:

$$NPV = \left[\sum_{t=1}^{5} \frac{\pounds\,250{,}000(1 + 0.03)^t}{(1 + 0.07)^t(1 + 0.03)^t}\right] - \pounds\,1{,}000{,}000$$

$$NPV = \left[\sum_{t=1}^{5} \frac{\pounds\,250{,}000}{(1 + 0.07)^t}\right] - \pounds\,1{,}000{,}000$$

With inflation included in both numerator and denominator we arrive back at our original calculation! *Consistency has been assured.* But this is misleading. Inflation does not impact all prices equally. While the real cost of capital can be calculated using the 3% inflation rate in the Fisher equation, there is little likelihood that each of the five years' cashflows would also be impacted by exactly 3%.

6.7 Sensitivity and scenario analysis

When using a discounted cashflow (DCF) technique to appraise a capital investment project, the selected discount rate should incorporate the appropriate degree of risk for the project under consideration. Riskier projects' cashflows should be discounted using a higher cost of capital. For larger firms it should be possible (and desirable) to use a market-determined cost of capital in their calculations. However, smaller firms and those with a more conservative outlook may prefer to make use of variations on DCF techniques for dealing with risk. This could be because they do not have the expertise to quantify the risk, or because the cost of quantifying risk in a scientific manner far outweighs the possible benefits.

The credibility of a DCF calculation depends to a large degree on the quality of the cashflow forecasts. Accurate cashflow forecasts lead to better decision-making. To compensate for the uncertainty of the future, variations on DCF techniques may be applied to give a clearer picture of the impact of the uncertainty. These variations are sensitivity and scenario analysis.

6.7.1 *Sensitivity analysis*

Sensitivity analysis is when a capital budgeting decision is recalculated to see how it reacts to changes in a single key variable. For example, if a firm is heavily reliant on financing its project through floating-rate debt, it may wish to consider how sensitive the accept/reject decision will be to changes in the rate of interest. The firm may calculate (e.g.) the project's *NPV* based on a series of different rates of interest. If *NPV* remains relatively stable regardless of the rate of interest, the project may be considered insensitive ('robust') to changes in that variable.

The key issue for a company is to identify which variables it considers crucial to the success of the project and examine how changes in them (individually) will impact the capital budgeting decision. While this will vary according to the nature of the characteristics of the investment project, there are some variables to which the investment decision is more likely to be sensitive. Typically, these would include the cost of capital and the sales forecast. The sales forecast, in particular, is often a crucial determinant of other cashflows used in the appraisal.

While it is beneficial to examine the sensitivity of the accept/reject decision in terms of a range of values for a key variable, it can also be costly in terms of both time and convenience (although use of spreadsheets can help remedy this). Consequently, many firms opt for a range of three values: one representing the 'truest' or 'baseline' estimate for the variable; a second, optimistic assumption, and a third, pessimistic assumption. There is no particular rule for use of sensitivity analysis; the company must make its judgement on the basis of the numbers which ensue. Nonetheless, because the use of sensitivity analysis offers additional information for making the final decision on a particular investment, it should enable the financial manager to make a better-informed judgement.

6.7.2 *Scenario analysis*

Scenario analysis is not unlike sensitivity analysis. The key difference being that sensitivity analysis considers the robustness of the investment decision to changes in a single key variable, scenario analysis considers the robustness of the investment decision to changes in a *range* of key variables. Once again, the calculations are often minimised to a consideration of a baseline scenario, an optimistic scenario, and a pessimistic scenario. Thus, for example, a pessimistic scenario may assume a worst-estimate case for the sales forecast, and the highest possible value for the cost of capital.

As with sensitivity analysis, there is no particular rule for use of scenario analysis. The firm must make its judgement on the basis of the numbers which ensue.

6.8 Investment appraisal: Introduction to newer techniques

In contrast to more traditional DCF techniques of capital budgeting, newer theoretical approaches have been suggested by financial economists. Perhaps the most clearly expounded is Dixit and Pindyck [1994] whose approach is based on the application of option-pricing theory to capital budgeting. They argue that their approach is superior to 'traditional' methods of capital budgeting because it provides an explanation of observable phenomena such as why firms often employ a hurdle rate cost of capital which is substantially higher than that observed in the market. Dixit and Pindyck note that investment decisions share three key characteristics to varying degrees:

- They are irreversible (partially or completely)
- There is uncertainty over the future rewards
- There is some leeway over the timing

Dixit and Pindyck argue that 'traditional' investment theory fails to recognise "the important qualitative and quantitative implications of the interaction between irreversibility, uncertainty, and the choice of timing." [1994: 1]. They explain that:

> a firm with an opportunity to invest is holding an "option" analogous to a financial call option—it has the right but not the obligation to buy an asset at some future time of its choosing. When a firm makes an irreversible investment expenditure, it exercises, or "kills," its option to invest. It gives up the possibility of waiting for new information to arrive that might affect the desirability or timing of the expenditure; it cannot disinvest should market conditions change adversely. This lost option value is an opportunity cost that must be included as part of the cost of the investment. [1994: 6]

According to Dixit and Pindyck, this opportunity cost can be quite large, and its omission from 'traditional' methods of capital budgeting explains the gap between existing theory and observed behaviour in practise. Like much of modern financial theory, this method of capital budgeting has yet to work its way from the arcane playing fields of the theoretician into the toolbox of the practitioner.

6.9 Sample questions

(1) Consider the following mutually exclusive projects:

Project	C_0	C_1	C_2	C_3	C_4	C_5
A	−160,000	200,000	0	0	0	0
B	−160,000	60,000	60,000	60,000	60,000	0
C	−160,000	40,000	40,000	40,000	40,000	40,000

(a) What is the payback period for each project?
(b) Which project is preferred according to the *NPV* criterion if the discount rate is 8%?

(c) How would the answer to (a) change if the discount rate was 5%?
(d) What is the Internal Rate of Return (*IRR*) for each project?

(2) *Société Nez de Caramel* manufactures *haute couture*. The company is considering investing in new AI-controlled production equipment, which will cost an initial sum of £ 20 million. The equipment is expected to last for five years, *after* which time it is expected to be sold to Ouvrières Chavs (a mass producer of clothing) for an estimated salvage value of £ 2 million. The equipment is expected to generate annual cash revenues of £ 9.5 million and will depreciate on a straight-line basis over the five years. Annual project-related expenses are expected to be £ 3.5 million. Assuming no taxes (for simplicity) and a required rate of return of 8%:
(a) Calculate the payback period for this investment?
(b) Calculate the Net Present Value (*NPV*) for this investment? How would this change if the discount rate increased to 14%?
(c) Calculate the Internal Rate of Return (*IRR*) for this investment?
(d) Would you recommend that Nez de Caramel undertake this investment? Explain fully

Chapter 7

(Financial) Investment Appraisal: Risk

7.1 Risk versus return

Risk is present throughout all existence. Benjamin Franklin is reputed to have said, "The only things in life which are certain are death and taxes", yet even these are uncertain with regard to their timing and magnitude respectively. Indeed, it might accurately be argued that the only thing in life which is certain is uncertainty!

All human decision-making involves taking risk into consideration. Even mundane everyday acts involve some form of risk. When crossing the road people explicitly acknowledge the risks involved by looking for oncoming traffic before crossing, trying to minimise risk of death or injury. When purchasing groceries people consider risk implicitly, by assuming that the foods bought will be safe, or that their safety is guaranteed by some organisation in authority. So, it is inevitable that in considering human decision-making in the corporate sphere the role of risk must be recognised explicitly.

Chapter 6 examined the process of capital investment appraisal, a company weighing up the relative costs and benefits of a capital investment. Because these benefits and costs take place in an unknown future, they can be only estimates; the actual values will likely differ from those estimates. Thus, there is an element of risk to capital budgeting. Each capital investment has its own inherent risk.

These risks must be fully reflected in the cost of capital applied in a Net Present Value appraisal of the investment. In this chapter risk is considered explicitly in a more scientific manner.

Chapter 4 explained how an interest rate (or 'yield') incorporates an element to compensate lenders for different kinds of risk. Thus, via interest rates the financial markets have a mechanism for 'pricing' risk. To understand risk, it must be considered from the objective overview of the financial marketplace, rather than from the subjective perspective of a single corporate entity. This means that in addition to considering the marketplace as a financial intermediary, it is necessary to consider the activities of all of the participants. Chapters 8 and 9 provide a detailed consideration of the demand side of the market for corporate funding. The remainder of this chapter is devoted to a consideration of the activities of the suppliers of funds: investors. It will offer insights into investor behaviour and also provide background technical information which will be useful in deriving the costs of capital (Chapter 8).

In the case of an (initial) offering by a corporation, investors are supplying funds to that corporation by purchasing the securities offered. This may be via the purchase of shares upon a company's flotation, or the purchase of corporate debt in the primary market. In either case, the primary aim of the investor is to earn a return on their funds, but also with an eye to the level of risk involved. This is as true for the individual investor as it is for the professional fund manager.

In this chapter the underlying assumption is that the market is efficient (Section 2.3.2), with all the consequent ramifications.

7.2 Portfolio theory

Possibly the most fundamental truism in all of finance is embodied by the risk-return trade-off. This shows that the 'price' of an investor desiring a higher expected return is the assumption of greater levels of risk. Lower risk involves the acceptance of lower levels of expected return. Thus, the two main characteristics of any financial asset will be its expected return (or yield) and its risk. The securities chosen to make up a portfolio are selected on the basis of their yield and risk characteristics.

7.2.1 *Yield (or expected return)*

A financial claim may be defined as a contract typically carrying an obligation on the issuer to make periodic payments (interest or dividends) and to redeem the claim at a stated value in any one of three ways:

(1) On demand;
(2) After a stated period of notice has been given; or
(3) On a given date or within a given range of dates.

It is entirely possible for one of the forms of payment to take a value of zero. One example might be the shares in a company which does not normally pay dividends (preferring to retain the profits for reinvestment within the firm).

Future periodic payments as well as that on redemption may be fixed or variable in value. For example, a bond may have a fixed rate of interest over its life and a fixed redemption value ('par') stated in advance. Alternatively, the interest may be paid at a variable rate. With an ordinary share in a listed company neither payment is fixed: dividends (the periodic payments) fluctuate according to the proportion of available profits which the directors decide to distribute to shareholders; the redemption value depends upon the market price of the share at the time of sale, or by a share of the realised assets should the company be wound up. Similarly, a deposit with a bank or building society possesses a fixed face value sum on redemption but a varying level of interest payments.

For the contractual right to receive either or both of these forms of future payment to rank as a financial claim the promise to pay must be unconditional. A life insurance policy, for example, justifies the title of a **financial claim** because it promises a given payment upon death or the prior attainment of a certain date. This is *not* the case with (e.g.) fire insurance, where payment is conditional, only occurring in the event of fire breaking out, which may not happen. Some contractual obligations to make future payments are not regarded as financial assets because they are not transferable from one owner to another. The payment of a wage or salary under a contract comes into this category.

The yield of a financial asset is the total of all expected future periodic payments plus the redemption payment. This is the *absolute* return on any financial asset. However, an investor will usually be more concerned with the value of their expected return relative to the purchase price of the asset, i.e. its *rate of return*. The percentage rate of return (or yield) of an asset is:

$$rate\ of\ return = \frac{receipt - expenditure}{expemditure}$$

where *receipt* is the sum of all future payments, both periodic and redemption, and *expenditure* refers to the purchase price of the asset. Typically, these values are unknown except in the present and the past, thus the *expected* rate of return is calculated and utilised. If the expected rate of return is positive then it would appear beneficial to purchase the particular financial asset (assuming transactions costs to be negligible, or zero), but this is not the whole story. If an investor can calculate the expected rates of return on all financial assets they can then be ranked according to their expected rates of return. At first glance it would seem reasonable to invest solely in the asset offering the highest expected rate of return, but this would indeed be unwise. This is because the risk of a financial asset—its second characteristic—must be considered in formulating investment selection strategy.

As noted, to induce investors to accept greater risk they must be compensated with greater expected rates of return, reflecting higher risk premiums. Consequently, there should be a positive relationship between the expected return on an asset and its level of risk. This might best be represented as:

$$k = r_f + \theta \tag{7.1}$$

where k is the expected return (also required rate of return, or cost of capital), r_f is the risk-free rate of return, and θ is the risk premium. This is shown graphically in Figure 7.1:

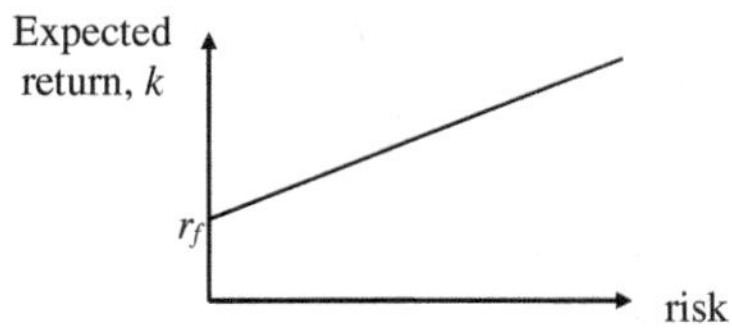

Figure 7.1. Risk versus return

7.2.2 *Risk and uncertainty*

While the yield on any (financial) asset is an unambiguous concept, it is more difficult to determine exactly what is meant by risk. In much of the literature 'risk' is used interchangeably with 'uncertainty', although they are by no means synonymous. The definitions first put forward by Frank Knight [1921] and John Maynard Keynes [1921] have been largely accepted since. The outcome of a decision is defined as involving *risk* if the probability of (considerable) loss is not small. The outcome of a decision is defined as *uncertain* if:

(1) the various pairs of possible outcomes are difficult to compare; or
(2) it is difficult to decide on a list of possible outcomes.

Consequently, for situations of risk there exists a well-defined probability function, while uncertainty implies that such a function is ill-defined, if it exists at all.

For Nobel Laureate Milton Friedman it is always possible to turn a situation of uncertainty into one of risk by assuming that the probability function is known at least subjectively. The apparent interchangeability of the two terms is typically based upon this view. It is one with which J. M. Keynes was very much at odds, especially in his later writings; referring to 'uncertainty' he argues:

> The sense in which I am using the term is that in which the prospect of a European war is uncertain, or the price of copper and the rate of interest twenty years hence, or the obsolescence of a new invention, or the position of private wealth-owners in the social system in 1970. About these matters there is no scientific basis on which to form any capable probability whatever. We simply do not know. [1936: 217]

Because of the very large amount of time-series data available on securities it can easily be argued that capital markets can be regarded as situations of risk. The plethora of historic data give rise to a set of probabilities for a large range of possible outcomes. It is on this basis that probability theory is used for modelling the impact of risk and (expected) return on investment behaviour.

Of course, the risk attached to any financial claim is not immutable. In part this is because the financial system is a highly dynamic sector of the economy, with intermediaries constantly seeking to innovate either to evade legislative constraints or to improve upon the competition. Thus, for example, with the appearance of new financial markets and the increased competition due to more trading on older markets, many financial assets experience diminishing marketability risk over time. Increasing internationalisation of the world's capital markets coupled with sensible deregulation should lead to higher potential returns for investors, partly in terms of a wider range of alternatives, as well as a diminution of risk within most of the various categories, and also because of the possibility of increased geographic portfolio diversification.

In addition to risk and uncertainty, more recent attention has been drawn to **Black Swan events**. Developed by Nicholas Nassim Taleb [2001, 2007], this metaphor is used to describe an event which is a complete surprise, something not even imaginable beforehand, which often has a major effect, and is often inappropriately rationalised *post hoc* with the benefit of hindsight. The term is based on a Latin expression which presumed that black swans did not exist. The phrase became reinterpreted as a reference to an unforeseen and consequential event after 1697 Dutch mariners discovered black swans in Australia!

7.2.3 *Risk and probability*

When considering risk most people will focus on the possibility of loss, i.e. 'downside risk'. Scientifically, risk deals with the probability of divergence from some 'normal' or 'expected' value. This divergence should include *both* downside risk (the risk of loss) as well as any 'upside potential' (the risk of gain). To quantify risk, begin by defining the expected return on a share, $E(R)$, as a weighted average of all of the possible returns, where the weights are the relevant probabilities:

$$E(R) = \sum_i p_I R_i \tag{7.2}$$

This weighted average, or expected return, is also referred to as the 'mean' of the distribution: μ or $\bar{R}$ in notation.

Example 7.1: For a stake (outlay) of £ 1,500, Ardiles Lotteries offers the chance of four possible prizes (outcomes) with the following corresponding probabilities:

Outcome number	Return, R	Probability, p	$p * R$
1	£ 1,000	0.1	£ 100
2	£ 2,000	0.2	£ 400
3	£ 3,000	0.4	£ 1,200
4	£ 4,000	0.3	£ 1,200
		$\sum p = 1.0$	$E(R) =$ £ 2,900

An initial outlay of £ 1,500 has an expected return of £ 2,900, which seems attractive at first glance.

More usually returns are expressed as *rates* of return (r), in percentages. Thus:

Table 7.1. Rates of return and probabilities

Outcome number	Rate of return, r	Probability, p	$p * r$
1	−0.05 or −5%	0.1	−0.005
2	0.02 or 2%	0.2	0.004
3	0.05 or 5%	0.4	0.02
4	0.07 or 7%	0.3	0.021
		$\sum p = 1.0$	$E(r) = 0.04$ or 4%

However, this ignores risk, which is quantified by the dispersion of the returns. This can be plotted as a probability distribution. Using data from Table 7.1 gives Figure 7.2:

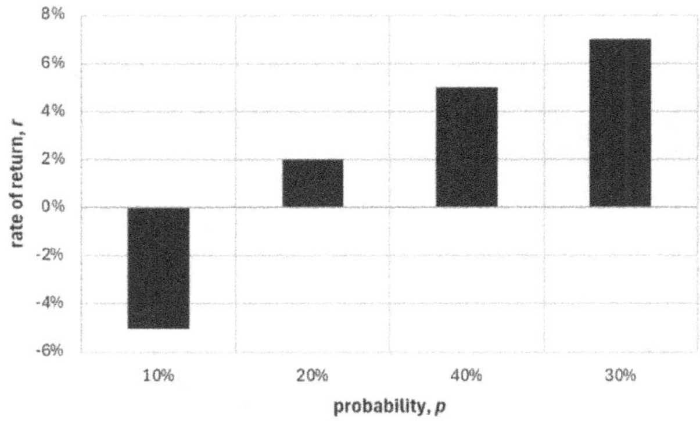

Figure 7.2. Rates of return and probabilities

In reality there are usually more than four possible outcomes for a given financial or economic variable, such as the return on a security. When there are a large number of possible outcomes the probability distribution will tend to look less discrete—more continuous as in Figure 7.3:

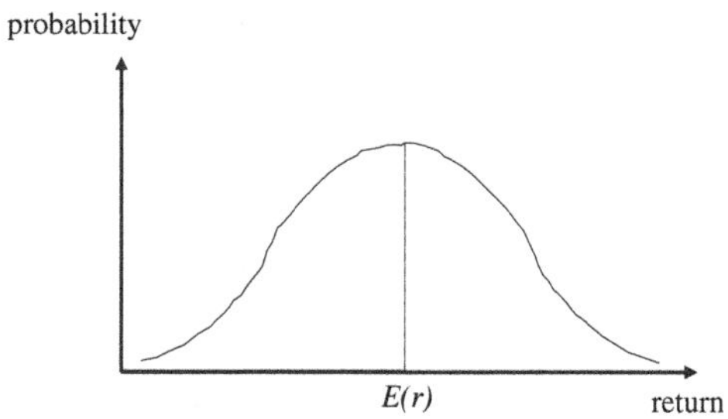

Figure 7.3. Probability distribution of rates of return

The lower the risk the narrower will be the dispersion of the curve. The greater the risk the flatter and more dispersed the curve. In the extreme, a completely certain outcome (probability = 100%) will appear as a single vertical line at its certain expected value, $E(r)$, going up to 100% probability. The dispersion of a probability distribution is quantified by making use of the statistical measure of standard deviation, σ:

$$\sigma = \sqrt{\sum_i p_i\{r_i - E(r)\}^2} \tag{7.3}$$

While perhaps daunting at first glance, this formula can be broken down into a series of simple calculations, each of which is individually straightforward:

(1) Calculate the expected return, $E(r) \equiv \bar{r} \equiv \mu$[1]
(2) Calculate the deviation of each possible return from the mean, $\{r_i - E(r)\}$
(3) Calculate the square of each deviation from the mean, $\{r_i - E(r)\}^2$
(4) Multiply each squared deviation by its probability, $p_i\{r_i - E(r)\}^2$
(5) Add these last up: $\sum_i p_i\{r_i - E(r)\}^2$
(6) Find the square root of this sum $\sqrt{\sum_i p_i\{r_i - E(r)\}^2}$.

This is best done using a simple table of calculations. Using data from Table 7.2:

Table 7.2. Calculation of standard deviation (risk), σ

Outcome number	**Rate of return, r**	**Probability, p**	$\{r_i - E(r)\}$	$\{r_i - E(r)\}^2$	$p_i\{r_i - E(r)\}^2$
1	−5%	0.1	−0.09	0.0081	0.0008
2	2%	0.2	−0.02	0.0004	0.0001
3	5%	0.4	0.01	0.0001	0.0000
4	7%	0.3	0.03	0.0009	0.0003
		$\sum p = 1.0$			$\sum = 0.0012$
					$\sigma = 0.03464$

The variance of the distribution is 0.0012 = 0.12%. The standard deviation, σ (= square root of the variance) is 0.03464 = 3.464%. This measures the risk of this share: the variation in its returns. A security with the same expected return but a higher standard deviation would be more risky, hence less attractive to a rational investor. For a financial asset it is usual for a security with higher risk to offer a higher expected return.

[1]Different authors use different ways of expressing expected return, from the *expectation operator*, $E(r)$, to 'r-bar', $\bar{r}$, and the mean, μ.

7.2.4 *The Markowitz approach*

The foregoing shows comparison of individual securities (or risky cash flows, returns on assets, etc.) using the statistical measures of mean (μ) and variance (or standard deviation, σ) for expected return and risk respectively. However, experience and observation show that investors generally do not purchase a single asset, preferring instead a *portfolio* of securities. At its simplest, the results of portfolio theory are little more than the time-honoured adage to avoid "putting all one's eggs into one basket". While the wisdom for holding a diversified portfolio of assets is almost as old as time, it was only with the pioneering work of Harry Markowitz [1952, 1959] and A. D. Roy [1958] that a sound theoretical explanation showed that any consideration of a portfolio needs to account for the interaction between the characteristics of the individual assets held in the portfolio. Consider the following mean-variance (μ-σ) characteristics:

	Mean, μ	**Variance, σ^2**	**Standard deviation, σ**
Asset A	0.20	0.2476	0.0613
Asset B	0.13	0.2433	0.0592

As expected, Asset A has both higher expected return (mean) and higher risk (as measured by its standard deviation). At first, this might seem to suggest that the best investment strategy would be to invest all of one's monies in Asset A; that there is little to gain by combining it with Asset B in a portfolio. Further analysis proves otherwise.

7.2.5 *Portfolio returns*

The expected return on a portfolio of assets is a weighted average of the expected returns on each of the individual securities. The weights are the proportions of the portfolio accounted for by each security, which must sum to one. Thus:

$$E(R_p) = w_1E(R_1) + w_2E(R_2) + w_3E(R_3) + w_4E(R_4)\ldots \quad (7.4a)$$

$$E(R_p) \equiv \mu_p = w_1\mu_1 + w_2\mu_2 + w_3\mu_3 + w_4\mu_4 \ldots \quad (7.4b)$$

where w_i is the proportion of Asset i in the portfolio (thus $\sum w_i = 1$), and μ_i is the expected return on asset i. Using summation notation:

$$E(R_p) = \sum_{i=1}^{N} w_i \cdot E(R_i) \tag{7.4c}$$

Or, using μ

$$\mu_p = \sum_{i=1}^{N} w_i \mu_i \tag{7.4d}$$

Example 7.2: Consider a two-asset portfolio consisting of £ 150 m worth of Asset X and £ 25 m worth of Asset Y. Thus, $w_X = 75\%$ and $w_Y = 25\%$. The expected return from this portfolio is

$$\mu_p \equiv E(R_p) = (0.75)(0.20) + (0.25)(0.13) = 0.1825 \quad \text{i.e. } 18.25\%.$$

A portfolio consisting of 50% asset X and 50% asset Y gives an expected return of

$$\mu_p \equiv E(R_p) = (0.5)(0.20) + (0.5)(0.13) = 0.165 \quad \text{i.e. } 16.5\%.$$

Regardless of the weights, the expected return on the portfolio always lies somewhere between the two individual asset expected returns. This confirms the notion that, based solely on returns, a portfolio consisting entirely of Asset X is preferred. But this neglects risk, the possible variance (standard deviation) in expected returns.

7.2.6 *Portfolio risk*

Intuition might suggest that the risk of a portfolio is a weighted average of the risks of the individual securities risks held in the portfolio. But this would be only partially correct. The risk on a portfolio of assets is more difficult to calculate, being based on a (seemingly) complex formula. In general, the portfolio risk depends on a few variables only:

- The risk of each individual security (its standard deviation, σ);
- The proportion of each security held in the portfolio (w_i); and
- The relationship between the various securities as measured by the covariance between their returns.

Thus, for a simple two-asset portfolio, risk is:

$$\sigma_p = \sqrt{(w_1^2\sigma_1^2 + w_2^2\sigma_2^2 + 2w_1w_2COV_{12})} \tag{7.5}$$

Where σ_p is the standard deviation of the portfolio, w_i represents the proportion of asset i held in the portfolio, σ_i is the risk of asset i measured by its standard deviation of returns, and COV_{12} is the covariance between the returns on asset 1 and asset 2. This latter term—the covariance—measures the degree to which the returns on the two assets move together, and is therefore related to the correlation coefficient, ρ, between the returns on any two assets:

$$COV_{12} = \sigma_1\sigma_2\rho_{12} \tag{7.6}$$

By selecting assets with low correlation of returns the overall risk of the portfolio can be reduced. This is because as the returns on (e.g.) asset 1 decline they will be offset by the returns asset 2 rising, keeping the overall return on the portfolio stable, i.e. with a low degree of variation.

Example 7.3: You recently had the good fortune to receive a financial windfall. After careful consideration of all the options, you decided to purchase a small portfolio of shares. You are impressed with the performance of two companies in particular—Greaves International plc and Chivers plc—and plan a two-asset portfolio of shares in those companies, which possess the following characteristics:

	Asset 1 (Greaves Int.)	**Asset 2 (Chivers plc)**
μ	0.12	0.08
σ	0.09	0.06
w	50%	50%

If you plan to allocate half of your portfolio to each asset ($w_1 = w_2 = 50\%$), what level of risk will you be assuming?

Suppose the correlation coefficient (ρ_{12}) between the individual asset returns is 1.0, i.e. the asset returns are perfectly (positively) correlated. The standard deviation of the portfolio would be

$$\sigma_p = \sqrt{(0.5^2 0.09^2 + 0.5^2 0.06^2 + 2(0.5)(0.5)COV_{12})}$$

Because $COV_{12} = \sigma_1\sigma_2\rho_{12}$ the standard deviation is

$$\sigma_p = \sqrt{(0.5^2 0.09^2 + 0.5^2 0.06^2 + 2(0.5)(0.5)(1.0)(0.09)(0.06))}$$

$$\sigma_p = 0.075$$

This combination offers a lower level of risk to the investor than for Greaves International ($\sigma = 0.09$), but marginally higher than that for Chivers plc ($\sigma = 0.06$). In practice it is highly unlikely to find two assets for a portfolio with perfectly correlated returns. Indeed, what a rational investor would ideally be seeking would be two assets with a *negative* correlation between their returns.

Suppose in Example 7.3 there had been a correlation coefficient (ρ) of -0.2? The standard deviation of returns on the two-asset portfolio would become 0.0488, a lower level of risk for the portfolio than for either of the individual assets of which the portfolio is composed.

A similar result occurs if the correlation coefficient is positive but lower than one. For example, a ρ_{12} of 0.1 results in a standard deviation of 0.0565, still lower than the risk for either of the two assets individually.

Using the data from Example 7.3 a graph of the portfolio risk (σ) resulting from different possible values for the correlation coefficient (ρ) between the individual investment returns shows a positive relationship as shown in Figure 7.4:

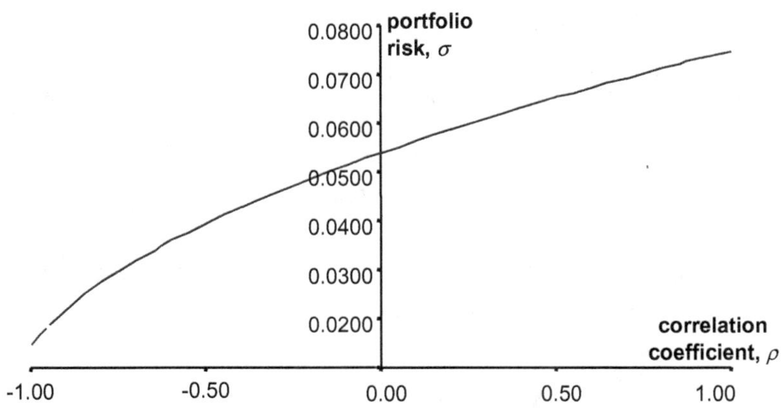

Figure 7.4. Risk (σ) vs correlation (ρ)

Another way of viewing this relationship is in risk-return (mean-standard deviation) space:

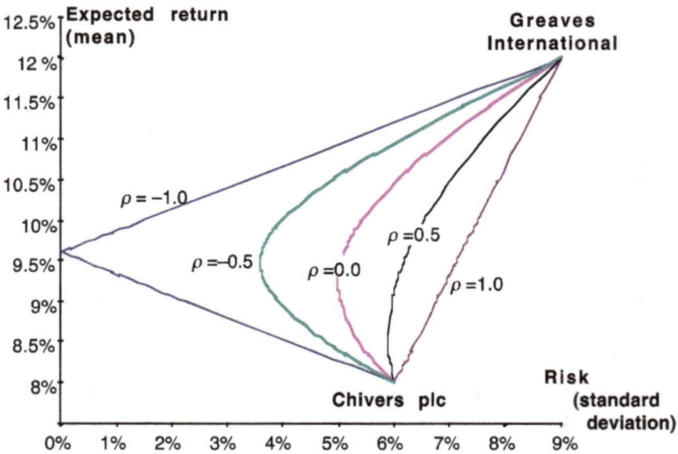

Figure 7.5. Expected return (μ or $E(R)$) vs risk (standard deviation, σ)

Again, using data from Example 7.3, the lines/curves between the two assets—Greaves International and Chivers plc—in Figure 7.5 show the variety of risk/return combinations which might occur with varying combinations of the two assets in a portfolio. When the $\rho =$ 1.0 these combinations lie on a straight line between the two assets. As ρ reduces the curve becomes more convex, and for any level of expected return the risk becomes lower. Ultimately, when $\rho = 1.0$ it becomes (theoretically) possible to reduce the risk of the two-asset portfolio to zero with an expected return of 9.6%.

The same principle also occurs for a multiple-asset portfolio (more than two assets). The general formula for portfolio risk, σ_p, is:

$$\sigma_p = \sqrt{\sum_{i=1}^{N}\sum_{j=1}^{N} w_i w_j \sigma_i \sigma_j \rho_{ij}} \tag{7.7}$$

where wi represents the proportion of the portfolio invested in asset i, σ is the standard deviation, and $-1 < \rho < +1$. Perhaps more clearly:

$$\sigma_p = \sqrt{\sum_{i=1}^{N} w_i^2 \sigma_i^2 + 2\sum_{i=1}^{N-1}\sum_{j=1}^{N} w_i w_j \sigma_i \sigma_j \rho_{ij}} \tag{7.8}$$

Example 7.4: You are considering investing in a portfolio consisting of three securities with the following characteristics:

p	Rate of return on		
	Security 1	**Security 2**	**Security 3**
0.1	0.25	0.25	0.1
0.4	0.2	0.15	0.15
0.4	0.15	0.2	0.2
0.1	0.1	0.1	0.25

The expected return on each of these three securities will be:

$$\mu_1 = 17.5\%, \quad \mu_2 = 17.5\%, \quad \mu_3 = 17.5\%$$

Using the formulas already explained, the risk (σ) for each of these securities:

$$\sigma_1 = 4.0311\%, \quad \sigma_2 = 4.0311\%, \quad \sigma_3 = 4.0311\%$$

There is little to choose between these three securities as they have *exactly* the same risk/return characteristics.

Intuition suggests that your portfolio will be the same regardless of the combination (weights) of these three securities. While the expected return of a portfolio of any combination of these assets will always yield 17.5%, the risk would differ.

Consider a portfolio consisting of one-quarter of Security 1, one-quarter of Security 3, and one-half of Security 3. The expected return of this portfolio would be:

$$\mu_p = (0.25 * \mu_1) + (0.5 * \mu_2) + (0.25 * \mu_3)$$
$$\mu_p = (0.25 * 0.175) + (0.5 * 0.175) + (0.25 * 0.175) = 17.5\%$$

Using equation 7.5 the risk attached to this portfolio would be:

$$\begin{aligned}\sigma_p^2 &= [(0.25^2 * 0.040311^2) + (0.5^2 * 0.040311^2) \\ &\quad + (0.25^2 * 0.040311^2)] + 2 * [(0.25 * 0.5 * 0.01) \\ &\quad + (0.5 * 0.25 * -0.01) + (0.25 * 0.25 * -0.02)] \\ \sigma_p &= 2.016\%\end{aligned}$$

The risk of a portfolio of all three assets is lower than any of the individual asset risks. This is largely due to the negative covariances between the returns of asset 2 and asset 3 ($COV_{23} = -0.01$), and between asset 1 and asset 3 ($COV_{12} = -0.02$). A portfolio split equally between the three securities (each accounting for one-third) has portfolio risk even lower, at 1.344%.

The implications from Example 7.4 are clear. To minimise the risk of any portfolio it is necessary to identify and include securities whose returns are (ideally) negatively correlated with those of existing securities in the portfolio. Once these securities have been identified, they should be combined in proportions which serves to minimise the risk, *ceteris paribus*. One way to consider this is via a simple 'thought experiment': imagine that you have a portfolio consisting of a single asset. This provides you with an expected return and a level of risk commensurate with those of the single asset *per se*. To reduce risk through diversification, add a second asset to the portfolio. It should be relatively easy to find a second asset with returns negatively correlated with those of the asset already in the portfolio. This will reduce the level of risk of the portfolio below that of either of the two assets of which it is comprised (see Example 7.4).

Diversify further by adding a third asset. Ideally, this should have returns correlated negatively with those on the two assets already in the portfolio; while possible, it will not be as easy as finding the second asset (see Example 7.4).

To further minimise risk via diversification, add an additional asset with returns negatively correlated with those assets already in the portfolio. The more of these latter there are, the more difficult it becomes to meet the criteria of negative correlation of returns. Thus, the more difficult it becomes to lower risk by the further addition of assets to the portfolio. This can be seen in Figure 7.6. Note the risk level never reaches zero!

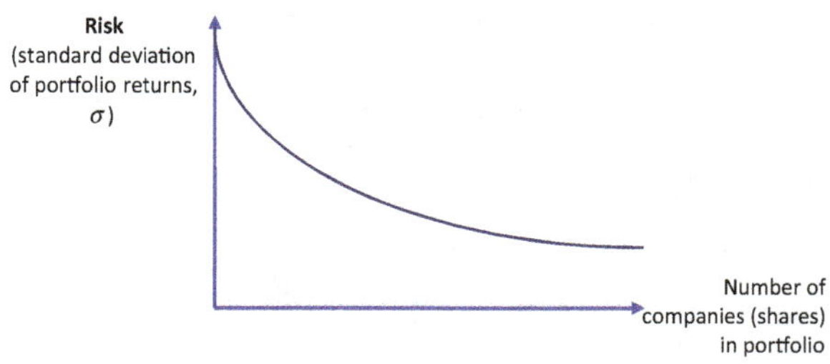

Figure 7.6. Portfolio risk vs number of shares

In summary, the Markowitz approach offers a good explanation of portfolio risk-reduction via diversification, something which has existed since long before Markowitz. In more recent literature it has also been called "mean-variance optimisation" (MVO), i.e. maximising expected return (mean) subject to risk (variance). However, it is not entirely practical, requiring calculation of the correlation coefficient between returns on all possible pairs of assets! While modern data access and personal computing would be able to handle this easily, in the late 1950s when these ideas were first in the public domain such technology did not yet exist. Theory and practice could not align. One workaround was to introduce a common measure, against which each individual asset's risk could be measured. Possibilities included a single benchmark security, or a benchmark portfolio. A benchmark portfolio might be the market portfolio: a portfolio consisting of every security available, in proportion to their overall availability.[2]

7.2.7 *Market risk*

To consider a market portfolio attention is focused specifically on market-traded investments, such as equity. Movements in share prices can be related to two major sources:

(1) **Unsystematic** (share-specific, or company-specific) information, i.e. that which will affect the company alone. Such information might include an increased level of company profits, death of the firm's key owner (especially if a charismatic figure or a person of great renown), the possibility of a takeover bid, or firm-specific industrial action.

[2]Every security available should include securities in every category: ordinary shares, preference shares, bonds, warrants, convertible bonds, and so on. If the ordinary shares issued by a given company represented 0.037% of the value of equity of all companies, the market portfolio's equity sector should also contain 0.037% of that share.

(2) **Systematic** (general market) information, i.e. that which tends to affect all companies, albeit to differing degrees, and not necessarily in the same direction. For example, macroeconomic policy changes, including such as changes in interest rates, or changes in the tax regime, etc.

For any given security, such as an ordinary share:

$$[\![\textit{Risk of a share}]\!] = \left[\!\!\left[\begin{array}{c}\textit{Systematic risk}\\(\textit{share market risk})\end{array}\right]\!\!\right] + \left[\!\!\left[\begin{array}{c}\textit{Unystematic risk}\\(\textit{share} - \textit{specific risk})\end{array}\right]\!\!\right]$$

And, for a portfolio:

$$[\![\textit{Risk of a portfolio}]\!] = \left[\!\!\left[\begin{array}{c}\textit{Systematic risk}\\(\textit{share market risk})\end{array}\right]\!\!\right] + \left[\!\!\left[\begin{array}{c}\textit{Unystematic risk}\\(\textit{portfolio} - \textit{specific risk})\end{array}\right]\!\!\right]$$

Through portfolio diversification it is possible to reduce the risk caused by unsystematic information, i.e. *diversification reduces unsystematic risk*. Systematic risk is market-wide: it cannot be reduced by diversification.[3] For reasons explained in the 'thought experiment' (immediately following Example 7.4), in practice there is likely to be a limit to risk reduction via diversification that can be achieved for a portfolio.

Although unsystematic risk for an individual company share can be substantial, it can be reduced by portfolio diversification. Figure 7.7 shows what many studies have revealed: it can be achieved with a portfolio of a relatively small number of securities—between fifteen and twenty appropriately selected shares. It also illustrates the relationship that exists between the risk for a given portfolio and the risk pertaining to the market *in toto*.

[3]Except, of course, via geographical diversification into other markets. In such a case the systematic risk applies globally, and not only to the local market. Local market 'systematic' risk can then be considered as another form of global unsystematic risk.

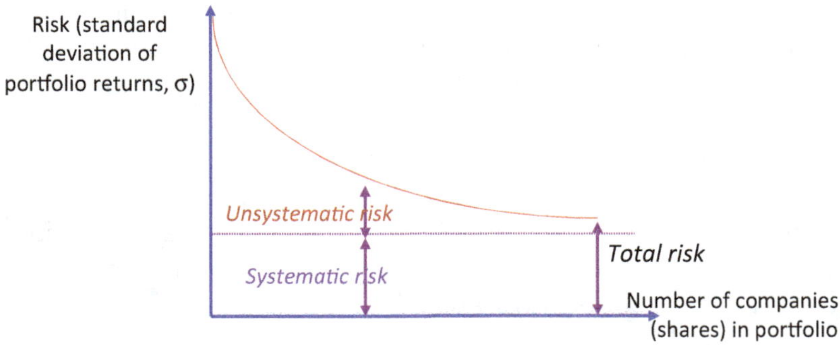

Figure 7.7. Systematic and unsystematic risk

It is the relationship between unsystematic risk and systematic risk which is the foundation of the Capital Asset Pricing Model (CAPM), the heart of which is the beta coefficient (β).

7.2.8 *The beta (β) coefficient*

The beta coefficient, β, measures the *relative* systematic risk of a share, i.e. the risk of a security relative to the market portfolio. Thus, the beta coefficient provides a single benchmark for easy comparison of a security's risk. It is no longer necessary to calculate the correlation coefficient of returns between each and every possible security combination. It is calculated as:

$$\beta_i = \frac{cov(r_i, r_M)}{var(r_M)} \tag{7.9}$$

where r_M indicates returns on the market portfolio, $var(r_M)$ is the variance of market returns, and $cov(r_i, r_M)$ is the covariance between returns on security i and returns on the market portfolio, M. A beta coefficient is sometimes described as a measure of security i's contribution to overall market risk. Market risk is the aggregate of the risks of all the securities in the market.

There are three possibilities for the value of β:

- $\beta_i = 1$ security i's returns will behave *exactly* as the returns on the market portfolio.

- $\beta_i > 1$ security i's returns are *more volatile* than those on the market. If the return on the market portfolio increases, security i's return also rises but in a greater proportion. Similarly for a decline in r_M.
- $\beta_i < 1$ security i's returns are *less volatile* than those on the market. If the return on the market portfolio increases, the return on security i rises but to a lesser degree. Similarly for a decline in r_M. Note that a negative beta ($\beta < 0$) is counter-cyclical the share's returns move opposite to those of the market.

One special case in this range occurs when $\beta = 0$. In this case the returns on the security are perfectly uncorrelated with the market return, thus the security has no market-related risk!

Logically, an investor who wished to follow ('track') the market should select a portfolio of securities with beta coefficient values close to one. If the market is in a 'bull phase', with share prices rising, then capital gains might be found by investing in securities with beta coefficients greater than one. This implies taking greater risk for potentially higher return. The risk-averse investor will prefer to hold a portfolio of securities with low beta coefficients.

In practice β coefficients are calculated using historical data, usually monthly observations over the previous five years. The data are used to estimate the total return—including dividends and any capital gain/loss—from investing in a security (r_i) and also from the relevant market index (r_M). These returns are then regressed against each other, the slope of the resulting regression line giving the beta coefficient (β). Figure 7.8 shows this graphically:

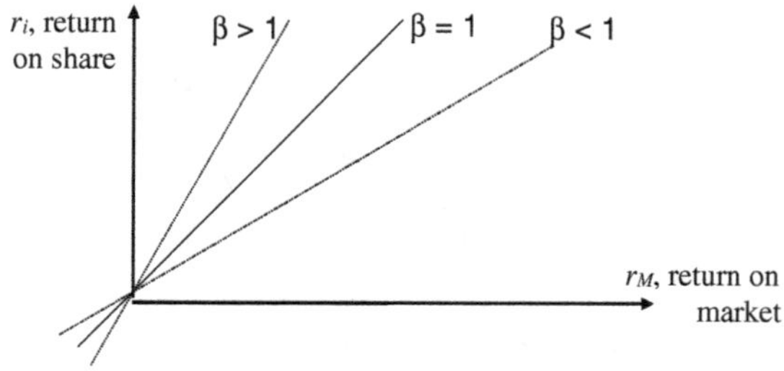

Figure 7.8. Beta coefficient, r_i vs r_M.

Note that $\beta = 1$ is a 45° line, where $r_i = r_M$ at every point on the line The regression equation for the line is $r_i = \alpha + \beta_i * r_M$ where β_i measures the slope of the line, and α is the intercept, which measures the **abnormal return**.[4] Theoretically, this should be zero. In practice it often has a value close to zero but may fluctuate between negative and positive values. $\alpha > 0$ is a 'buy' signal. If (many) investors respond to this then the share price will rise in response to the increased demand, leading to a reduction in its rate of return, lowering it towards 0. Similarly, but opposite, if $\alpha < 0$. Arbitrage ensures a value close to zero.

Although it is feasible to for an individual to collect data and calculate beta coefficients, it is not necessary. There are established providers who sell the results of such calculations. In the UK there is a monopoly, with the London Business School's Risk Measurement Service (London Share Price Database | Finance | London Business School) which, in addition to beta coefficients. London Business School also provides other statistical information on UK companies via its London Share Price Database (LSPD: London Share Price Database).

In the USA there is competition among beta providers, with highly competitive prices. Such providers include ABG Analytics (Stock Betas List for S&P 100 Large-Cap Stocks (abg-analytics.com)). Free access is available at Total Beta (nyu.edu). And there are the global providers including Bloomberg, Reuters and Refinitiv (LSEG).

Beta coefficients tend to be calculated mostly for the equity markets, largely due to ease-of-access, combined with the huge volume of data available. Indeed, some commentators give the impression that beta coefficients only apply to equity markets. In the UK, the FT Actuaries All-Share Index is used as a proxy for the market. The five-year beta has long been the most common, although it is feasible to estimate beta over a shorter period. Betas apparently increase in volatility as the length of the period reduces, although that may

[4]It is an abnormal return because if $\alpha > 0$ then $r_i > 0$ when $r_M = 0$, i.e. the share offers a positive return even when there is zero return on the market portfolio.

simply reflect current market conditions. Some financial information providers supply beta estimates based on five days to provide an extremely short-term view of market conditions.

7.3 The Capital Asset Pricing Model (CAPM)

Before World War II (1939–1945) it was intuitively understood that investor risk could be reduced by holding a diversified portfolio of assets. With the advent of the 1950s, the application of statistical and other quantitative methods to financial behaviour began to offer theoretical insights that had previously been missing. The work of Markowitz [1952, 1959], Roy [1958], and Tobin [1958] provided the foundations for modern portfolio theory.[5] Although these pioneering expositions provided a sound theoretical background, they could not be exploited practically: they required each security in a portfolio to be compared with every other possible security in terms of correlation of returns. This difficulty was eliminated in the 1960s with the work of Sharpe [1964], Lintner [1965] and Mossin [1966], resulting in the **Capital Asset Pricing Model**. The CAPM provides a simplifying device—the beta coefficient, β—for comparing each security's return with a single yardstick: the return on the market portfolio *in toto*. The CAPM is a single-factor model.

The Capital Asset Pricing Model assumes that:

(1) The market is efficient, and
(2) Investors live in a 'mean-variance' world (i.e. they measure return and risk by mean and variance respectively), with more return preferred to less, and lower risk preferred to higher.

Consequently, it is possible for a range of investments in both individual stocks and (more importantly) portfolios to be plotted in terms of their mean-variance characteristics:

[5] Although it has been more than 70 years, these ideas continue to be referred to as *modern* portfolio theory.

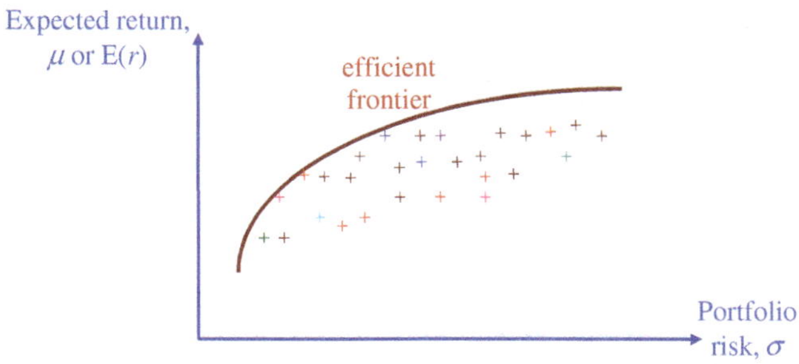

Figure 7.9. The efficient frontier in μ/σ space

In Figure 7.9 each + symbol represents a portfolio in terms of its mean-variance (μ/σ) characteristics. An **efficient portfolio** is one with:

- Highest expected return (μ) for a given risk level (σ), or
- Lowest risk (σ) for a given expected return (μ).

Some portfolios will be efficient, including single security portfolios. Given that rational investors prefer higher expected returns and lower levels of risk, efficient portfolios should dominate those which are inefficient. The locus of efficient portfolios is the efficient frontier.

Assuming the market is efficient, arbitrage will ensure that portfolios with low returns and high risks are sold, driving down their price and increasing their return. Ultimately this arbitrage should result in all portfolios on the efficient frontier. Where on the frontier an investor would choose depends entirely on their risk-aversion: a 'risk-lover' would tend to opt for the top right (higher μ, but also high σ), while a more risk-averse investor would be towards the left-hand end of the frontier (lower μ, but also lower σ). How far left would depend on the investor's degree of risk-aversion.

Introducing a risk-free investment (i.e. one with no variation in its return, $\sigma = 0$), which may be held in addition to a portfolio of risky assets, adds the Efficient Market Line (EML), as shown in Figure 7.10:

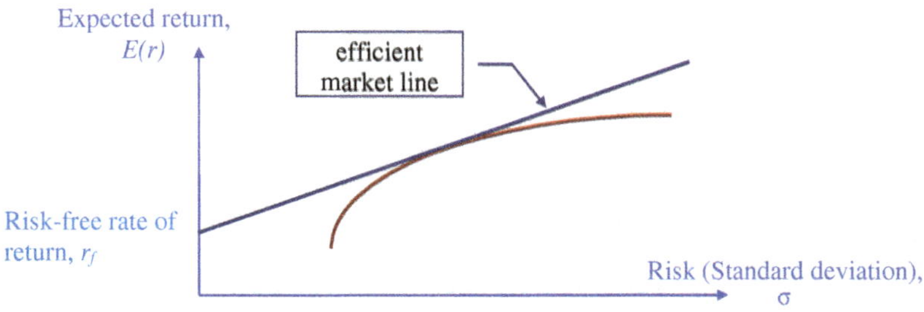

Figure 7.10. The Efficient Market Line (EML)

The EML is possible due to the introduction of a risk-free asset. This means that an investor is no longer restricted to portfolios on the efficient frontier. It is now possible to achieve a better risk-return combination using a portfolio of the risk-free investment plus any investment on the efficient frontier. The equation of the EML is:

$$E(r_p) = r_f + \left(\frac{E(r_m) - r_f}{\sigma_m}\right) * \sigma_p \qquad (7.10)$$

where p refers to some efficient portfolio, and m indicates the market (index) portfolio. $E(r_m) - r_f$ is the **market-risk premium**, measuring the additional return to the market portfolio over-and-above the risk-free rate of return, r_f. Equation 7.10 can be rewritten using μ instead of $E(r)$:

$$\mu_p = \mu_f + \left(\frac{\mu_m - \mu_f}{\sigma_m}\right) * \sigma_p$$

This should also hold for the market portfolio:

$$E(r_m) = r_f + \left(\frac{E(r_m) - r_f}{\sigma_m}\right) * \sigma_m \qquad (7.11)$$

This shows clearly that the market portfolio lies on the EML *and also* on the efficient frontier: the terms σ_m cancel each other, as do the r_f, leaving the truism that $E(r_m) = E(r_m)$. The only place this can occur is at their point of tangency.

The market portfolio consists of all shares with the following characteristics:

- The expected return on the market is a weighted average of the individual share expected returns, $E(r_m) = \sum w_i \cdot E(r_i)$, where the weights sum to one, $\sum w_i = 1$.
- The risk (variance) of the portfolio is a weighted sum of the covariances, $\sigma_m^2 = \sum w_i \cdot \sigma_{im}$, where $\sigma_{im} = cov(r_{i_i} m)$.

Using these, equation 7.10 can be expanded to:

$$E(r_p) = \sum w_i \cdot E(r_i) = \sum_i w_i r_f + \left(\frac{E(r_m) - r_f}{\sigma_m^2}\right) * \sum_i w_i \sigma_{im}$$

Alternatively:

$$\sum w_i * \left\{E(r_i) - r_f + \left(\frac{E(r_m) - r_f}{\sigma_m^2}\right) * \sigma_{im}\right\} = 0$$

In an efficient market, where individual shares are bought and sold, the only practical solution to this equation is:

$$E(r_i) - r_f + \left(\frac{E(r_m) - r_f}{\sigma_m^2}\right) * \sigma_{im} = 0$$

for all shares. Using the definition of β above this becomes:

$$E(r_i) = r_f + [E(r_m) - r_f] * \beta_i \tag{7.12}$$

which is the **fundamental equation of the Capital Asset Pricing Model** and describes the Securities Market Line (Figure 7.11). The expected return on an investment is related to:

- A risk-free return (proxied by e.g. the return on 90-day government bills)
- An additional premium the stock market provides over and above the risk-free rate, $E(r_m) - r_f$
- The individual variability of each share's return relative to the market average, β

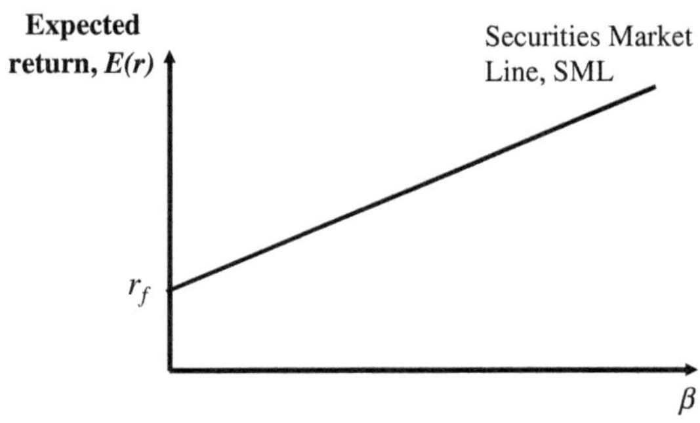

Figure 7.11. The Securities Market Line

The SML shows the positive relationship between a portfolio's expected return, $E(r)$, and it's risk as measured by β. The slope of the EML is the market risk premium, $E(r_m) - r_f$.

Example 7.5: The expected return on the market portfolio, $E(r_m) = 16\%$, and $r_f = 7\%$. The market risk premium, $E(r_m) - r_f$ (will be 9%).

For a portfolio with $\beta = 1$, the market risk premium should equal the market risk premium. A security with $\beta = 2$ should be twice as risky as the market average, and so its market risk premium should be twice the market risk premium. Using Equation 7.12

$$E(r_i) = r_f + [E(r_m) - r_f] * \beta_i$$
$$E(r_i) = 7\% + [16\% - 7\%] * 2 = 25\%$$

The importance of CAPM as part of modern financial theory should not be underestimated. While the underlying assumptions are quite rigorous (and some might argue unrealistic) it goes a long way to providing an explanatory framework for relating risk and return, which provides a useful tool for analysing many situations.

Note that the beta of a portfolio can be calculated as the weighted average of the betas of the individual shares, with the weights reflecting the individual asset values:

$$\beta_p = \sum_i w_i \beta_i \tag{7.13}$$

where β_p = the portfolio beta, β_i represents the betas for the individual shares, and w_i represents the relevant weights. This enables the investor to choose assets for their portfolio which will achieve their target portfolio beta.

7.3.1 *The risk-free rate: Afterthoughts*

The two main methodological difficulties in using CAPM are defining the market portfolio and finding a proxy for the risk-free rate. The market portfolio has traditionally been proxied by the relevant market index—Dow Jones, S&P, FTSE, etc—despite academic criticisms. The risk-free rate can be defined as the rate of return on a hypothetical investment making all contracted payments with certainty over a finite time-horizon. The risk-free rate has traditionally been proxied by the yield on government bonds, largely on the basis that these are default risk-free (in high-income economies, at least).

Theoretically, it can be argued that the risk-free proxy should be the return on short-term government bonds (bills, such as T-bills in the USA or short gilts in the UK). This is because they have the lowest purchasing power risk: inflation has less impact in the short run. However, in a low inflationary environment longer term bonds may be no more risk than bills with regard to inflation. In fact, the evidence suggests that the price of bills (and hence their rate of return) is more volatile than the return on longer-term bonds.

In the UK the Bank of England publishes **SONIA** (the Sterling Overnight Index Average rate), the UK's risk-free reference rate. It is a measure of the rate of interest paid on eligible short-term wholesale funds in the sterling unsecured deposit market.

In the USA it has become customary for business valuation to use the long-term yield on US Treasury bonds as the risk-free rate of return, primarily because the risk of the US government defaulting is virtually zero. For other valuations, especially with short term horizons such as option pricing, a short-term rate such as the interbank lending rate is often considered preferable.

7.3.2 *Value additivity*

A company can reasonably be described as a portfolio of the (real) investment projects it undertakes. Imagine a company consisting of only two projects, A and B. The market value of the firm will be $PV(\text{A}+\text{B}) = PV(\text{A}) + PV(\text{B})$. This may seem a little too obvious. Using CAPM, assume that:

- Each project lasts for only one year generating a cash flow of £ 100 at the end of the year
- Project A has a β of 1.0, project B has a β of 2
- The risk-free rate (r_f) is 10% *per annum*, and the market risk premium $[E(r_m) - r_f]$ is 8% *per annum*

The expected return on project A is $E(r_i) = r_f + [E(r_m) - r_f] * \beta_i = 10\% + [8\%] * 1 = 18\%$. This results in $PV(\text{A}) = \frac{£\,100}{1.18} = £\,84.75$.

The expected return on project B is $E(r_i) = r_f + [E(r_m) - r_f] * \beta_i = 10\% + [8\%] * 2 = 26\%$. This results in $PV(\text{B}) = \frac{£\,100}{1.26} = £\,79.37$.

Because of value additivity, $PV(\text{A} + \text{B}) = £84.75 + £79.37 = £164.12$.

Alternatively, using CAPM, first calculate the β of (A + B) using a weighted average:

$$\beta_{\text{A+B}} = \beta_{\text{A}} * \left[\frac{PV(\text{A})}{PV(\text{A}+\text{B})}\right] + \beta_{\text{B}} * \left[\frac{PV(\text{B})}{PV(\text{A}+\text{B})}\right] = 1.484$$

Second, calculate the expected return:

$$E(r_{\text{A+B}}) = r_f + [E(r_m) - r_f] * \beta_i = 0.1 + [0.08] * 1.484 = 21.87\%$$

Finally, calculate the present value:

$$\boldsymbol{PV(\text{A}+\text{B}) = \frac{£\,200}{[1 + E(r_{\text{A+B}})]} = £\,164.12}$$

7.3.3 *Introduction to the Arbitrage Pricing Theory (APT)*

While CAPM offers theoretical and practical insights beyond those of its progenitor, it is certainly not immune to criticism. There have been substantial criticisms concerning the credibility of its underlying assumptions. These include investors having quadratic utility functions, or that the probability distribution of returns is normal.

Additionally, CAPM is dependent upon the existence of a market portfolio of all risky assets.

The difficulty of finding a truly accurate proxy for a risk-free rate of return is noted in Section 7.3.1.1. Empirical studies have found that beta coefficients for individual securities tend not to be stable, while those for portfolios were for long sample periods and adequate trading volume.

One response to these criticisms by academics was to offer an alternative asset pricing theory which required only limited, credible assumptions and would also be regarded as intuitive. This resulted in the **Arbitrage Pricing Theory** (APT). While CAPM is a single-factor model—relating the expected return on a stock (or portfolio) to the market portfolio—APT is a *multi-factor* model which relies heavily on the principles of arbitrage. First developed by Ross [1976], APT is built on three main assumptions:

(1) Perfect capital markets
(2) Investors prefer more wealth to less wealth under certainty
(3) The stochastic process generating asset returns can be represented by the (linear) N-factor model $r_j = a_j + b_{j1}f_1 + b_{j2}f_2 + b_{j3}f_3 + \cdots + b_{jN}f_N + \varepsilon_j$

for all $j = 1 \ldots N$, where r_j is the return on asset j, a_j is a constant for asset j, f_j represents factor scores, b_{jk} represents the reaction of asset j's returns to movements in f_j, ε_j represents a unique effect on asset j's returns (i.e. an effect which only impacts asset j), and N is the total number of assets.

Thus, APT posits that the returns on any given asset will be determined by a series of factors common to all assets (*systematic* factors, represented by fj), and by factors unique to any given asset (*unsystematic* factors, represented by ε_j). It is assumed that f are uncorrelated with each other, and also with ε_j. The means of f and ε are assumed to be zero.

Because investors are assumed rational, they will choose to diversify their portfolio to eliminate risk via ε_j. Market equilibrium occurs when arbitrage will no longer yield better returns or lower risk. At this point, the expected return on asset j, $E(r_j)$ would be a linear function of the various factors (not yet specified):

$$E(r_j) = r_f + b_{j1}RP_1 + b_{j2}RP_2 + b_{j3}RP_{31} + b_{j4}RP_{41} + \cdots + b_{jN}RP_N$$

where r_f is the risk-free rate of return, and $RP_i = (f_i - r_f)$ are the risk premiums for each of the common factors identified.

By looking explicitly at common factors, APT recognises that some share returns will be more sensitive than others to given factors, avoiding the CAPM assumption that this is all implicit in the return on the market portfolio.

APT does not pre-specify the factors in advance. Rather, it requires accurate determination of the relevant factors using an advanced statistical technique: factor analysis.[6] Chen, Roll and Ross [1986] identified four main macroeconomics factors as significant in explaining security returns:

- Unanticipated changes in inflation,
- Unanticipated changes in GNP, usually proxied by an industrial production index,
- Unanticipated changes in investor confidence, due to changes in the default (risk) premium in corporate bonds,
- Unanticipated shifts in the yield curve (the term structure of interest rates).

Apart from their usefulness in calculating the cost of capital (which is also the expected return), both CAPM and APT allow investors to determine if securities or portfolios are under- or over-priced and act accordingly (buy or sell). Of course, in an efficient market such mis-pricing would not last for very long at all.

7.4 Time diversification: A footnote

Note that Markowitz, CAPM and APT are all static models. They consider the construction of a portfolio for a single period of time. There have been attempts to expand the time horizon of these models for multi-period time horizons, but these are quite complicated and

[6]For the brave, there is an excellent guide to factor analysis at stats.oarc.ucla.edu/spss/seminars/introduction-to-factor-analysis/a-practical-introduction-to-factor-analysis/.

not really suitable for an introductory book like this. However, there is a simple adage which states that "time diversifies risk". Attributed to Peter Bernstein and Jeremy Siegel, this notion is of particular relevance to the wealth management industry which takes a much longer time-horizon than investment management, which is more focused on asset allocation.

Put simply, time diversification is that idea that the volatility of risky assets declines over increasingly lengthy periods of time, i.e. longer investment horizons. If true, one of the key implications is that younger investors should hold a larger percentage of riskier assets (e.g. shares) in their portfolios than older investors, because they have more time for good years in the future to offset any more recent bad years of investment returns. More broadly:

- Over the longer run, an investor can be reasonably sure a higher-volatility portfolio will earn more than a lower-volatility portfolio.
- The longer the investment horizon the larger the percentage of a portfolio that should be invested in equity and other higher-return assets (which will also involve higher risk).

One way of showing this to be true is the relationship between long-run risk and short-run risk:

$$\sigma_{annualised\ return\ over\ T\ periods} = \frac{\sigma_{annual\ return}}{\sqrt{T}} \tag{7.14}$$

Thus, for example if an equity fund has a standard deviation of 25% p.a. has a total standard deviation over four years of $\frac{25\%}{\sqrt{4}} = 12.5\%$. This clearly illustrates risk reduction via time diversification.

7.5 Sample questions

The following questions can be solved either 'by hand' or using a spreadsheet. A good way to ensure your understanding is to use both methods to cross check your answers.

(1) Characteristics of the securities held in a portfolio are:

Securities	Beta (β)	Expected Return	Percentage held
Share A	1.1	14%	26%
Share B	0.8	10%	18%
Share C	1.7	18%	31%
Treasury Bill	0	2%	25%

(a) Calculate the expected return and beta (β) of this portfolio.
(b) How does the risk of this portfolio compare with that of the market portfolio?

(2) A portfolio manager has £ 100,000,000 to manage. She can choose to invest in shares and/or bonds. Cash is also available for lending or borrowing. She has the following information about future returns:

- Average expected return on stocks = 15% per annum
- Average expected return on bonds = 6% per annum
- Average standard deviation on stock returns = 5.5% per annum
- Average standard deviation on bond returns = 2.5% per annum

(a) Compute the expected return and standard deviation of returns for the following three portfolios if the correlation coefficient between stocks and bonds is 0.5:

(i) Portfolio is 33% bonds and 67% shares
(ii) Portfolio is 50% bonds and 50% shares
(iii) Portfolio is 67% bonds and 33% shares

(b) Compute the expected return and standard deviation of returns for the same three portfolios if the correlation coefficient (ρ) between stocks and bonds is equal to 0.
(c) If the portfolio manager is a 'risk lover' and wants to maximize her expected return, which portfolio would you recommend?
(d) In theory, how far can she increase her expected return? Explain fully.

Chapter 8

The Cost of Capital

Possibly the most important concept in all of finance is *valuation*, in theory and in practice. Any stream of cash flows can be the subject of valuation. In previous chapters we made extensive use of Net Present Value for valuation purposes: for debt (Chapter 4), equity (Chapter 5), and (real) investment projects (Chapter 6). Calculation of NPV requires calculation of an appropriate discount rate, usually determined in the financial markets. To the provider of funds—the investor—the discount rate represents a *required rate of return*; to the corporation seeking funds, the discount rate represents its *cost of capital*, the cost of acquiring or using funds. Naturally, cost refers to *opportunity cost*. There are a number of ways of defining the cost of capital, including:

- The minimum return expected by an investor in order to remain in an existing investment (or be tempted into a new one)
- The minimum rate of return which the firm must earn on its new investments to cover its investment costs. It reflects the return which might have been earned from alternative investments of equal risk.

The funding for a company's investments can be acquired from either internal or external sources. Traditionally, three major sources are recognised:

- Equity
- Debt
- Retained earnings

Retained earnings are an internal source of funds, while debt and equity are raised from external sources. For very large investments a company usually needs to raise specific fresh funding. For most purposes a company would consider a pool of funds for investment, without breaking down the sources. Regardless, different sources of capital usually have different costs, which should be calculated on an after-tax basis. Before considering the company's overall (or weighted average) cost of capital, we consider them individually.

8.1 The cost of debt

Stated simply, the cost of debt is the cost incurred by a firm when it acquires funds by borrowing. This applies whether the borrowing is from a bank or from the issue of bonds. If a company can borrow funds at 9% then, by definition, its *component cost of debt* (k_d) is 9%. For example, if a firm borrows £ 100,000 for one year, paying the suppliers of those funds £ 9,000 annual interest, then:

$$k_d = \frac{interest}{principal} = \frac{\text{£}\,9,000}{\text{£}\,100{,}000} = 9\% \tag{8.1}$$

The simplicity of this approach ignores certain complicating factors, such as multi-year borrowing and corporate taxation. When funds are borrowed on a multi-year basis, the cost of debt should be calculated using the bond valuation formula (Formula 4.1):

$$P_B = \left[\sum_{T}^{t=1} \frac{c_t}{(1+k_d)^t}\right] + \left[\frac{M}{(1+k_d)^T}\right] \tag{8.2}$$

where c_t is the coupon payment at time t, M is the capital (principal) repayment at maturity, and P_B is the issue price (or money raised). The yield-to-maturity, k_d, (also known as redemption yield, or *IRR*) is the cost of debt. This can be rewritten, using the annuity formula for the coupon payments:

$$P_B = \mathrm{c}\left[\frac{1}{k_d} - \frac{1}{k_d(1+k_d)^t}\right] + \left[\frac{M}{(k_d)^t}\right] \tag{8.3}$$

This approach easily incorporates many different kinds of debt, including discount bonds, and can even be extended to include embedded option structures as well.

Because interest is normally paid out before tax, it is neccesary to adjust the cost of debt. One way is to estimate the after-tax cost of debt, k_d^* as:

$$k_d^* = k_d(1-\tau) \tag{8.4}$$

where k_d is the pre-tax cost of debt, calculated as above, and τ is the (marginal) rate of corporate income tax. The impact of interest being tax-deductible is known as the **tax-shield effect**.

The main drawback is that this approach is completely historic. The cost of existing debt is calculated without reference to contemporary economic conditions. For a company considering new investment it would be more logical to use the cost of *new* debt. It can be argued on theoretical grounds that the incremental cost (i.e. the marginal cost) of taking on new debt should be considered, especially as this may cause an increase in the cost of existing debt: it increases the risk. The higher the level of debt, the greater the risk that a company will default in part or in full. If the company has existing debt which it can choose to use for a particular investment (or redeem the debt), the current cost of replacement is the sensible option. Only if there is an existing facility with spare capacity should the historic cost of debt be used.

Some companies prefer to subdivide their debt by maturity and estimate the cost of each maturity band separately. Using this approach the total cost of debt would be a weighted average of the various debts issued, which is both sensible and acceptable, especially from a yield curve perspective.

8.2 The cost of equity

There are two main techniques for calculating the cost of equity capital: using the equity valuation model (Chapter 5) or using the Capital Asset Pricing Model (Chapter 7).

In the same way that the cost of debt can be calculated by 'inverting' the bond valuation formula, the cost of equity can also be obtained by 'inverting' the equity valuation formula. This involves forecasting the future stream of dividend payments. Like any forecast, this is fraught with difficulty. It makes sense to simplify the model and assume the future path dividends are likely to take.

This can be done by reference to the company's stated dividend payout policy, or by extrapolating the path of its recent dividend payments. One such simplifying approach is to calculate the cost of equity using (Gordon's) constant growth model (Equation 5.9) which gives:

$$k_e = \frac{D_1}{P_0} + g \tag{8.5}$$

This shows the cost of equity capital, k_e, (return on equity) consisting of two elements: an expected dividend yield, D_1/P_0, and the growth rate of dividends, g. Some analysts prefer to distinguish between existing equity and new (or external) equity, as the latter involves the additional costs of flotation.

A second method of estimating the cost of equity capital is to use the Capital Asset Pricing Model (CAPM):

$$k_e = r_f + \beta[E(r_M) - r_f] \tag{8.6}$$

The cost of equity, k_e, is related to current market conditions via $E(r_M)$. It assumes the company has not changed its type of business or its size (scale) over the period of beta (β) estimation. If the company is private or does not have a long record of results, then applying this formula will be more difficult. Under such circumstances it becomes necessary to work with proxies.

Note that there are key differences between these two approaches:

- The equity (dividend) valuation model is forward-looking, based on expected future dividends. CAPM looks backwards, using historical data.
- The equity (dividend) valuation model is based on fundamentals. CAPM is based on market factors.

Because CAPM is backward-looking while the equity valuation model is forward-looking, they are likely to give quite different values. In practice both are used, although CAPM tends to have more adherents. Although there have been very few studies of this, Graham and Harvey [2001] discovered 74 per cent of (392) companies using CAPM to estimate the cost of capital. Despite its limitations, the model remains widely used by academics and analysts.

Companies should estimate their costs on an after-tax basis, as seen above for the cost of debt, k_d. For CAPM to be used on a post-tax basis, then the pre-tax risk-free rate, r_f, needs to be adjusted to $r_f * (1 - \tau)$, where τ is the marginal tax rate for the firm (*not* the historic or actual tax rate). Similarly for the market risk premium, $[E(r_M) - r_f]$.

Finally, it is worth noting that the cost of equity capital will always be greater than the cost of debt capital: $k_e > k_d$. This is because cashflows from debt (interest payments, capital repayments) are much less risky from the investor perspective than cashflows from equity (dividends, possible capital gains). Consequently, investors will require a higher expected return from equity than from debt, thus a higher cost of equity from the perspective of the firm. Additionally, because debt is typically subject to a **tax-shield effect**, being effectively tax-deductible (Section 8.1), then the risk premium on equity is increased in consequence.

Since 2008, Pablo Fernandez and colleagues from IESE Business School (University of Navarra) have been publishing the results of surveys of market-risk premium and risk-free rate in 96 countries. AT the time of writing the latest results were published in March 2024. The survey is based on the results of an email sent to

> "more than 14,000 email addresses of finance and economics professors, analysts and managers of companies obtained from previous correspondence, papers and webs of companies and universities".

It is perhaps not surprising that a wide range of results are recorded for the many different countries, with higher-income economies typically showing both lower market-risk premium and risk-free rates than middle and lower-income economies. For 2024 the market-risk premium ranges between a low of 5.2% (Canada) and a high of 22.7% (Ghana). The respective figures for the risk-free rate are 1.1% (Japan) and 18.7% (Egypt). However, even within a given country there is a wide range of different values offered by survey respondents. Perhaps surprisingly, USA respondents range between 3% and 16% for the market-risk premium, and 1.5% to 10% for the risk-free rate. Similar figures for the UK are between 4% and 8% for the market-risk premium, and 2% to 6% for the risk-free rate. Similar figures for the expected return on equity, $k_e = r_f + [MRP]$, show similar ranges, both across countries and within. The authors also compare current survey results with those of past surveys. One of their most interesting conclusions is:

> "that many market participants (equity investors, investment banks, analysts, companies...) do not use standard theory (such as a standard representative consumer asset pricing model...) for determining their Required Equity Premium, but rather, they use historical data and advice from textbooks and finance professors. Many investors still use historical data and textbook prescriptions to estimate the required and the expected equity premium." [2024: 12]

8.3 Other costs of capital

8.3.1 *The cost of retained earnings*

Some people like to make the case that the cost of retained earnings is zero, i.e. retained earnings are a free source of funds. This is, of course, nonsense, not least because it ignores *opportunity cost.* Theoretically, if there no transaction costs or taxes, then a company could (i) distribute all of its earnings in the form of dividends, and (ii) simultaneously request from its shareholders more funds, at the cost of equity capital, k_e. While this has an intuitive appeal, it is not something which companies tend to do. The main reason why (at least some) earnings are retained is to avoid the expense and delay such a procedure would entail. The logical equivalence is why the cost of retained earnings are also k_e. The only cost advantage of retained earnings is such items as:

- Issue and flotation expenses, as noted above
- The discount on newly-issued shares re: current price which needs to be taken into account.

Analogously, it has been (incorrectly) argued that depreciation should be regarded as a source of funds and be treated in a similar way to retained earnings. The purpose of depreciation is to record (in some way or other) the expiration of an earlier investment. Therefore depreciation is (theoretical) revenue put aside to maintain the existing structure of the company. It does not represent the method of originally funding the investment. Thus, depreciation is not a free source of funds, unless the decision has been made not to maintain the structure and should not be included in the cost of financing. The usual argument is that if funds are provided from the depreciation account, they are charged at the average cost of capital, calculated using all three sources of funds.

8.4 Tying it all together: The weighted average cost of capital (WACC)

The most common conceptual model for calculating the cost of capital is the Weighted Average Cost of Capital (WACC). This is a weighted average of the costs of the various individual sources of capital:

$$WACC \equiv k = \sum_i \pi_i k_i \tag{8.7}$$

where k_i are the individual sources of capital, and π_i represents the corresponding proportions. If the only sources of capital are debt and equity:

$$WACC \equiv k = \pi_d k_d + \pi_e k_e \tag{8.8}$$

Where π_e is the proportion of equity in the total capital, and π_d is the proportion of debt in the total capital. Obviously $\pi_d + \pi_e = 1$.

As well as practical problems, there are some theoretical issues that need to be addressed. For example, how are the weights (π_i) to be estimated? The technique usually employed is to use data from the company accounts:

$$\pi_d = \frac{D}{D+E} \quad \text{and} \quad \pi_e = \frac{E}{D+E} \tag{8.9}$$

where

E = value of equity = (shares issued) $*$ (current market price) and
D = market value of existing debt.

Some analysts prefer to use book values rather than market values, in which case:

E = total book value of equity (including premia accounts, retained earnings, etc) and
D = book value of medium- and long-term debt (i.e. *not* working capital).

If WACC is the discount rate used to assess future activities then market values, which are current, must be more relevant. However, if the company is more interested in measuring existing investments or past performance, then book values, which are historic, are more appropriate. What *cannot* be done is combine the two. This would be the cause of confusion, because while the changing value of equity through its share price is well understood the fact that debt also has a varying value for a given level of future interest payments is not always so well comprehended.

Further, a reminder that dividends are paid net of tax, unlike interest which is tax-relievable. Although the usual adjustment is to estimate the post-tax cost of debt as $k_d^* = k_d(1-\tau)$, a better alternative theoretically is to modify the value of debt, D, to $D(1-\tau)$, recognising the fact that the effective post-tax level of debt is lower, relative to the post-tax level of equity.

Proof. Assume interest paid is iD, where i is the interest rate and D is value of debt. The saving in tax is τiD per annum. The PV of these savings is:

$$\sum_{t=1}^{\infty} \frac{\tau iD}{(1+r)^t} = \frac{\tau iD}{r} = \tau D$$

assuming that $r \approx i$. Thus, the total tax benefit of the debt is τD, i.e. the net level of debt is $D(1-\tau)$.
QED

Note that there is a strong (implicit) assumption in WACC that the current level of leverage (however measured) will continue, i.e. any new investment will be funded using the same mix of debt and equity. Yet, there is no reason why this should be the case. One alternative is to use the Marginal Cost of Capital (MCC: "the cost of the last dollar of capital raised."), which considers the marginal cost of new capital (both debt and equity) and includes both the cost of raising the new money and any cost or benefit on the market value of the existing financing. In theory this is calculated as:

$$\begin{bmatrix}\text{total cost of all financing}\\ \text{including new investment}\end{bmatrix} \textit{less} \begin{bmatrix}\text{total cost of}\\ \text{old financing}\end{bmatrix}$$

In practice MCC is seldom used unless the new investment is so large as to fundamentally impact the entire company. Furthermore, most investments are financed from existing funds, in which it is impossible to identify the precise mix of debt and equity. Fund-raising seldom, if ever, occurs simultaneously for debt and equity; rather it occurs sequentially, so that the leverage ratio is often fluctuating.

8.5 Afterthought: The cost of capital and ESG

It is clear the cost of capital should reflect the riskiness of the projects which the funding is for, or the riskiness of the company *per se*. One of the overarching characteristics of the 21st century has been an increasing focus on the importance of ESG: environmental, social and governance aspects of business activity. Usually more the domain of 'responsible' investing, it has been argued that ESG ought to also be reflected in a company's cost of capital. Companies with good records in ESG should be 'rewarded' with lower costs of capital than those for whom ESG is seen as an 'unnecessary' burden. ESG is sometimes referred to in the corporate context as "sustainability". Going deeper, the three 'pillars' of ESG can be detailed as:

(1) **Environmental:** impact on climate change, including greenhouse gas emissions, loss of biodiversity, pollution mitigation, energy efficiency, water management, and deforestation/reforestation.
(2) **Social:** employee safety and health, general working conditions, diversity, equity and inclusion (DEI), and, perhaps more controversially, war, conflict and humanitarian crises.
(3) **Governance:** prevention of bribery and other forms of corruption, DEI on Boards of Directors, management structure, executive compensation, cybersecurity, and transparency/privacy.

In theory, companies which successfully pursue these goals should be able to fund their capital at lower cost as they are perceived as being at lower risk. As is so often the case, a new lexicon has developed, in particular talk of 'green interest' and its opposite 'brown' interest and companies. Among central banks, the ECB has been considering implementing 'green' interest rates but has recognised that "Eurozone banks are already charging higher interest rates to "brown" companies than to greener ones." Polluters are paying higher interest rates, ECB finds (ft.com) [August 16 2024].

In the same manner that some consumers are expressing their wish for more 'ethical' products from companies, it is likely that shareholders will become increasingly activist in demanding more attention to ESG issues from companies. Suppliers of capital will also be aware of this and seek to allocate their funds to greener rather than brown companies. This trend is likely to be all the more marked for pension funds, whose membership can be more vocal and impactful than shareholders generally.

8.6 Sample questions

(1) Brian's Drive-Thru Brain Surgery Inc. (BDBS) currently has no debt. Its cost of equity capital is 15%. BDBS are planning on issuing a series of bonds. The pre-tax cost of debt, k_d, is 8%. Proceeds from the bonds will be used to buy back(retire) some outstanding equity. This will result in the ratio of debt to total capital rising from 0.0 to 0.30. The cost of equity capital, k_e, is currently 18%. If the corporate tax rate is 50%:

   (a) What is the weighted average cost of capital (WACC), assuming a tax-shield effect?
   (b) Assuming k_e is 18%, k_d is 8 %, and there are no personal income taxes, what is the weighted average cost of capital?
   (c) Is your answer to (b) consistent with the Modigliani and Miller Hypothesis? Explain fully.

(2) The following data is for The Albatross Corporation. Calculate its cost of capital (WACC), explaining fully your approach.

Share price	£ 40.00
Dividend per share	£ 4.00
Number of outstanding shares	15,000,000
Estimated earnings growth	8%
Estimated dividend growth	5%
Book value of debt	£ 250,000,000
Book value of equity	£ 350,000,000
Treasury Bill rate	3.5%
10-year Treasury bond rate	4.5%
Beta (β)	1.25
Equity risk premium	8.0%
Historic cost of debt	7.0%
Marginal cost of debt	5.5%
Historic tax rate	45%
Marginal tax rate	42%

Chapter 9

The Capital Structure Conundrum

9.1 Value and the cost of capital

Chapter 2 clearly established that the objective of the firm is to maximise shareholder wealth by maximising the value of the firm. This is achieved *indirectly* by a company focusing on efficient, competitive and profitable delivery of its products or services. It was also clearly established that the value of a company is the discounted value of its expected stream of future cashflows. Chapter 8 covered the determination of the relevant discount rate: the weighted average cost of capital (WACC). The capital structure of a company is its mix of its sources of capital. With only two external sources the capital structure is the proportions of debt and equity used as sources of funds. The capital structure may be measured by either of two financial ratios:

- The debt/equity ratio, $[D/E]$
- The debt/total assets ratio, $[D/(D+E)]$

Considering debt and equity as separate sources of corporate funding was based on the implicit assumption that the amounts of debt and equity were fixed. The same applies to WACC. Because the objective of the company and its directors is to maximise its long-run value, this can only be achieved if funds are obtained at the lowest overall long-run cost. Because the cost of equity, k_e, is *always* less than the cost of debt, k_d which, in turn, is less than the post-tax cost of debt, k_d^*, several questions arise

- Is there any relationship between the capital structure of a company and the cost of the individual sources of funds?
- Is there an 'optimal' capital structure, such that the overall cost of funds is minimised?
- To what extent does the capital structure of the firm impact its WACC and hence its value? Or, alternatively, does the value of the firm depend on its capital structure?

9.2 The 'traditional' view

At its simplest, the 'traditional' view is that a company's capital structure *is* significant in determining its cost of capital and will consequently affect the value of the firm. Begin with a company financed wholly by equity. Because $k_e > k_d$, as the company acquires more debt it will find its cost of capital diminish. At some point, WACC will increase. Thus, there will be an 'optimal' debt/equity ratio, giving the lowest WACC, hence maximising the value of the firm for a given stream of cashflows. This is shown diagrammatically in Figure 9.1:

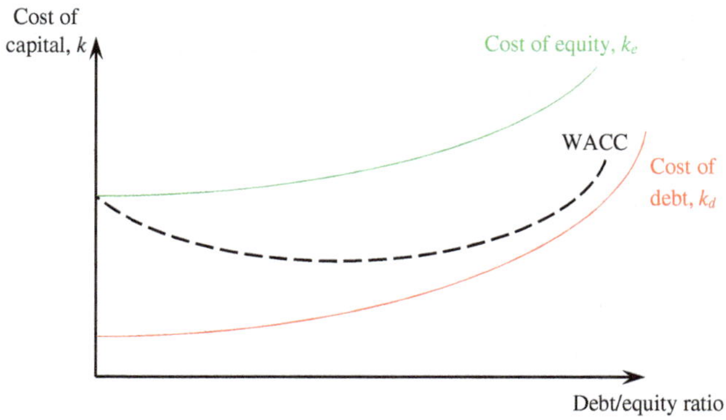

Figure 9.1. WACC and capital structure: The 'traditional view'

The rationale for a U-shaped WACC curve is straightforward: because the cost of debt, k_d, is lower than the cost of equity, k_e, taking on additional debt (i.e. increasing leverage) will initially lower the weighted average cost of capital. However, further increases in debt will raise the cost of capital due to increasing risk: both (potential) external providers of funds and current shareholders will demand higher return on their funds to compensate them for the increased risk of the additional debt.

To examine the traditional view in a little more detail, consider a company funded solely by equity, an *unlevered* company. The cost of capital is exactly the cost of equity, $WACC = k_e$. Now, suppose the company increases its leverage slightly, i.e. the company acquires a little debt. The cost of capital will decrease because:

- The post-tax cost of debt is less than the cost of equity (as explained earlier): $k_d^* < k_e$
- The cost of equity has remained constant.

The second assumption is crucial. According to the CAPM, the cost of equity depends upon its riskiness, i.e. the variability of its expected rate of return. In general, the expected return from an investment increases as the level of risk increases. Thus, as the company moves from zero leverage to a small, positive level, the shareholders' perceived risk increases. This is because by law interest has to be paid out from gross earnings irrespective of the financial fortunes of the company, hence the variability of profit-after-tax (PAT) must increase with the leverage of the company. Additionally, if the company goes into liquidation, debtholders take priority over equityholders. Consequently, for these two reasons the risk of equity investment increases with leverage. This suggests that as the company's leverage increases—even by a small amount—the cost of equity should also increase. However, according to the traditional view, in practice *for low levels of leverage shareholders do not perceive any increase in their risk*. The second assumption is acceptable as a matter of practicality.

Nonetheless, if the level of debt increases further then at some point shareholders will become concerned about their risks. Thus, their required return will rise to compensate them accordingly. If debt increases further, debtholders themselves become increasingly nervous and require greater return.

Taking the views of debtholders and shareholders together, the traditional view that as a function of leverage, the cost of capital first decreases with low leverage levels and then increases with the level of leverage. The implication is that there must be an optimal level of leverage corresponding to a minimum cost of capital. Trying to find this optimal debt/equity ratio which corresponds to the minimum WACC is another matter altogether.

9.3 Modigliani and Miller (MM)

While the 'traditional view' of capital structure has a strong intuitive appeal, Modigliani and Miller [1958] were the first to offer a rigorous scientific analysis of the relationship between leverage and the cost of capital, and hence the value of the firm. In contrast with the 'traditional view' MM showed that the cost of capital was independent on the company's leverage. Their analysis was based on a series of assumptions—which some consider rather restrictive—permitting full arbitrage to occur:

(1) Perfect capital markets exist, where companies and individuals can borrow without limit at the same rate of interest.
(2) There are no taxes or transactions costs.
(3) Personal and corporate borrowing are perfect substitutes.
(4) Other firms exist having the same business (systematic) risk, but different leverage.
(5) All projects, cash flows, debt, etc, can be regarded as perpetuities.

Intuitively, MM argued that the value of the firm—as with the value of any other asset—depended upon the capitalised value of the income stream the firm generated by its activities, and not by the manner in which its activities were financed. There is a separation of the investment decision from the financing decision. This argument can be outlined as follows:

- Given perfect markets, shareholders perceive an increase in their risk even at very low levels of leverage.
- Consequently, shareholders will demand increased return by way of compensation.
- The existence of arbitrage (Assumption 3 above) means that this increased return will *exactly* offset the benefits to the company

of cheaper debt, thereby keeping the average cost of capital constant, and equal to the required rate of return on equity of an unleveraged (no debt) company. This appears diagrammatically as in Figure 9.2:

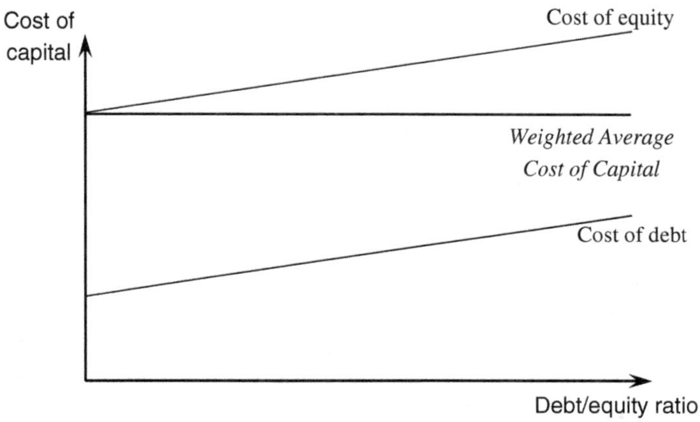

Figure 9.2. WACC and capital structure: The Modigliani and Miller view

Example 9.1: Consider two companies in the same (business) risk class: Jennings Ltd and Clemence Ltd. Both companies have annual earnings before interest of £ 1 million, but different capital structures. The companies are valued on the market as follows:

	Jennings Ltd.	**Clemence Ltd.**
Equity	£ 5,000,000	£ 4,000,000
Debt @ 8%	–	£ 2,000,000
	£ 5,000,000	£ 6,000,000

Now, suppose Bill Brown owns 5% of Clemence's equity. Ignoring taxes, his annual income would be calculated as:

Earnings of Clemence Ltd.	£ 1,000,000
less interest (8% of £ 2 m)	£ 160,000
	£ 840,000
Bill Brown's income = £ 840,000 $*$ 5% =	£ 42,000

Suppose Bill Brown sold his equity for £ 200,000 (= 5% * £ 4 m), and then borrowed £ 100,000 from the market to maintain his financial risk at the same level. If he bought 6% of Jennings Ltd with the £ 300,000, his annual earnings would become:

Earnings from Jennings Ltd. (£ 1,000,000 * 6%)	£ 60,000
less interest payable (£ 100,000 @ 8%)	£ 8,000
Bill Brown's income =	£ 52,000

Thus, Bill Brown can increase his return while maintaining his exposure to business and financial risk.

Modigliani and Miller [1958] would claim this result as untenable. If Bill Brown can increase his return, then other investors are also likely to take advantage of the situation. (Perfect) market forces of supply and demand would ensure that arbitrage occurs, ultimately driving down the value of Clemence's equity and increasing the value of Jennings' equity, until the value of the two companies become identical. Thus, according to MM, the value of the company (i.e. the sum of total equity plus total market value of debt) is independent of the capital structure of the firm, as shown in Figure 9.3:

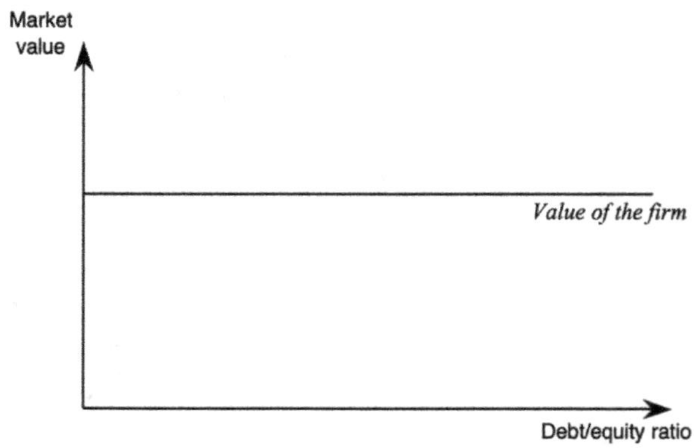

Figure 9.3. Debt/equity ratio (leverage) and the value of the firm

To reiterate, the key implication of MM is that the debt/equity ratio is irrelevant. The proportions of debt to equity which the firm seeks to obtain its funding do not matter.

9.3.1 *Critique of Modigliani and Miller*

Modigliani and Miller [1958] has been subject to strong criticism, not least because of the restrictive assumptions on which it is based. Additionally, empirical evidence suggests that Boards of Directors do *not* consider their debt/equity ratio to be irrelevant. Indeed, there is a range of academic literature which suggests that the cost of capital is strongly influenced by the composition of the Board of Directors, e.g. its size, the number of female directors, the number of independent directors, and the degree of managerial ownership.

The perfect market assumption is often a source for criticism, although its use as a methodologically sound simplification is acknowledged. It is widely used in theoretical models in finance, partly because imperfect markets produce intractable models, while the assumption offers a useful starting point from which practical imperfections may be added afterwards.

Ironically, some MM critics continue to make use of the Capital Asset Pricing Model (CAPM) in their own work, conveniently ignoring the fact that it is also the result of the perfect markets assumption.

Regardless of the many criticisms, the original MM theory is important for several reasons. In the first instance, it has formed the basis for much theoretical thinking in financial management. Following criticism, the original model has been modified to take account of less restrictive assumptions (see below). It has also led to a continuing debate on the importance of company capital structure, a debate in which "the jury is still out".

9.3.2 *MM modifications*

The original MM theory has subsequently been modified in response to some of the more relevant criticisms it faced. Most importantly, the tax-shield effect (see Section 8.3), is included to emphasise the importance of corporate taxation:

$$\begin{aligned} \textit{value of a company, } V = {} & (\textit{its value with no taxes}) \\ & + PV(\textit{tax shield on interest}) \end{aligned}$$

Thus, if the value of a company without taxes is independent of its debt (leverage) and, given that the value of the tax-shield increases with the level of debt *ad infinitum*, a company should implement the highest level of leverage possible, thereby maximising the value of the company. Figure 9.4 shows this graphically:

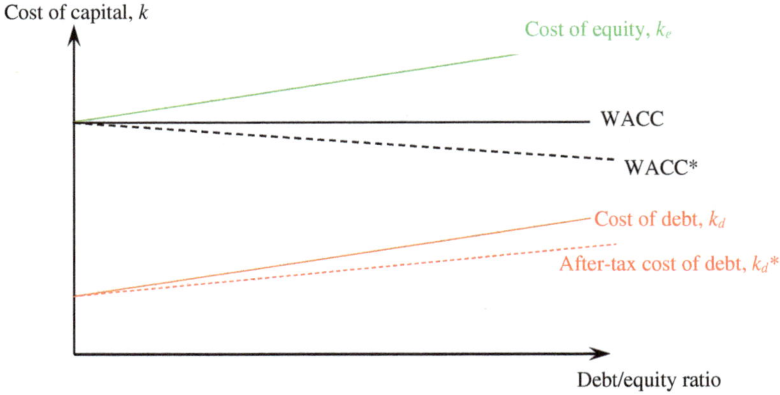

Figure 9.4. MM with corporate taxation

The inclusion of corporate taxation gives a new, after-tax cost of debt curve, k_d^*, (dotted line) which has a shallower slope than its original pre-tax variant, k_d (solid line). This lower post-tax cost of debt gives rise to an amended weighted average cost of capital curve, WACC* (dotted line), which is downward sloping. Thus, the more debt the company acquires, the lower is its weighted average cost of capital, and hence the higher the value of the company. Were this true in reality it would make sense for companies to borrow as much as possible. Lenders would also realise this, and seek to lend as much as possible to enance corporate value. This is obviously not the way things operate in the real world!

The reason is because the above does not include the **costs of financial distress**, i.e. the cost (risk) of potential bankruptcy that occurs with increasing debt. As leverage increases, suppliers of funds—, bondholders, shareholders, general trade creditors, customers, etc—become increasingly nervous about dealing with the company. In particular they will be worried about the company's ability to meet its interest and debt principal repayments. This will manifest itself in lost sales, loss of goodwill, etc. Shareholders will also view such potential losses as an increasing threat, which serves to reduce the value of the firm. Incorporating the costs of financial distress gives:

$$\begin{aligned} \textit{value of a company, } V = {} & (\textit{its value with no taxes}) \\ & + PV(\textit{tax shield on interest}) \\ & - PV(\textit{costs of financial distress}) \end{aligned}$$

suggesting again that there is an optimum leverage level which minimises the cost of capital, thereby maximising the value of the company. Figure 9.5 shows this graphically:

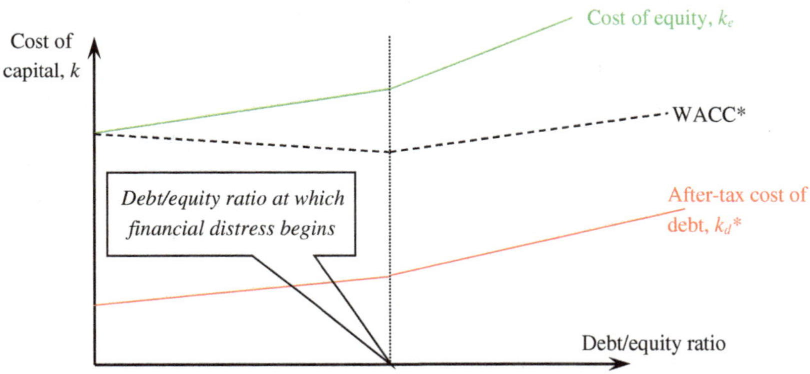

Figure 9.5. MM with corporate taxation and financial distress

Both the cost of debt and cost of equity curves now 'kink' upwards at the point where the costs of financial distress begin. This gives rise to a V-shaped weighted average cost of capital curve (WACC*), leading to the same conclusion as the traditional viewpoint with which this discussion began!

Miller [1977] took the debate further, introducing personal taxation into the model. In essence, Miller introduces a 'clientele effect', suggesting that the tax benefits of debt for any particular company depends on the personal tax positions of both its shareholders and its debtholders (lenders). The implication is that firms will tend to attract investors who are 'suited' to the firm's existing capital structure. If this were so, then it would make sense for firms to try to maintain their existing capital structure, as any changes might act as an incentive for shareholders and debtholders to sell their securities in the firm.

9.4 A final thought

For many students this subject is often one of the most difficult and hence unsatisfying especially for those studying finance for the first time, because there are no definite conclusions: "the jury is still out". Further, much of the work in this area assumes that the company is a 'price-taker' (implied by perfect markets), facing whatever costs of capital the market serves up. This is often extended to the implicit (simplifying) assumption that there is no change in market costs over time. However, even casual observation suggests that companies determine the mix in which they raise new capital based on current and anticipated market conditions. Consequently, it may be that changes in a company's cost of capital have more to do with market conditions, both now and in the future, than anything else. That makes it one of the most fruitful areas for analysis, and a subject in which a great deal of research remains to be done, both in theory and in practice.

9.5 Sample questions

(1) The Bottle of Beer Company has several bond issues outstanding, each making semi-annual interest payments. The bonds are listed in the following table. If the corporate tax rate is 28%, what is the after-tax cost of debt for Bottle of Beer?

Bond	Coupon rate	Maturity	Yield-to-maturity	Face value	Market value
1	5.3%	June 2025	1.3%	£ 100,000	£ 105,000
2	5.0%	June 2026	2.4%	£ 165,000	£ 175,000
3	7.0%	June 2029	2.6%	£ 110,000	£ 130,000

(2) Smiling Daily plc has £ 200 million of equity and $100 million of debt. It recently issued bonds at 9%. The company's beta (β) is 1.125. Assuming a corporate tax rate of 30%, a risk-free rate of 6% and an expected return on the market portfolio of 14%, calculate Smiling Daily's weighted average cost of capital (WACC). How will this be impacted if the corporate tax rate was reduced to 28%?

(3) Corporate Treasurer, Tudor Weigh, has recently been asked to determine the appropriate weighted average cost of capital (WACC) for Solly's Carpet Emporium. Solly's has outstanding debt of £ 10 million, ordinary shares of £ 30 million, both at market value and no preference shares. Its cost of equity is 12%, cost of debt is 8% and faces a marginal tax rate of 40%. Assuming Solly's ratios reflect its target capital structure, what is it's WACC?

(4) Brain Damage plc is a software development company. It has a capital structure comprised of 60% equity and 40% debt. In order to finance several capital projects, Brain Damage plans to raise £ 1.6 million by issuing ordinary shares and debt in proportion to its current capital structure. The debt will be issued at par with a 9% coupon and flotation costs on the equity issue are estimated at 3.5%. Ordinary shares currently sell for £ 21.40 per share. Brain Damage's last dividend was £ 1.80 and is expected to grow at 7% in perpetuity. If the corporate tax rate is 40% what is Brain Damage's cost of capital?

Chapter 10

Financial Forecasting

"Never make predictions, especially about the future."
"There are two kinds of forecasters: those who don't know,
and those who don't know they don't know."
John Kenneth Galbraith

10.1 Why forecast?

Everyone makes predictions. The future is unknown, uncertain. Making forecasts, either implicitly or explicitly, is how human beings deal with uncertainty. If forecasts are important for normal everyday activities, they must be at least as important for business (and government) decision-making. Almost all forecasts assume that the future will be similar to the past, so our forecasts are basically extrapolations of the past into the future.

Financial forecasting is a key element in Financial Planning and Analysis (F P & A). This umbrella term incorporates the entire range of planning, forecasting, budgeting, and other analytical activities which support a company's decision-making to ensure its overall financial health. It is usual for F P & A to be part of a broader financial management system. This includes core financial processes, including accounting, revenue management, cashflow management, governance, risk and compliance (GRC). F P & A can also be part of a standalone analytics solution integrated with other business systems, such as Enterprise Resource Planning (ERP). More recently

F P & A has developed beyond the use of spreadsheets into contemporary, cloud-based solutions, which increasingly use Artificial Intelligence (AI), automation, and advanced analytics designed to deal with the financial challenges of a rapidly changing world of uncertainty.

While many companies—such as Gartner, SAP, and others—offer proprietary software for F P & A, these tend to be expensive solutions only feasible for very large corporations. This Chapter focuses exclusively on the use of spreadsheets, offering some insight into the processes involved in F P & A, primarily focusing on the F P.

10.1.1 *A short note on profits*

In Chapter 1 the primary objective for a company was clearly established as *value maximisation.* Nonetheless, in the real world and in the short run companies tend to focus on profits, partly because it is on those profits that taxes will be levied. And, of course, it is out of profits that shareholders receive dividends. Thus, current or expected profits might be seen as an indicator of value maximisation.

In accounting, company profits are the difference between sales revenues (or turnover) and explicit costs, both measured in current monetary terms. However, **accounting profits** differ from **economic profits**. Economic profits include both implicit and explicit costs. Implicit costs include **normal profits:** the minimum profit a company can achieve to justify its continued operation in a competitive market. The inclusion of implicit costs means that economic profits tend to be lower than accounting profits. Economic profits are sometimes referred to as 'surplus value'.

But how do profits come about? One view is that profits are *the reward to entrepreneurs for taking a risk and 'correctly' predicting the future.* This applies to decisions such as which products to sell (relates to sales), and the mix of factors of production to be employed (relates to costs). Which products or services a company decides to sell needs to include some estimate of *how much* it expects to sell. This **sales forecast** gives an entrepreneur some idea of how much revenue they can expect to generate from those sales. It also contributes to estimating how much it will cost to manufacture and distribute the products: a costs forecast. Thus, the starting point of any business forecasting is the sales forecast. The dependability of any financial forecast depends crucially on the soundness of the sales forecast (Section 10.3).

10.1.2 *Forecasting, prediction and financial modelling*

If future sales are expected to grow the company may need to increase capacity by increasing its capital stock. Chapter 6 examined this process—capital budgeting—under the implicit assumption that real investment was required. This Chapter goes a little deeper, using financial forecasting to determine if more capital stock is required, and how much. If more capital stock is required, it will require funding. Financial forecasting helps determine this.

Although the terms 'forecasting' and 'prediction' are often used interchangeably, there is a significant difference between them. Both are used to estimate future outcomes; both rely heavily on the (implicit) assumption that past trends and patterns are likely to continue in the future (hardly surprising given the past is the *only* guide as to what might happen in the future!).

Prediction is a process of making an 'educated guess' about a specific future outcome without reliance on historical data or statistical methods. It tends to be short-term, often involving making assumptions based on intuition, 'expert' opinion, or even subjective judgment. It is an approach which lends itself to such areas as sporting predictions ('fantasy football' comes to mind) and even astrology!

Forecasting is considered the more scientific approach. It is the process of estimating future events or trends making full use of both historical data—usually time-series—and statistical methods, while also accounting for external factors and uncertainties. It usually has a longer time frame than prediction. The aim is to provide the most accurate estimate of future outcomes possible, hence its use in business decision making. This Chapter considers some basic, introductory techniques of financial forecasting. A lot of financial forecasting is incorporated under the umbrella term of **financial modelling**.

Before the advent of the personal computer and spreadsheet technology in the early 1980s, financial forecasting was very difficult. Although the necessary data might have been available it would have been analogue (non-digital), and largely paper based, making its use time-consuming, tedious. The ubiquity of the internet since the late

1990s has made long-distance information transfer much more possible than before. Software such as SQL (Structured Query Language) enables data to be acquired and used in analytical software, from Excel to SPSS (www.ibm.com/products/spss-statistics) and beyond, often in real time. The entire industry of 'big data analytics' has been built on this foundation.

10.2 Forecasting and budgeting

Financial forecasting is particularly useful helping companies plan their budgets and adapt to changing circumstances. The budgeting process must include both planning and control elements.

10.2.1 *Budgeting, planning and control*

At its simplest a budget is a plan of spending and income. Almost everyone has one. For many it is completely informal, a woolly set of thoughts. For others it is more controlled and detail-oriented: anything from a set of hand-written pages to a full-blown spreadsheet. For an individual it is normal to think first of income and then determine how to spend it. For a company, the chronological order might differ: 'you have to speculate (spend) to accumulate'. For a government it will be much more complex, with dynamic chronological interactions between income and spending (see Figure 2.1).

A company **budget** is a formal statement of what is to be done in the future. It forms part of a company's **financial plan**. The financial plan should include projected versions of the Balance Sheet, Income Statement and cash flow statement.

A formal budgeting process and ensuing budget provides a company with a tool for obtaining the most productive and profitable use of its resources. Because larger companies often have separate, but linked, budgets for different functions within the company, a budget can help clarify intra-firm relationships, helping improve internal coordination. As well as planning and control (see below), a budget can provide management with a continuous monitoring system, allowing it to react to changing circumstances. A useful budget requires a realistic understanding of the company's activities and serves company decision-making; the company—and especially its employees—should not become a slave to the budget. This can only happen if the budget is not 'set in stone' but subject to regular revisions in the face of changing circumstances. A budget which is overly rigorous will be unachievable; if it is unrealistic or too generous it will set targets which are all too easily achieved. The **control process** consists of three steps:

(1) Performance standards are established in advance.
(2) Performance is evaluated relative to the standards.
(3) Corrective action is taken if performance is above or below standard.

Company budgets are usually prepared using one or more of the financial forecasting techniques which follow after Section 10.3.

10.3 Sales forecasting

Sales forecasting is a process of using previous sales figures and other historic data to estimate a business' future sales. Sales can be forecast for any future time-period: monthly, quarterly, semi-annually, or annually. A good sales forecast provides information a business can use to make intelligent, informed decisions. It is notable that the further into the future a forecast is made the less likely it is to turn out to be accurate.

A sales forecast estimates the volume of goods and/or services a business can sell over the forecast period. This can help with estimating the costs of producing and distributing those goods and/or services, and thus potential profit. As with forecasting in general, the process involves extrapolating from historic data, primarily previous sales. Other factors which might impact futures sales include:

- **The macroeconomy:** the position of the economy in the business cycle—e.g. likely to grow, or likely to shrink—is a key determinant of sales for most companies.
- **The relevant industry or market:** the market for a company's goods and services may not necessarily grow or decline with the macroeconomy. It may be less than perfectly correlated. Similarly, there may be new companies entering the industry impacting the

degree of competition, thereby affecting sales. A useful sales forecast will include some estimate of percentage growth or shrinkage in the market.

- **Regulatory changes:** the prospect of new laws or regulations may impact future sales, either positively or negatively.
- **New products:** From time to time a company will change the range of its product offerings. A company launching new products hopes to increase sales, although there is always the possibility of cannibalizing sales of existing products. These and any changes in costs which may arise need to be considered in making the sales forecast.
- **Marketing:** Companies engage in marketing to boost sales. There will be historic data on the impact of the marketing spend on sales, which can be used in building the sales forecast. Any planned changes to the marketing spend—new campaigns, more advertising, changes to sales staff, etc.—need to be part of the sales forecast.

All relevant factors (above) should be included in any statistically based sales forecast.

10.3.1 *Sales forecasting: established companies*

Sales forecasting for an established company tends to be more straightforward than for a new company or projecting sales for a new product line. An established company will already have historic sales and other data (e.g. GDP) enabling it to project sales. They are likely to have some knowledge of how their sales have been impacted by both the macroeconomy and conditions in their industry. This is particularly true for a company with repeat customers or clients.

10.3.2 *Sales forecasting: new companies, new products*

A new company, or an existing company with new products, will find much greater difficulty building a sales forecast as there is little or no historic data. Without pre-existing sales data, unless there is comparable data available the first step in forecasting sales is to conduct research into the target market. This involves both sides of the market: demand—numbers of potential customers and the underlying demographics—and supply side—especially competitors, the likely degree of competition.

10.3.3 *Sales forecasting: using Excel*

Although proprietary statistical software exists a more general approach can be taken using a spreadsheet. For example, Microsoft's Excel provides a series of simple tools as well as a range of functions which can be applied to historic sales data.

Assuming that the historic data follows a simple linear trend, or even an exponential growth trend, it can be extended simply using the "fill handle" (square on the bottom right hand of a selection of cells):

With a linear trend the 'step value'—the difference between the first and next value in the series—is applied to create the projected values. If the data exhibit a growth trend apply the same procedure as for a linear trend but select two or more cells of historic data before dragging the fill handle.

Another way to consider the historic data with a view to creating a sales forecast is to use Excel's graphic tools, such as **TRENDLINE** or **MOVING AVERAGE** to create a two-dimensional chart. Alternatively, more recent versions of Excel include an **Analyse Data** button on the toolbar:

In the Mac version this appears on the right-hand side of the toolbar. With the relevant data selected the Analyse Data button will reveal any relationships between the data series, enabling further analysis without too much effort.

There are a number of key functions in Excel which can be used for forecasting sales in Excel. These include:

- FORECAST: calculates, or predicts, a future value along a linear trend by using existing values. The formula appears as:

  = **FORECAST(x,known_ys,known_xs)**, where

  - **x** is the data point for which you want to predict a value and must be a numeric value
  - **Known_ys** is the dependent array or range of numeric data
  - **Known_xs** is the independent array or range of numeric data. The variance of **Known_xs** must not be zero.

- TREND: returns numbers in a linear trend matching known data points, using the least squares method. The formula is:

  = **TREND(known_ys,known_xs,new_xs,const)**, where

  - **Known_ys** is a range or array of y-values that you already know in the relationship y = mx + b
  - **Known_xs** is an optional range or array of x-values that you know in the relationship y = mx + b, an array the same size as Known_y's.
  - **New_xs** is a range or array of new x-values for which you want TREND to return corresponding y-values.
  - **Const** is a logical value: the constant b is calculated normally if Const = TRUE or omitted; b is set equal to 0 if Const = FALSE.

- GROWTH: calculates predicted exponential growth using existing data. The formula appears as:

  = **GROWTH(known_ys,known_xs,new_xs,const)**, where

  - **Known_ys** is the set of y-values that you already know in the relationship y = b*m^x, an array or range of positive numbers
  - **Known_xs** is an optional set of x-values that you may already know in the relationship y = b*m^x, an array or range the same size as **Known_ys**
  - **New_xs** are new x-values for which you want GROWTH to return corresponding y-values
  - **Const** is a logical value: the constant b is calculated normally if Const = TRUE; b is set equal to 1 if Const = FALSE or omitted.

10.4 Per cent of sales forecasting

Per cent of sales forecasting assumes that *almost* all Balance Sheet line items vary directly in relation to sales. Other items may vary with sales, but not directly. Some items will not vary at all with sales, e.g. equity. There are three simple steps to this method:

- Identify balance sheet items which vary (directly) with sales.
- Calculate each item as a percentage of the firm's current annual sales.
- Calculate their future values as a percentage of projected future sales.

Note that some items tend to remain constant from year to year, e.g. long-term debt, share premium account (unless more funds have been raised in the intervening period). For those line items which vary with sales, but not directly, it is important to make the simplest assumption about how much they might change, the key being the 'K.I.S.S. principle' (*"Keep It Simple, Stupid"*).

Because *Assets* = *Liabilities* + *Equity* (*or Net Worth*) it is unlikely that the forecast Balance Sheet will automatically balance. Thus, while most items can be forecast on a 'per cent of sales' basis, there is a need for a 'balancing item' (also known as a 'plug') to ensure that the forecast Balance Sheet actually balances. Typically, analysts will use 'short-term debt' as the plug. However, if balance requires that to be negative then 'cash' or 'marketable securities' (on the other side of the Balance Sheet) will be used instead as the plug.

Example 10.1: A simple 'per cent of sales' forecasting illustration
Consider the following Balance Sheet:

		(£ millions)	
Assets		**Liabilities**	
Cash	£ 10	Accounts Payable	£ 50
Receivables	£ 85	Accrued Wages and Taxes	£ 25
Inventory	£ 100	Bonds	£ 70
Net Fixed Assets	£ 150	Ordinary Shares	£ 100
		Retained Earnings	£ 100
Total Assets	**£ 345**	**Total Liabilities and equity**	**£ 345**

Assuming current sales (turnover) of £ 500 million, then the Balance Sheet showing line items as a percentage of sales is:

(per cent of sales)			
Assets		**Liabilities**	
Cash	2 %	Accounts Payable	10 %
Receivables	17 %	Accrued Wages and Taxes	5 %
Inventory	20 %	Bonds	N/A
Net Current Assets	**39 %**		
Net Fixed Assets	30 %	Ordinary Shares	N/A
		Retained Earnings	N/A
Total Assets	**69 %**	**Total Liabilities and equity**	**15 %**

Suppose forecast sales for the following year has been estimated at £ 600 million, then the projected Balance Sheet would appear as:

(*£* millions)			
Assets		**Liabilities**	
Cash	£ 12	Accounts Payable	£ 60
Receivables	£ 102	Accrued Wages and Taxes	£ 30
Inventory	£ 120	Bonds	£ 70
Net Current Assets	***£* 234**		
Net Fixed Assets	£ 180	Ordinary Shares	£ 100
		Retained Earnings	£ 100
Total Assets	***£* 414**	**Total Liabilities and equity**	***£* 360**

This assumes no change to the previous year's data for Bonds, Ordinary Shares and Retained Earnings. While logical for Bonds and Ordinary Shares, it is illogical for Retained Earnings: increased sales usually lead to increased profits which would typically impact Retained Earnings, which we address below.

It should also be noted that cash is unlikely to vary directly with sales, unless the company is primarily cash-sales. If cash is reduced (hypothetically) to zero, Total Assets = £ 402 which is still much higher than Total Liabilities and equity.

Obviously, £ 414 million $\neq$ £ 380 million—*the Balance Sheet does not balance*. Equally obviously, Net Fixed Assets cannot increase from £ 150 million to £ 180 million without funding. Because Net Fixed Assets are capital expenditures, they require a long-term commitment and consequently are unlikely to be financed by short-term debt. In terms of the Balance Sheet funding must come from either an issue of more Ordinary Shares, more Bonds, and/or Retained Earnings. It is unlikely that Retained Earnings will be a constant percentage of sales, year to year. However, assuming for simplicity that profits remain a constant percentage of sales—e.g. 10%—and an unchanged dividend payout ratio—e.g. 30%—leads to forecast profits of £ 60 million, of which £ 42 million will be retained. This leads to the following revised forecast Balance Sheet:

		(£ millions)	
Assets		**Liabilities**	
Cash	£ 12	Accounts Payable	£ 60
Receivables	£ 102	Accrued Wages and Taxes	£ 30
Inventory	£ 120	Bonds	£ 70
Net Current Assets	**£ 234**		
Net Fixed Assets	£ 180	Ordinary Shares	£ 100
		Retained Earnings	£ 142
Total Assets	**£ 414**	**Total Liabilities and equity**	**£ 402**

This reduces the imbalance to £ 12 million, which will need to be raised via a rights issue of Ordinary Shares or Bonds.

It is also possible to calculate the amount of **external funds required** (EFR) to fund a sales increase. Assuming that the company is close to or at capacity, as shown above the amount of funding from external sources is:

$$\begin{aligned}&\textit{External Funding Required}\\&\quad = (\textit{Total Assets}) - (\textit{Total Liabilities} + \textit{Equity})\end{aligned}$$

This is also equivalent to the 'plug', the amount required to balance the Balance Sheet. The amount of time such funding requires in practice is considerable, involving accountants, lawyers, and the stock exchange itself in the case of a listed company. This is why financial forecasting is crucial, so that such things can be planned well ahead of time.

A more detailed formula is:

$$EFR = \frac{A}{S_0}(\Delta S) - \frac{D}{S_0}(\Delta S) - mbS_1 \tag{10.1}$$

where

S_0 = current sales and S_1 = sales forecast for next year
thus, $= \Delta S$ the forecast change in sales
A = all assets which increase with sales
thus, $\frac{A}{S_0}$ = total assets which increase with sales as a % of sales
D = liabilities which increase 'spontaneously' with sales (typically short-term)
thus, $\frac{D}{S_0}$ = liabilities which increase with sales as a % of sales
m = profit margin on sales (so mS_1 = forecast profits)
b = earnings retention ratio (so mbS_1 = forecast retained earnings)

Applying the data from Example 10.1 to Equation 10.1 gives:

$$EFR = \frac{345}{500}(100) - \frac{75}{500}(100) - (m * b * 600)$$

The profit margin, m, depends on the previous data from the company's income statement, while the earnings retention ratio, b, is largely dependent on the company's dividend policy. Assuming a profit margin of 10% and an earnings retention ratio of 50% gives:

$$\begin{aligned} EFR &= [0.69 * (100)] - [0.15 * (100)] - (0.1 * 0.5 * 600) \\ &= £\ 54.00m \end{aligned}$$

Assuming the profit margin of 10%, it can easily be determined using Excel how EFR will change if the earnings retention ratio changes. In fact, an earnings retention ratio of 90% will require no additional external funding. Similarly, a higher profit margin would reduce the amount of EFR. For example, if $m = 25\%$ and $b = 50\%$ then:

$$\begin{aligned} EFR &= [0.69 * (100)] - [0.15 * (100)] - (0.25 * 0.5 * 600) \\ &= -£\ 21.00m \end{aligned}$$

In this case the EFR is negative; no additional external funding is required. In fact, an additional £12m is generated from the sales growth. This might be used to retire debt, or pay an exceptional dividend to shareholders, or even buy back existing shares.

10.5 Regression (linear) forecasting

Short-term forecasting (e.g. 'per cent of sales') is subject to strict constraints. Per cent of sales assumes that many Balance Sheet items remain the same percentage of sales over time. While this might be feasible from one year to the next, it is unlikely to remain the same over longer periods of time. Using regression avoids making prior assumptions about the relationship between a Balance Sheet item and company sales. Instead, future line items are projected based on past relationships revealed by regression. There are two basic steps:

- Estimate the (linear) relationship between sales and Balance Sheet items using regression analysis
- Use the estimated relationship to calculate future Balance Sheet items based on the sales projection.

Example 10.2: Forecasting inventory
Consider the following annual data for inventory (Y) against sales (X)

	(£ thousands)		**Inventory/Sales ratio**	**Inventory/Sales**
	Inventory (Y)	**Sales (X)**	**(Y/X)**	**ratio (Y/X) %**
2012	403	4,560	0.088	8.8
2013	461	4,962	0.093	9.3
2014	506	5,728	0.088	8.8
2015	507	6,477	0.078	7.8
2016	665	8,480	0.078	7.8
2017	1,087	17,924	0.061	6.1
2018	1,165	17,524	0.066	6.6
2019	1,278	20,181	0.063	6.3
2020	1,438	21,752	0.066	6.6
2022	1,216	24,106	0.050	5.0

Although there is some year-on-year variability it is clear that over the decade, 2012–2022, inventory is slowly declining as a percentage of sales, making it a completely unsuitable candidate for per cent of sales forecasting.

Using the Analyse Data tool in the Excel toolbar on the data above reveals the following:

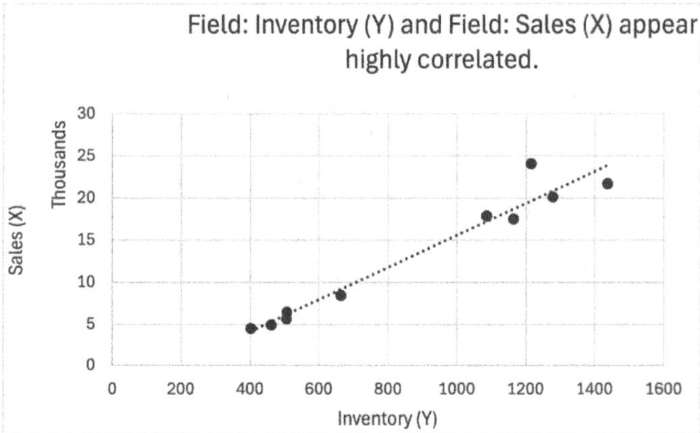

Using Excel's Regression tool (click on Data Analysis on the right side of the menu bar), the relationship is estimated as: **Inventory (Y) = 215.79 + 0.0499 Sales (X)** with a very high correlation coefficient of 0.9496 (almost 95%). For this example, if we assume that the sales forecast for 2025 is £ 32,543,000, then Inventory for 2025 will be [215.79 + 0.0499*32,543] = £ 1,843,000.

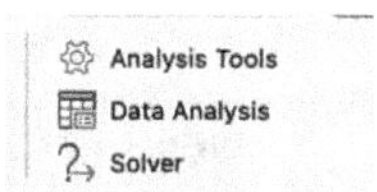

Using the same approach as Example 10.1, other Balance Sheet items can be forecast. Each is then inserted into a projected Balance Sheet, with the 'balancing item' being either cash or short-term debt/securities (as previously noted).

10.6 Concluding comments

This chapter has reviewed some basic techniques for financial forecasting. It is not possible in an introductory textbook to go into greater depth; there are several specialist books available for those who wish to examine the subject more closely. Equally, there are also professional software packages which are in regular use in larger companies. If you have found this Chapter interesting and especially if you think you might enjoy a career in F P & A then you should begin by playing with Excel and applying the techniques above to the historic data of real companies. Once that itch has been scratched you can go deeper by using the more sophisticated versions of these techniques explained in specialist books. Good luck!

10.7 Sample questions

(1) Select a company of your choice. Using Excel (or your preferred spreadsheet app) build a column of annual sales (revenues, turnover) for a minimum of five years (ten would be even better). Using either the FILL HANDLE, or one of FORECAST, TREND, or GROWTH functions create sales forecasts for the next three years.

(2) Build a second column of the company's 'home country' GDP. Repeat (1) using annual sales as the 'y' variable and GDP as the 'x' variable. Compare and contrast your results from (1) and (2). Why might there be differences?

(3) Using data from your chosen company:

    a. Identify balance sheet items which vary (directly) with sales.
    b. Calculate each item as a percentage of the firm's current annual sales.
    c. Calculate their future values as a percentage of projected future sales, from your results to both (1) and (2) above.

(4) Using your historic data and your forecasts, calculate the amount external funding required (EFR). If EFR is calculated as negative, what would you recommend to the company?

Chapter 11

Further Topics in Finance

Previous chapters examined a range of the key tools and ideas which have become established as part of the toolbox of finance. Ideas such as Net Present Value (*NPV*) have become tried, tested and trusted. Some debates continue, e.g. Modigliani and Miller's [1958] view of the relevance of the debt-to-equity ratio for value maximisation. This chapter brings this introductory journey towards a close, with consideration of some slightly more advanced applications of the tools and ideas previously considered.

11.1 Valuation of companies

In Chapters 4–6, discounted cashflow (DCF) techniques such as *NPV* and *IRR* were applied to the valuation of bonds, shares, and investment projects (capital budgeting). Because a company is a portfolio of its investment projects, it is logical to apply *NPV* to estimate the value of a company.

Finance theory explains that the value of an asset is the discounted value of the expected stream of cash flows the asset generates. Consequently, the value of a company should be the discounted value of the cash flows the company is expected to generate. But, to which stream of cash flows should *NPV* be applied? From the shareholders' perspective, should it be the expected stream of dividend payments? Perhaps, but this is the perspective of a single group of stakeholders in the company. Surely, finance theory would indicate that *NPV* be calculated from the cash flows from *all* of the company's expected earnings (profits), whether distributed as dividends or retained for reinvestment within the firm. Ultimately, the value of the firm is best calculated using the discounted value of its forecasted *free cash flows.*

11.1.1 *Free cash flows*

Free cash flow is defined as **cash not retained and reinvested** in the company, i.e. cash paid out as dividends: dividend per share equals free cash flow per share. Alternatively, free cash flow can be defined as the amount of cash a company available to pay out to investors after paying for all the investments necessary for growth. Thus:

$$\textit{Free cash flow } (FCF) = [\textit{Revenues} - \textit{Costs}] - \textit{Investments}$$

where ***Investments*** is the company's spending on capital equipment (including property), sometimes referred to as **capital expenditures** (capex). Because [*Revenues* – *Costs*] represents the company's ***Cash Flow from Operations***, *CFO*, free cash flow can be written as:

$$\begin{aligned}\textit{Free cash flow } (FCF) = \textit{ Cash Flow from Operations } (CFO)\\ - \textit{Investments}\end{aligned}$$

Note that it is entirely possible for a rapidly-growing business, one with a very high level of capital expenditure, to have a negative free cash flow.

Free cash flow is similar to earnings. The key difference is that *FCF* omits 'book entry' (i.e. non-cash) expenses, and accounts for capital spending when it actually occurs rather than depreciating it over several years. The major difference between earnings and *FCF* is that depreciation accounts for sunk costs of the past, whereas *FCF* attempts to capture all of the real cash outlays of the present. A company's *FCF* represents a real measure of value added, but when used as an analytic device, caution is recommended. It would be a mistake to judge a company purely on its *FCF*, especially without full regard to its level of capital investment.

11.1.2 *EVA and MVA*

Also known as residual value, **Economic Value Added** (*EVA*) is a proprietary concept defined by consulting firm Stern-Stewart (www.sternstewart.com). Closely equivalent to the concept of economic profit (which itself differs from the accounting concept of profit), *EVA* is the return a business makes on invested capital, minus the cost of capital times the amount of invested capital. Thus, *EVA* is a measure of the surplus value created by an investment, or a company (i.e. a portfolio of the investments it undertakes). Thus:

$$\begin{aligned} EVA = {} & (\textit{return on capital} - \textit{cost of capital}) \\ & * (\textit{capital invested in project}) \end{aligned}$$

where ***return on capital*** is the true cash flow return on capital, and ***cost of capital*** is the weighted average of the costs of the various funding instruments used to finance the investment (*WACC*).

It is also possible to define *EVA* as the "*after-tax cash flow generated by a business minus the cost of the capital it has deployed to generate that cash flow*" (cf. the definition of economic profit). It is therefore apparent that *EVA* underlies true shareholder value. Note that *EVA* is measured in terms of a single currency (e.g. GBP, EUR, USD, etc.), not in percentage terms. *EVA* is close in underlying theory to the construction of the *NPV* of a capital budgeting project.

EVA can be used to estimate company valuation. The present value of a company can be written in terms of the *EVA* of those projects already in place and the present value of the *EVA* of future projects. Thus:

$$\begin{aligned} \textit{Company value} &= (\textit{Value of assets in place}) \\ &\quad + (\textit{Value of future growth}) \\ \textit{Company value} &= [\textit{Investment in existing assets} \\ &\quad + NPV(\textit{assets in place})] + NPV(\textit{future projects}) \\ \textit{Company value} &= [I + NPV(\textit{assets in place})] + \sum_{j=1}^{N} NPV_j \end{aligned}$$

where I = the capital invested in assets already in place, and there are expected to be N projects yielding surplus value (or excess returns) in the future.

Market value added (MVA) is current market value of a company less the capital contributed by its investors:

$$MVA = V - K$$

where MVA is market value added, V is the market value of the firm, (i.e. the value of the company's debt and equity), and K is the amount of capital invested in the firm.

A positive MVA indicates a company which has added value. A negative MVA indicates a company with reduced value (value has been destroyed). MVA needs to be greater than the expected return on the market portfolio ($E(R_m)$)—which represents what the company's investors might have achieved, their opportunity cost—adjusted for the company's leverage relative to the market.

MVA can also be defined as the present value of a series of EVA values. It is economically equivalent to traditional NPV, evaluating the after-tax cash flow profile of a project using the cost of capital as the discount rate.

11.2 Corporate Restructuring: M&A

Chapter 1 examined the relationships between the various stakeholder groups of a company and the agency costs which can arise. Companies can try to reconcile management objectives with those of shareholders through the design of executive compensation packages. This is an internal form of corporate control. There are also external mechanisms which incentivise managers to act in the best interests of their shareholders. Sometimes referred to as the 'market for corporate control', these consist of the possibility (threat?) of various kinds of merger or acquisition (takeover). A merger or takeover should occur only if there is a strong expectation that the new entity will be greater than the sum of its individual parts. In other words, a merger or takeover should result in value being added, either because of synergies or due to improved management. Unsurprisingly, expectations are not always met: the outcome can be better or worse than expected.

A **merger** is a 'friendly' process of combining two or more separate companies into a new, single entity. The Boards of Directors will usually have negotiated the mutual benefits they believe will derive from the merger before recommending it to shareholders for approval. Typically, the shares of one company will be exchanged for the shares of the other at a rate commensurate with their relative market prices. There are three main kinds of merger:

(1) A **horizontal merger** is when two firms in the same line of business combine. This might become the subject of monopoly (antitrust) enquiries, especially if it concerns two already-large firms. One key motive for such a merger is the expectation that it will yield economies of scale benefits. These occur when a firm can operate at increasingly lower per unit costs as it produces increasingly more. Economies of scale are the underlying rationale for the production line method, favoured by manufacturing.
(2) A **vertical merger** is when a company merges with (e.g.) one of its suppliers, or vice versa. Vertical integration brings both supply of and demand for given products within a single company. Proponents argue that it enables better control and coordination than might otherwise be the case. But this can only be the case if there is some kind of market failure. In recent years vertical integration has fallen out of favour, with companies increasingly resorting to **outsourcing**: using outside suppliers with expertise beyond the company's core competencies.
(3) A **conglomerate merger** is one which is not either (1) or (2). Specifically, it involves the combination of two firms in entirely different lines of business. It represents diversification within a company (the merged entity). Diversification in this manner is often considered to be a dubious motive because it can be achieved in a less costly way by individual investors adjusting (diversifying) their own share portfolios.

An **acquisition** or **takeover** occurs when one company purchases another. The purchased company can be subsumed into the buying company, similar to a merger. Alternatively, the purchased company can keep its previous identity, effectively becoming a subsidiary of the purchasing company.

One motivation for merger or acquisition activity is 'surplus funds'. Finance theory explains that a firm which has fully exploited all possible investment projects yet still finds itself with cash, these funds—surplus to requirement—should be returned to shareholders, either through a share buyback or a bonus dividend. In practice this is not always the case, with managers seeking to enhance their own reputations (or perhaps believing they are doing good for the firm) by using the surplus cash for a cash-funded merger or takeover. In part, there is an incentive for this kind of activity, as cash-rich firms are often seen as takeover targets, with the cash surplus acting as a 'honey pot'.

Recent decades have seen increasing numbers of divestitures and spinoffs, with companies selling off parts of their business. **Spinoffs** are particularly prolific in high-tech companies, with more advanced units within a company being spun off to free them from the corporate constraints that occur within the existing (large) company. Often, the parent company will maintain some degree of ownership through a significant shareholding in the newly independent entity. Sometimes a company will divest itself of units which are outside its area of core competence, perhaps describing them as being of 'poor fit' with the firm's strategic direction.

11.2.1 *Leveraged buyouts (LBOs)*

There are two key differences between a leveraged buyout (LBO) and the more normal kind of acquisition:

(1) A large proportion of the purchase price is financed using debt. It is often the case that such debt is considered as 'junk'. Although the term can be viewed as pejorative, in this context it implies little more than the fact that the bonds are rated below investment grade (see Table 4.1) due to the higher risk involved.
(2) The shares in the LBO are removed from trading on the open market; they become private shares.

Often, the shares in an LBO are held privately by a small group of investors. These are usually institutional investors, i.e. financial institutions. In some cases, the LBO is arranged by the company's management, in which case it is referred to as a Management Buyout (MBO).

11.2.2 *Mergers and macroeconomics*

11.2.2.1 *Merger waves*

Merger activity tends to come in waves [Gaughan 2018, Chapter 2], relatively short periods of time when they occur in abundance. Merger waves tend to occur when share prices are buoyant, something which happens towards the top of the macroeconomic business cycle (an economic ‘boom’). In the USA there have been merger waves at the very beginning of the 20th century, followed by the 1920s, between 1967 and 1969, as well as during the stock market boom years during the 1980s and the 1990s. Although there is a strong correlation between share prices and merger waves researchers have found it hard to discover a common set of reasons. Certainly, when the stock market is booming there is a greater possibility for shares in some companies to be considered overvalued, making them prime targets for takeover or merger activity. It is also the case that high share prices may lead even the most rational of analysts to be swayed by the apparent buoyant value of the merged entity, which could ultimately turn out to be overvalued when the stock market boom recedes.

11.2.3 *Merger evaluation*

As with any investment, the key to the success of a merger or acquisition is its ability to generate added value: are the two companies worth more as a single entity than separately? Expressed simply:

$$\begin{aligned}&(\textit{Estimated gain from merger/acquisition})\\&\quad = PV(\textit{net accrued benefits})\\&\qquad - (\textit{cost of merger/acquisition})\end{aligned}$$

The *net accrued benefits* arise from extra revenues and/or reduced costs resulting from the merger or acquisition. Their estimation is often the hardest part of the calculation. In a takeover, the more important calculation is determining a reasonable value for the target firm (the subject of the takeover bid). For a listed company (i.e. shares listed on a stock exchange) it might seem that the value of the company should be the price of each share multiplied by the number of shares. However, if offered, it is unlikely that such a price would be attractive to shareholders of the target company. Consequently, the share price of a takeover target often rises substantially. This can even be the case when the takeover is little more than a rumour, but then in efficient markets all information—even unsubstantiated rumour—is discounted into the current price.

Because a merger or takeover normally requires the agreement of both sets of shareholders, it is important that benefits can be seen to accrue to both groups. Some of this will be embodied in the complex (legal) terms under which the merger or acquisition is drafted. But not all of the benefits and costs can be readily determined in monetary terms. One key example is that bringing together managers from two different corporate cultures, which has often been noted as a major source of post-merger difficulty. When the merger or takeover is cross-border, involving companies in different countries, these difficulties are typically even greater.

11.2.3.1 *Winners and losers*

The primary objective of any company is to maximise returns to the shareholders. In theory, then, a merger ought to generate increased benefits to the shareholders of both firms involved, and a takeover should benefit the shareholders of both the acquiring firm and the acquired firm. At the very least, a merger or takeover should generate enough benefits overall that the losses sustained by some shareholders will be outweighed by the gains of the other group of shareholders. The evidence suggests that shareholders of a firm which is the subject of a takeover bid are likely to be winners, at least in the short-run.

11.2.3.2 *Tactics*

There are two methods by which one company can make an offer to merge or acquire another:

- 'Friendly' discussions between the acquiring company and the target.
- The acquiring firm directly approaches the shareholders of the target firm with a tender offer, often referred to as a 'hostile' takeover.

Companies which are takeover targets, or believe they are potential targets, have several means at their disposal for trying to deter or prevent a hostile takeover:

(1) **Poison pill** refers to any tactic employed by the target firm to avoid being acquired. This could include offering existing shareholders the right to buy additional shares at an attractive price if the acquiring company has a large shareholding.
(2) **White knight**. A target company may prefer to be acquired by a different company from one which has already made its acquisitive aspirations known. The friendly potential acquirer is referred to as a 'white knight'.
(3) **Shark repellent** refers to changes made to the company's Memorandum and Articles of Association (USA: corporate charter) to defend against hostile takeovers. One common repellent is to amend the Memorandum so that a takeover requires approval by a supermajority of (e.g.) 80% of shareholders, rather than the more common simple majority (51%).

11.3 Pensions

Pensions have too often been little more than an afterthought in mainstream corporate finance. No longer! The combined impact of changing demographics (to an ageing society) and lack of pension fund investment in UK shares has increased the profile of UK pension funds.

Although an occupational pension fund is a separate legal entity from its 'parent' company, any financial pressures on the pension fund will affect the company, and vice versa. Parent companies sometimes find themselves beneficiaries from exceptional performance by the pension fund. However, sometimes companies are adversely affected by the financial position of their pension fund. The combined effects of an ageing population for decades together with a declining equities market has meant that:

(i) pension funds end up paying out more money to pensioners, and
(ii) receiving less money both by way of contributions from working members and also less money from investment income.

This has primarily impacted **defined benefit** (DB) pension funds. According to the Office for National Statistics (ONS):

> "Membership of defined contribution (DC) occupational pension schemes was 22.4 million at the end of 2019, compared with 18.3 million for funded defined benefit and hybrid (DBH) pension schemes."

For many years the UK has experienced a shift from DB to DC schemes, primarily due to financial pressures resulting from changing demographics. DB pension schemes promise workers in advance a specific (monthly) benefit upon retirement. The amount is based on the fund member's earnings-based contributions and number of years in service. These benefits must be met regardless of the investment performance of the pension fund. Consequently, during any period of poor investment performance it may be necessary for the employer to make 'top up' contributions to the pension fund if it is in actuarial deficit. During years of good or excellent investment performance the pension fund may be in actuarial surplus, and the employer can reclaim some of the surplus, either directly or via a 'contributions holiday', in which the employer makes no further contributions for a period of time.

Under a defined benefit (DB) scheme almost all of the risk falls upon the parent company employer. The demographic shift to an ageing population and the poor performance of the capital markets has meant that defined benefit schemes have become increasingly unattractive to employers, with many companies closing their DB schemes to new entrants and establishing **defined contribution** (DC) schemes instead. The 2004 Pensions Act established the Pension Protection Fund (PPF) to provide a safety net in the event that a DB scheme was unable to pay the necessary defined benefits.

Also known as **money purchase** schemes, DC schemes do *not* promise workers a predetermined amount of pension benefits. Instead, the amount of the pension depends on:

(iii) the contributions made into the fund on their behalf—usually by both employer and employee—and
(iv) the investment returns earned on those monies.

Under a DC scheme risk is borne entirely by the workers. DC schemes are less affected directly by demographic shifts; the pensions paid are entirely dependent upon the state of the capital markets in which the fund is invested.

While many pension funds try to 'sit tight' during capital market declines, the problem for the parent companies has been exacerbated by changes in the way in which companies account for their pension liabilities.

11.3.1 *Accounting for pensions: FRS 17 and more*

Because a pension is part of an employee's remuneration—pensions are regarded as 'deferred wages'—it needs to be included in company accounts. In the UK pension contributions come from both employer and employee. A company's pension contributions to a pension fund are an ongoing liability, not least because they need to be paid for the pension fund member's working lifetime. Like wages, pension contributions are a cost to the company.

Before FRS 1 (1996) UK companies accounted for their pension liabilities under the SSAP 24 accounting standard. This allowed companies to 'smooth' their pension liabilities over several years. This was superseded by FRS 7 in June 2003. This accounting standard was designed to show the cost of a company's commitment to fund employee pensions on an annual basis. Similar to America's FAS 87 (December 1985: fasb.org/page/PageContent?pageId=/reference-library/superseded-standards/status-of-statement-no-87.html&bcpath=tff), it was praised by some for introducing "valuable consistency and transparency". However, following its introduction there was a succession of bad news stories revealing severe underfunding of many UK pension funds, especially those of top companies. Because FRS 17 required *annual* disclosure of a pension fund's surplus or deficit, which are subject to the short-term vagaries of capital market performance. Consequently, companies were pressured into taking short-term actions regarding their pension funds, which too easily conflicted with longer-term objectives.

Mandatory from 1st January 2027, the International Accounting Standards Board (IASB) introduced IFRS 18. This is a revised standard for presenting and disclosing financial statements, replacing IAS 1: *Presentation of Financial Statements* (1997). It aims to enhance comparability and transparency by standardising reporting practices across companies. Companies are permitted to adopt IFRS 18 early.

The primary changes are to the Income Statement (Profit and Loss), although there are also changes to the Statement of Financial Position and the Statement of Changes in Cash Flows. The new standard does not impact Net Profit but does affect how it is itemised and disclosed. Like the use of cashflows in capital budgeting, it focuses on Operating, Investing, and Financing activities, together with updated rules for disclosing non-GAAP performance measures. Specifically, IFRS 18 requires income and expenditure to be classified into one of the following categories:

- Operating
- Investing
- Financing
- Income taxes
- Discontinued operations

In addition, there are two new mandatory subheadings:

- Operating profit
- Profit before financing and income tax.

Because IFRS 18 introduces a more structured Income (P&L) Statement it impacts where pension costs must be shown. Items such as service costs, administration expenses, and any special event costs related to pensions (such as settlements) must be included within the Operating category. Net interest costs or credits associated with defined benefit pension liabilities must be included in the Financing category.

11.4 A (very) brief introduction to International Finance

For much of history most business transacted was local. Although international trade has seemingly always been a feature of human economic activity, it was largely the province of travelling merchants. Today, business of every size is increasingly involved in international transactions. The telegraph, then the telephone, then radio shrank the world by making communications easier and cheaper.

Today, the internet has made international trade completely accessible, made even faster by fibre optics. The ubiquity of the world wide web and social media means that even a small business—traditionally focused solely on its local market—can now sell to customers or buy products from all over the world. An added stimulus to cross-border transactions has been the ever-increasing credibility of the common European currency, the euro (€), throughout most of the countries of the European Union, with no need to change currencies. Such possibilities give smaller EU-based companies a taste for operating outside their more traditional national boundaries, encouraging them to go beyond EU countries. International transactions are essentially:

- **International trade:** either buying from abroad (importing) or selling to overseas customers (exporting), or both.
- **International finance:** at its broadest this is the purchase or sale of overseas currency (foreign exchange), and also includes financing activities across national boundaries (including both loan transactions and equity transactions).

Focus here is the latter. It should be noted that the key driver of international finance is international trade. The tools required for analysing and making international financial decisions are extensions of the same tools applied in the domestic context.

11.4.1 *Foreign exchange (forex or fx)*

Foreign exchange is the exchange of one country's money for that of another country.[1] The usual motive is to buy goods or services from overseas (import) or to sell them (export). Foreign exchange is a centuries-old set of transactions, with its origins probably predating that of coinage (c. 500 BCE). As the volume of international transactions has increased so has the need for foreign exchange markets.

[1]In some cases, 'region' should be used instead of 'country', the obvious example being the eurozone, currently 20 of the 27 EU countries. Other formal currency unions include the CFA franc zone, the CFP franc zone, and the Eastern Carribean dollar zone.

11.4.1.1 *Spot (or cash) markets*

For individuals or companies in one country to purchase goods and services from another country, they must first acquire the currency of that other country. Exchanging one currency for another *now* is referred to as a **spot transaction**. The price of an overseas currency in terms of the home country's currency is the **spot exchange rate**. If the UK is the 'home country' and the USA (e.g.) is the overseas country, then the exchange rate is how many UK pounds (GBP) it takes to buy one dollar (USD) expressed as a **direct quote**.[2] An **indirect quote** is how many USD it takes to buy a GBP. The indirect quote is simply the reciprocal of the direct quote. In the global foreign exchange (forex) markets most currencies are quoted on an indirect basis, with the exception of the GBP and the euro (EUR: €).

The exchange rate between two currencies is a price, determined by the interaction of supply and demand. The demand for any overseas currency is a derived demand: derived from the demand for the underlying commodities—goods, services and securities—that the currency can buy. Some degree of the demand for overseas currency will be for speculative purposes. The supply of a given currency reflects demand for overseas currencies; it is with 'home currency' that payment is made for the overseas currency.

Figure 11.1 shows the (stylised) market for USD priced in terms of GBP. The equilibrium exchange rate—where the supply and demand curves intersect—is GBP 1.50 per USD. Anything which causes either the USD demand curve or the USD supply curve to shift will cause a change in the equilibrium exchange rate. International demand for a 'home country' currency depends on the following:

- Overseas demand for 'home country' products (goods, services).
- Overseas demand for 'home country' financial assets (securities).

[2] All national currencies have a three-letter code as defined by the International Organization for Standardization (ISO) under the ISO 4217 standard. The first two letters are the ISO 3166-1 alpha-2 code for the country, while the third letter typically represents the first letter of the currency's name. See: Complete World Currency List: Names, Codes & Symbols (eurochange.co.uk)

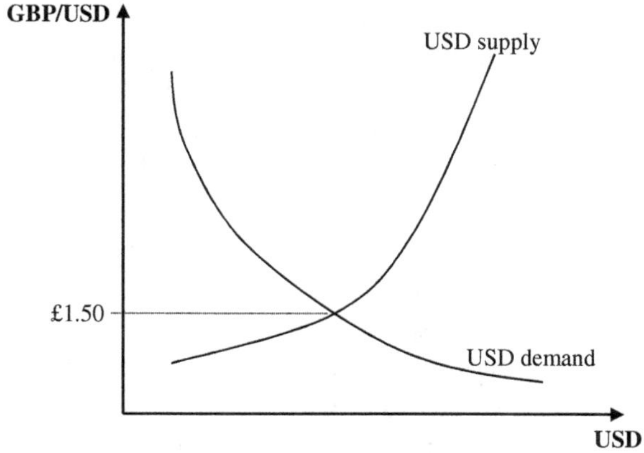

Figure 11.1. A foreign exchange market, USD/GBP

- Transfer payments (those for which there is no counterbalancing transaction. Includes gifts, interest or dividend payments, etc.) into the 'home country'.
- Speculative demand for 'home country' currency.

Suppose it became more fashionable in the UK to wear US clothing. This would lead to an increased demand for USD to import these items into the UK. In Figure 11.1 the USD demand curve would shift *to the right*, increasing the USD exchange rate (i.e. making the USD more expensive to purchase with GBP). The USD would have **appreciated** against the GBP; the GBP would have **depreciated** against the USD.

Because overseas currency is paid for using 'home country' currency, the supply curve of 'home' currency reflects the demand for overseas currency. Thus, the factors which shift the demand curve for overseas currency will shift the supply curve for 'home' currency:

- 'Home country' demand for overseas products (goods, services).
- 'Home country' demand for overseas financial assets (securities).
- Transfer payments (those for which there is no counterbalancing transaction. Includes gifts, interest or dividend payments, etc.) out of the 'home country'.
- Speculative demand for overseas currency.

Measured by trading volume, the forex markets are the largest financial markets in the world. They are also the most liquid. The main participants are the larger international banks. Because trading occurs around the world in a range of financial centres, formal forex trading occurs on a 24/5 basis, i.e. Monday through Friday typically. According to the Bank for International Settlements (BIS), April 2022 showed average daily turnover at USD 75 trillion (2004: USD 1.9 trillion). USD 2.1 trillion was spot transactions, with USD 5.4 trillion in forwards, swaps and other derivatives. At the time of writing, the forex markets in London remain the largest by volume, accounting for 38.1% of the global total, making it by most important centre for foreign exchange trading in the world. Forex trading elsewhere in April 2022 was USA 19.4%, Singapore 9.4%, Hong Kong 7.1%, and Japan 4.4%, with the vast majority of trading being spot forex transactions.

11.4.1.2 *Derivatives*

A derivative is a financial contract with no intrinsic value. A derivative's value *is derived from* the value of some underlying asset, either real or financial. In Chapter 5 (Section 5.6) equity options were introduced. The value of an equity option depends on the value of its underlying shares. Similarly, there are also **call** and **put options** on foreign exchange (i.e. overseas currency). Additionally, there are **forward rate agreements** and **futures** contracts on overseas currency, discussed below.

The primary use for which derivatives were designed was to hedge risk. Forex derivatives are designed primarily to hedge exchange rate risk, i.e. to reduce the impact of the volatility of exchange rate fluctuations on the company. Of course, they can also be used to achieve other objectives. Derivatives are often used speculatively, to try to leverage up rates of return. However, when speculative activity goes wrong it often does so spectacularly. It is a result of this that a great deal of criticism of derivatives originates.

Forward Markets and Hedging

A **forward rate agreement**, or **forward contract**, is an agreement for the delivery of a currency at a specified time in the future, at a price (exchange rate) specified now, known as the **forward rate**.

By engaging in a forward rate agreement, both counterparties contractually lock themselves into a fixed price for the exchange of currencies, thereby removing the chance of any loss or gain due to future movement in the exchange rate.

A forward contract can be drawn up between any two counterparties, for any mutually agreeable size, currency, and expiration. Although there is no formal market *per se* for forward contracts, they are traded directly bank-to-bank the **interbank market**. Transactions costs take the form of a bid-ask spread. Because forward contracts are tailored to the needs of the two counterparties, they are usually for large transactions.

A **futures contract** is a standardised forward rate agreement, and works in much the same manner, allowing exchange rate risk to be hedged by 'locking in' the exchange rate. Standardisation is via highly uniform contracts—size of contract and standard expiration dates, usually the third Wednesday of March, June, September and December—making them more tradeable, hence more liquid, than a similar forward contract. Futures contracts are usually for a much smaller size than forward contracts. Transaction costs are via commission paid to brokers; there is no bid-ask spread.

The futures market consists of a central marketplace, including both a primary and secondary market, as well as a clearing corporation. In London this is currently ICE Futures Europe (originally LIFFE, the London International Financial Futures Exchange). In the USA it is the International Monetary Market (IMM) division of the Chicago Mercantile Exchange.

In practice, a futures contract is between the counterparty and the exchange. Futures contracts are marked-to-market on a daily basis. This means that at the close of each day's trading settlement is made between counterparties, with a new one-day contract being written for the next day. This takes place each day for the life of the futures contract and reduces the possibility of default risk. It also makes it much easier for the counterparties to monitor their position on a day-to-day basis.

Currency Options

Currency options are similar to equity options, the main difference being the underlying asset: a currency pair rather than shares in a company. A currency **call option** gives the holder the right, but not the obligation, to buy the underlying currency at a specified exchange rate on or before a given date. A currency **put option** gives the holder the right, but not the obligation, the right to sell the underlying currency.

Currency options offer the ability to hedge exchange rate risk, but with added flexibility. The option offers a fixed price at which the currency can be bought (call) or sold (put) if the option is exercised, but if the underlying exchange rate unexpectedly moves in a more favourable direction the option can be left to expire, unexercised, and the overseas currency bought or sold on the spot market at a more favourable rate.

In Summary

The international financial markets discussed here do not deal with long-term financing. They are concerned with **treasury management**: short-term funds management dealing with the management of exchange rate risk.

Futures and options can both be used to help managers hedge exchange rate risk. Ultimately, the position taken in the option or futures market depends on the position in the spot market being hedged. There is no doubt that futures offer a more perfect hedge, as they fully 'lock in' the exchange rate. However, options offer the manager a greater degree of flexibility in the form of the ability to 'walk away' if an exchange rate moves favourably, rather than unfavourably as anticipated. Options enable the manager to reduce their downside risk, yet at the same time allow the ability to take advantage of any upside potential. Such flexibility comes at a price, with the option typically being more expensive than the futures approach.

11.4.1.3 *Euromarkets and others*

As well as forex markets there are other international financial markets. The bond and equity markets in other countries can provide a source of international capital for the largest of companies. In addition, there are the **euromarkets**. More accurately referred to as xeno-markets or external-markets, a euromarket is a market for loans in a given currency outside the jurisdiction of the country in whose currency the loan is denominated. Thus, the eurodollar market is for dollar-denominated loans outside of the USA, and therefore not subject to U.S. regulation. Unsurprisingly, the eurodollar market is the largest of the euromarkets. The lack of regulation makes the euromarkets a particularly attractive (and low-cost) means for raising funds, despite the drawback of the extra risk entailed with zero regulation.

11.4.1.4 *Exchange rate relationships*

Market diagrams (supply and demand) can help analyse changes to predict the future movement of exchange rate. It is also possible to distil the bulk of the information into a handful of basic exchange rate relationships. In most cases, these relate changes in exchange rates to movements in underlying macroeconomic factors in the relevant countries. As with so many ideas within finance, the concept of arbitrage underlies much of what follows.

Purchasing Power Parity (PPP)

Absolute Purchasing Power Parity is an intuitively simple idea: the price of a basket of goods in one country should be equivalent to the price in another country when converted via the exchange rate. Also known as "the Law of One Price" (LoOP), it is based on the simple premise that were it not true there would be incentive for profit-seekers to buy commodities in the low-price country and then sell them in the high-price country for a riskless arbitrage profit. If such arbitrage occurred it would raise prices in the low-price country (due to increased demand) and lower prices in the high-price country (due to increased supply), thereby bringing prices across countries into a PPP equilibrium.

One of the most interesting uses made of Absolute PPP is *The Economist*'s "Big Mac standard". (www.economist.com/interactive/big-mac-index) The Big Mac is used, light-heartedly, as a proxy basket of goods with comparison being made between its exchange-rate adjusted price in different countries. Unsurprisingly, the price of a Big Mac varies greatly between countries, suggesting that Absolute PPP does not hold. Of course, it is virtually impossible to arbitrage the Big Mac, partly because it is perishable, and partly because it is a branded good.

While Absolute PPP is a static view of the relationship between prices and the exchange rate, **Relative PPP** takes a more dynamic view. Here the suggestion is that the exchange rate should adjust to reflect changes in the price levels (inflation) of the two countries. Thus:

$$\textit{Future spot rate} = \textit{spot rate} * \left[\frac{1 + \textit{inflation rate}_A}{1 + \textit{inflation rate}_B}\right] \tag{11.1}$$

If the inflation rate is measured on an annual basis, then this equation says that the spot rate one year from now (future spot) should equal the current spot rate multiplied by the ratio between the two countries' inflation rates. One key implication is that a country with a relatively high rate of inflation should find its currency depreciating.

Example 11.1: A UK-based company is planning to export 1 million USD of its products to the USA one year from now, pricing them in USD to make them more attractive to US buyers. Using Equation 11.1 the company can calculate what the spot exchange rate will be one year from now. Assuming the rate of inflation is 2.1% in the UK and 1.7% in the USA, and the current spot rate is 1.31 USD/GBP:

$$\textit{Future spot rate} = 1.31 * \left[\frac{1 + 1.7\%}{1 + 2.1\%}\right] = 1.3049$$

As predicted the USD appreciates, so the GBP depreciates: a single USD now buys 1.3049 GBP, whereas it had previously taken 1.31. Had the UK company opted for payment now they would have received GBP (1 million/1.31) = GBP 763,358.78. Payment in one year would be GBP (1 million/1.3049) = GBP 766,342.25, almost GBP 1,000 more.

Bearing in mind the issue of *dimensional consistency*, this formula can be adapted for different time periods, primarily by using the relevant inflation rate: e.g. quarterly for three-months, etc.

Using the Relative PPP formula allows a company to make forecasts of the path of future spot exchange rates. This enables a company to determine when to sell its products internationally and also where.

Interest Rates and Exchange Rates

Theoretically, arbitrage should ensure **interest rate parity**, i.e. that interest rates adjusted for the exchange rates in different countries are the same for loans of similar risk. The only difference between interest rates in different countries ought to be for the different sovereign (political) risks involved. This should happen as investors seek to maximise the return on their investment funds by placing them where they can earn the highest possible rate of return. Of course, large investors will also seek to diversify their risks by holding a portfolio of bonds from different countries. For example, consider an investor who can place one million pounds of investment funds in the UK—a high-income developed economy—at a rate of interest of 6% or in country B—a less-developed economy—at a rate of interest of 15%. The obvious answer would be to opt for the higher rate of interest, *ceteris paribus*, but other things are rarely constant. To make the investment, the funds will first need to be converted into country B's at a known (spot) rate of exchange. When the investment is eventually liquidated (as it must surely be), the funds will need to be repatriated at the then-existing rate of exchange. That the rate of exchange is likely to be different at the end of the investment could mean that any gain on the rate of interest could be countered by an adverse change in the exchange rate. Were this not the case then it would be simple to make riskless arbitrage profits by borrowing in the low-interest country and lending in the high-interest country. This is known as the 'carry trade'. This can only occur when there is less than full arbitrage between two currencies and their respective interest rates. Despite Equation 11.2, this situation can occur when (e.g.) there is a difference in monetary policy between two countries leading to medium-term differences in interest rates which are not reflected in changes in exchange rates.

The result of this maximising behaviour ought to be a clear relationship between the interest rates and exchange rates in any two countries, i.e. **interest rate parity**. This can be stated mathematically:

$$Forward\ exchange\ rate = spot\ rate * \left[\frac{1 + Interest_A}{1 + Interest_B}\right] \tag{11.2}$$

i.e. differences in interest rates should be offset by differences between spot and forward exchange rates.

Example 11.2: At the time of writing the GBP spot rate is USD 1.26. Interest rates (ten-year Treasury) are 4.38% in the UK and 4.41% in the USA. While the difference is not a significant margin, for the larger investor there is enough difference to warrant 'buying low and selling high'. Using this data in Equation 11.2:

$$Forward\ exchange\ rate = 1.26 * \left[\frac{1 + 4.38\%}{1 + 4.41\%}\right] = 1.2596$$

As predicted the USD is expected to appreciate, with the GBP expected to depreciate.

Because the forward exchange rate is an (imperfect) predictor of the future spot rate, Equation 11.2 can be used in helping companies determine when to buy or sell products internationally, and also where.

Inflation and Exchange Rates

Relative PPP shows the relationship between exchange rate movements and the relative inflation rates of any two countries. Similarly, for the relationship between interest rates and exchange rates. What has yet to be taken introduced is the relationship between interest rates and inflation: the Fisher Effect (Chapter 4, Section 4.5).

Combining the Fisher Effect with Relative PPP gives the **International Fisher Effect**. In one sense the International Fisher Effect is little more than an extension of the Fisher Effect to the international arena: while nominal interest rates would *not* be expected to be the same in different countries, real interest rates *should* be equal across countries. Were this not the case, there would be the possibility of arbitrage profits. If exploited, this would serve to equalise the real rates of interest in different countries. However, it is also possible for any differences in real interest rates across countries to be offset by exchange rate differences. Thus:

$$Future\ spot\ rate = spot\ rate * \left[\frac{1 + Interest_A}{1 + Interest_B}\right] \tag{11.3}$$

Equation 11.3 shows that currencies with higher nominal interest rates (due to relatively high inflation rates) should find their currencies depreciating. This can also be stated as *the spot exchange rate should change equally but opposite to any change in interest rate differences between two economies.*

Example 11.3: Applying the data from Example 11.2 gives:

$$Future\ spot\ rate = 1.26 * \left[\frac{1 + 4.38\%}{1 + 4.41\%}\right] = 1.2596$$

Again, as predicted the USD is expected to appreciate, with the GBP expected to depreciate. As with the previous examples in this Chapter, this forecast of the spot rate can be used by business to guide its decision-making, especially with regard to imports and/or exports.

These three relationships can be summarised in a diagram (Figure 11.2):

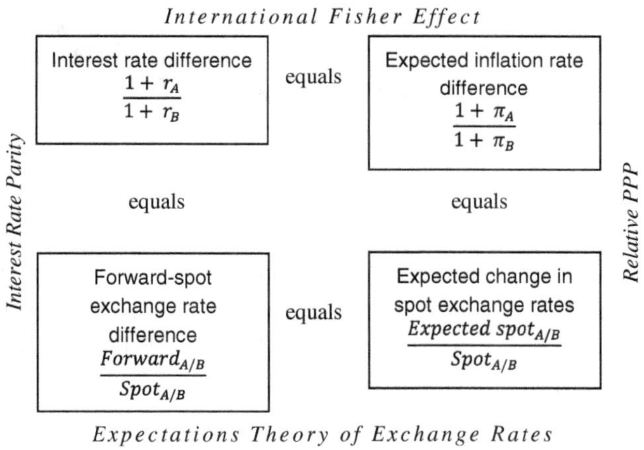

Figure 11.2. Exchange rate relationships

There is also a fourth relationship, between the forward-spot differential and the *expected change* in the spot exchange rate over time, i.e. the **Expectations Theory**. Because the future path of the exchange rate is unknown, the best guidance is the forward exchange rate. The forward exchange rate essentially offers an average of the forecasts of the path of the exchange rate by all the 'players' in the market. However, note that if the forex market is efficient, then the exchange rate will follow a random walk.

This theory does not suggest that financial managers can forecast the future spot exchange rate with impeccable certainty. Rather, it suggests that while forecasts will sometimes prove too low and sometimes too high, there will be no tendency of bias in either direction. Thus, forecasts will prove to be correct *on average*, i.e the forward rate will equal the future spot rate on average.

Each and every one of these four relationships can be used as the basis for predicting exchange rates. In practice, finance departments will tend to use more sophisticated variants, and even cocktails of the above. Nonetheless, even if forex markets are efficient, it is necessary to have some means of forecasting exchange rates in order to make rational financial (business) decisions. Exchange rate forecasts help managers determine which countries to sell into (export), and which countries to buy from (import). Forecasts are also useful in assessing whether to raise capital at home or from capital markets overseas. Some forecast of the path of the relevant exchange rate is required in order to determine whether or not to use a hedging tool, such as a forward, future or option. Indeed, on the basis of the forex forecast the financial manager can determine which of these tools will best serve the needs of the firm.

11.4.2 *International capital budgeting*

A company operating in more than one country will appraise international capital expenditure in the same way they would appraise domestic capital budgeting (Chapter 6). In both cases, the best tool is to make use of NPV. The key question is whether the appraisal should be from the viewpoint of the project *per se* (as is typically the case with domestic capital budgeting) or from the viewpoint of the parent company? The importance of this question has to do with the fact that there are possible differences between the net cash flows of the project *per se* and those project cash flows which are available for repatriation to the parent company. The usual answer is: appraise the project from the parent company viewpoint.

For example, suppose a manufacturing company is considering building an extra factory for production, an expansion investment. There are two mutually exclusive options: build the factory at home (i.e. in the home country) or build the factory overseas (a foreign direct investment, FDI). The first step is to forecast the two sets of cash flows. If each of these was in the relevant currency an immediate comparison would be invalid. One way of making the cash flows comparable would be to convert them into a single currency. Which currency should be used typically would depend on the currency in which the capital had been raised:

- If the funding for the project had been raised domestically then the overseas cash flows should be converted into 'home currency' using forecasts of the exchange rate (or forward exchange rates, if they exist).
- If the funding for the project had been raised 'locally' (i.e. overseas), then the cash flows should be converted into the overseas currency using the forecasted exchange rate (or forward rates, if they exist).
- However, if exchange rate hedging is to take place, it is possible to calculate the entire *NPV* in the relevant currency, and then convert it at the current exchange rate.

In practice, the parent company is often based in a high-income economy, while the potential FDI projects are located in low- or middle-income economies. Thus, cash flows tend to be calculated in the currency of the parent company's 'home country'. In some cases, the very large multinational corporations tend to conduct all of their analyses in one of the major global currencies, such as the USD or the EUR. Because the cashflows are generated in the future they are converted (where possible) using future exchange rates (see Section 11.4.1.4 above).

11.4.2.1 *International cost of capital*

Just as there may be an issue concerning which currency should be used for denominating investment project cash flows, there is also an issue regarding calculation of the cost of capital for international capital budgeting. It is logical to use the same currency for both WACC and cashflows. However, what if cashflows are in one currency but the capital raised is in a different currency? One possibility is to convert the overseas cost of capital into the domestic rate, or *vice versa*. Another possibility is when the funds have all been raised in the domestic capital markets, in which case the company's domestic WACC is applicable.

The total funding required for a new investment (measured in parent company currency, comes from three possible sources:

- P = parent company funding
- E_f = subsidiary retained earnings
- D_f = foreign debt

Thus, total funding for (new) investment, $I = P + E_f + D_f$.

It follows that the WACC for an overseas investment project will be a weighted average of the home cost of capital (funds raised at home, e.g. P) and the overseas cost of capital (funds raised overseas, E_f and D_f). Assuming that the funds raised at home are costed at the company's existing cost of equity, k_e, and funds raised overseas are in the form of debt:

$$WACC_{overseas\ projects} \equiv k = (1 - L)k_e + L * r_d(1 - \tau) \qquad (11.4)$$

where

L = proportion of funds raised overseas, thus $(1 - L)$ = proportion of finds raised at home
r_d = overseas cost of debt
τ = the overseas tax rate

Of course, while entirely likely, it may not be the case the home funds are from equity while overseas funds are raised via debt. Theoretically, a company could raise both debt and equity at home and also overseas. This gives rise to:

$$WACC_{overseas\ projects} \equiv k = (1 - L)k_{home} + L * k_{overseas} \qquad (11.5)$$

This can be expanded to a general formula for WACC for overseas projects:

$$\begin{aligned} WACC_{overseas\,projects} \equiv k = (1 - L)(\pi_{e\,home}\,k_{e\,home} + \pi_{d\,home}\,k_{d\,home}) \\ + L(\pi_{e\ overseas}\,k_{e\ overseas} + \pi_{d\ overseas}\,k_{d\ overseas}) \end{aligned} \qquad (11.6)$$

where

$\pi_{e\,home}$ = proportion of funds raised at home via equity
$\pi_{e\,overseas}$ = proportion of funds raised overseas via equity

$\pi_{d\,home}$ = proportion of funds raised at home via debt
$\pi_{d\,home}$ = proportion of funds raised at home via debt

and $(\pi_{e\,home} + \pi_{d\ home}) + (\pi_{e\,overseas} + \pi_{d\,overseas}) = 1$. Of course, any of the π's can take a value of 0. If $\pi_{e\,overseas} = 0$ and $\pi_{d\,home} = 0$ then Equation 11.6 can be restated as Equation 11.5. The values for each π can be calculated as explained in Chapters 4 and 5.

11.5 The limitations of finance

The tools of finance considered in this book play an important role in helping corporate decision-makers arrive at robust and trustworthy conclusions. As with any tool, the conclusions at which executives arrive are only as trustworthy as the manner in which the tools themselves are used. For a tool to operate most effectively it has to be applied appropriately: it is absurd to use a hacksaw to knock a nail into a wall (as my late father might have said)! The proper use of financial tools in decision-making depends on a full understanding of what the tool can deliver and where its shortcomings lie. If decisions suggested by the use of financial tools were infallible, there would be no need for any human input; a computer might be programmed—or AI!—to apply the relevant financial tools to the corporate and market data that come in. It would be possible to successfully run a business using only computer-generated decisions.

Business should not become overly reliant on the tools of finance. They should be used judiciously with their output as one important element—guidance—for decision-making. Actual decisions should be made partly on the basis of the objective advice proffered by using financial tools combined with an element of judgement. This latter should come primarily from experience and is therefore somewhat subjective. Ultimately, all finance decisions should be part-art and part-science.

Chapter 12

The Future of Finance

Previous chapters have focused on applying finance theory to the two main pillars of finance: (i) valuation (of bonds, shares, etc.) and (ii) the construction of investment portfolios, partly with a view to calculating the cost of capital. At the time of writing, it seems unlikely that finance theory will develop entirely new themes or theories, rather than develop and enrich what is already in place. However, the application of new developments in technology to finance theory and practice is inevitable. In what follows consideration is given to existing new developments: fintech!

12.1 Fintech

Financial technology—*fintech*—is an umbrella term for the application of technological innovations to finance. This includes products and services as well as 'under the hood' systems.

Included in fintech are innovations in payment systems (including cryptocurrencies), credit markets (including P2P lending), and insurance, with Blockchain-assisted smart contracts playing a role. In many ways, crowdfunding—funding a project or venture from many sources (mostly individuals), typically via the internet—should also be included under the fintech umbrella, given that the first documented use of the term 'fintech' is in a 1967 *Boston Globe* article, "Fin-Tech New Source of Seed Money."

At its heart fintech is the use of technology to provide new and improved financial services. Part of the motivation for the emergence of fintech is that, while information technology has made everything—from computers to cars—cheaper and more functional, the unit cost of financial intermediation barely changed in more than a century. According to Philippon (2014), the unit cost of financial intermediation in the USA remained about 2% over 130 years. One promise of fintech is unveiling ways lower the cost of financial services, to overcome financial contracting frictions, and thus improve consumer welfare. According to Thakor (2020), the Financial Stability Board (FSB) defines fintech as:

> "...technologically enabled financial innovation that could result in new business models, applications, processes, or products with an associated material effect on financial markets and institutions, and the provision of financial services."

a definition also adopted by the Basel Committee on Banking Supervision (BCBS).

Fintech companies are sometimes startups. Established companies in both finance and technology sectors have embraced it with varying degrees of enthusiasm. As with any new technology, the primary objective of fintech is to improve and/or replace more traditional financial products and services, to reduce costs, and/or increase revenues.

Unsurprisingly, fintech includes a wide range of technological advances. Probably the oldest, and most widely adopted, is mobile banking. Building on web-based banking, in high-income economies the banking app on a smartphone (and often on associated digital watches) has become ubiquitous. Such apps also play a role as part of modern digital payments systems: e.g. in Kenya M-PESA—a branchless banking service—has been active since 2007 (www.vodafone.com/m-pesa). Other fintech applications include online lending platforms, many of which are peer-to-peer (P2P), as well as those aimed at fundraising, such as Crowdfunder (www.crowdfunder.co.uk) or GoFundMe (www.gofundme.com). Possibly the most high-profile are cryptocurrencies, an example of a blockchain-based application. With the ever-increasing development of Artificial Intelligence (AI) many financial companies are moving to 'robo-advisers', replacing their human counterparts. At the time of writing this is still in its infancy.

12.1.1 *A brief history of fintech*

Broadly, technology refers to the application of knowledge, especially scientific knowledge, to achieve practical objectives. Nowadays there is a tendency to think of technology as being primarily the application of computers (including both hardware and software) and electronic equipment. This includes not only fintech but also e.g. biotech.

The use of technology in the financial sector is not new. Its origins can be traced back to the 19th century, when banks and some financial markets began to make use of new developments in communications technology, particularly the telegraph. Literally meaning "writing at a distance" (from ancient Greek: *τῆλε*: 'at a distance' and *γράφειν* 'to write', the term was coined by Claude Chappe, the French inventor of the semaphore telegraph.

Revolutionising long-distance communications, the telegraph provided a conduit for the transmission of information in a faster and more efficient manner than previously. As well as the rapid transmission of financial (and other) news over long distances, the telegraph made possible money transfer via the equivalent of a telegraphic cheque.

The effectiveness of overland telegraph rapidly became apparent, especially in the UK and USA. The feasibility of submarine telegraph soon followed: a link between Dover and Calais was completed in 1851. Laying submarine cables in the Atlantic (1865–1866) went further (physically and metaphorically), enabling cross-border communications over even greater distances. Before this, communication between the UK and USA was by mail only, although the advent of fast steamships made this faster than by sailboat. By the early 20th century radiotelegraphy (wireless telegraphy using radio) had been perfected, reducing the need for telegraphy using cables, at least over relatively short distances.[1]

In 1918 using the telegraph, Federal Reserve Banks in the USA established the Fedwire Funds Service. This early form of electronic funds transfer facilitated secure transfers between member banks.

With the mid-20th century dominated by the disruption of two World Wars (1914–1918; 1939–1945) the next significant fintech

[1]A contemporary parallel to this is the shift over recent decades away from the landline telephone as mobile phones have become ever more ubiquitous.

development occurred in the 1950s. Heralding an era of consumer financial services, Diners Club International (www.dinersclub.com) introduced the first universal credit card in 1950. This set the stage for a major reshaping of consumer credit and spending, starting with the launch of American Express (www.americanexpress.com) cards in 1958, followed by BankAmericard (rebranded as Visa in 1976) in 1959. The now-ubiquitous credit card industry was born. Mastercard (originally Master Charge, then MasterCard) was founded in 1966.

12.1.2 *Fintech: Birth of the digital era (1960s–1970s)*

The shift from analogue to digital technology began in the early 1960s. For the financial services sector this became evident on 27th June 1967 when Barclays (www.barclays.co.uk) opened the world's first Automated Teller Machine (ATM; in UK vernacular the 'hole in the wall') in Enfield, north London.[2] Originally inspired by the ingenuity of self-service vending machines, ATMs revolutionised access to cash and other basic banking services. The downside has been a reduction of in-bank over-the-counter services and, more recently, the closure of several bank branches.

In 1968 the Inter Bank Computer Bureau was established in the UK, enabling the electronic transfer of funds. This led to the UK's first automated clearing house system, BACS (Bankers' Automated Clearing Services: www.bacs.co.uk), enabling electronic funds transfers (EFTs) between banks. In the USA the first EFT system was ACH (Automated Clearing House) in 1972. Operated by the Federal Reserve Bank of San Francisco the aim was to replace check (cheque) payments. In 2012 the World Bank identified 98 ACH systems operating in various countries.

Further developments followed quickly. In the USA in 1971 NASDAQ (www.nasdaq.com) established the world's first digital stock exchange. Since then, most of the world's stock markets have switched to digital trading, replacing the more traditional 'open outcry' trading pits.

In 1973 SWIFT (Society for Worldwide Interbank Financial Telecommunication: www.swift.com) was set up to standardise

[2]home.barclays/news/2017/06/from-the-archives-the-atm-is-50.

secure global communications between financial institutions. The SWIFT system rapidly became the global standard for international money and security transfers. For good or for ill, in more recent years SWIFT has become a political football, becoming a component of sanctions against some countries. In 2023 the Russian Federation banned the use of SWIFT, establishing its own alternative.

12.1.3 *Digital financial services begin (since 1980)*

The final two decades of the 20th century saw the rise of digital financial services and the beginning of global online banking. The key was communications infrastructure switching from the slow and ponderous (analogue) 'dial-up' to early broadband (digital). One notable breakthrough was Michael Bloomberg's Innovative Market Systems (now Bloomberg LP), which introduced the first Bloomberg Terminal in 1982. This proprietary computer software system enabled professional users to monitor and analyse financial market data in real-time. Users use the Terminal to access news and also for trading. It quickly became ubiquitous in the financial services workplace, with the only notable competition being Reuters, who introduced their 3000 Xtra System in 1999. This was decommissioned in 2013, ultimately being replaced by the *Thomson Reuters Eikon* platform. Thus, duopoly continues today.

Preceded in some countries by telephone banking, the early 1980s saw the emergence of online banking. In 1981 four major New York-based banks (Citibank, Chase Manhattan, Chemical Bank and Manufacturers Hanover) introduced home banking using a proprietary videotex service, although it never really caught on. In the UK the Bank of Scotland was first to offer online banking. "Homelink" allowed customers to transfer money, pay bills, and view statements using telephones and televisions.

The late 1980s saw the development of Electronic Data Interchange (EDI) standards. This enabled businesses to exchange financial documents, thereby streamlining business-to-business (B2B) transactions.

Probably the first internet banking website was offered by Stanford Federal Credit Union in 1994. Other banks followed, so that internet banking became commonplace by the end of the 20th century (millennium bug notwithstanding!).

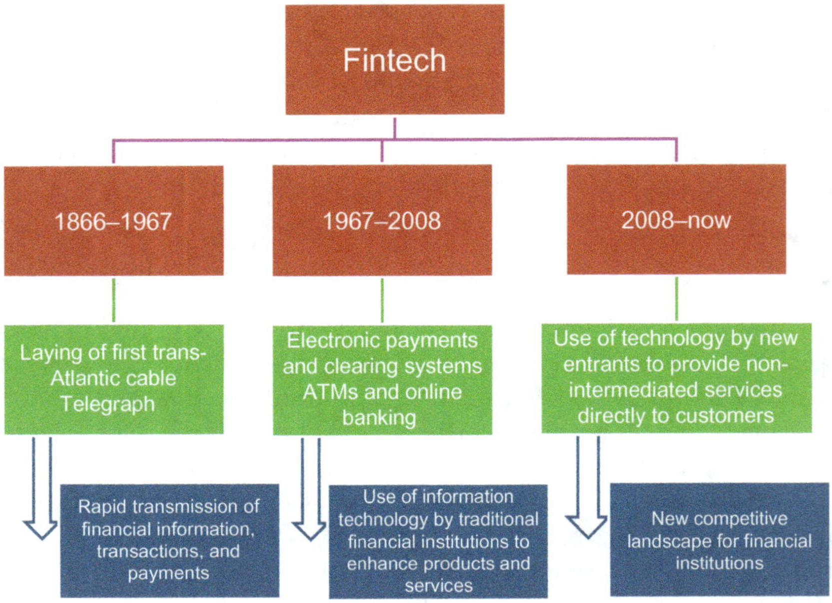

Figure 12.1. The three phases of fintech (adapted from *Consumers International* 2017)

In 1992 E*trade (etrade.com, part of Morgan Stanley) began offering online financial trading to consumers. In 1998 PayPal (paypal.com) established a secure, user-friendly online payment system. Both developments spawned a wave of innovation and imitators, enabling further fintech developments which continue to today. Figure 12.1 shows the three historical phases of fintech development.

While technological developments continued throughout the 1990s and into the 2000s, the COVID-19 pandemic (c. December 2019–c. May 2023) gave fintech a huge boost on the demand side. The pandemic created global havoc, with many countries implementing a series of lockdowns (requiring people to remain at home, including working from home) and social distancing measures. This required individuals and businesses to rapidly adopt remote digital communications channels. The surge in demand for software such as Zoom (zoom.com) and Microsoft Teams was matched by a surge in demand for mobile fintech platforms for both payment—remote banking, contactless payments, and digital lending—as the ability to use cash was often forbidden to minimise COVID transmission. Similarly for trading in nearly all financial (and some other) assets. This shift to digital finance also provided a stimulus to the adoption of blockchain technology. Central banks considered the issuance of digital currencies (still ongoing!), while decentralized finance opened doors for further innovation including non-fungible tokens (NFTs). These are unique digital assets—"cryptographic tokens"—which can be traded online. Each NFT represents a digital or real-world asset, recorded on a blockchain which certifies ownership and authenticity.

At the time of writing (December 2024) the promise of Artificial Intelligence (AI) is yet to become truly manifest, its development continues from its embryonic state. Several companies have been established to develop AI, often with the backing of US giant tech companies (Microsoft, Meta, etc). Perhaps these will have become part of fintech by the time this edition is on bookshelves!

As fintech continues to develop so do the potential fears of any negative fallout which might result. Governments throughout the world continue to review fintech developments, especially AI, with a mind to introducing regulation to prevent any wrongful use of the technology.

12.2 Digital finance

Digital finance is the process of applying new *digital* technologies in the financial sector. It consists of a wide range of technology-enabled services, from online banking and mobile payments (including digital wallets: e.g. Apple Pay) to POS (point of sale) terminals and cryptocurrencies. As has always been the case with applying new technology to production, the primary objective is to reduce costs and/or increase revenues through greater efficiency, enhancing the reach and speed of financial services. This makes finance more accessible to the general public, potentially reducing financial exclusion. To ensure the fairness of digital finance it needs a structure in place to ensure it is inclusive, safe and secure (e.g. data protection), private and sustainable. This may be internal, or it may require outside regulation.

There is a subtle difference between *digital finance* and *fintech*: the former is concerned with widespread digitisation of financial services while the latter is concerned with the application of digital technologies enabling, innovating, and disrupting commercial activities in finance.

12.2.1 *Digital payments systems*

In retail transactions the most high-profile aspect of digital finance has been the rapid growth of digital payments systems. One key driver behind this has been the mass adoption of smartphones during the 21st century. One of the first payment systems to make use of smartphones was Square (squareup.com), who in 2009 introduced a mobile credit card reader for small business. In 2011 the Google Wallet was introduced, followed by Apple Pay in 2014. These user-friendly, consumer-friendly, secure payments solution have rapidly become a feature of modern life. This author uses his Apple Wallet to store credit and debit cards, loyalty cards from a number of retail chains, and also his football club's season ticket!

Less apparent to the ordinary person has been the development and growth of peer-to-peer (P2P) payment applications. These applications conduct fast, direct transfers through mobile devices, significantly reducing the friction in personal financial transactions, while making it simpler for people to split bills, share costs, or send money to family or friends.

12.2.2 *Cryptocurrencies*

For many, cryptocurrency is a mystery, one which seems to promise untold riches to those 'in the know'. However, it is worth noting the old adage: "if something appears to be too good to be true, it probably is"!

Cryptocurrency, or *crypto*, is a digital asset which operates via a decentralized computer network. This means that there is no over-arching central authority which maintains or regulates crypto. Ownership of individual crypto assets ('coins') are stored in a decentralised digital ledger (a computer database), which uses strong cryptographic techniques to record secure transactions, verify ownership, and control the creation of additional coins. A crypto coin can be considered to be a fungible blockchain token, because crypto depends on blockchain as the underlying technological architecture for its existence (see Section 12.2.2.1 below).

Cryptocurrency is NOT currency: it possesses none of the functions of money.[3] In particular, the variability of its value makes it unsuitable to act as money. In some jurisdictions it has been classified as 'commodities' or 'securities', subject to the same legislation as those assets.

Probably the most well-known cryptocurrency is Bitcoin (BTC; ₿). The first decentralized cryptocurrency, it was invented in 2008 by the anonymous "Satoshi Nakamoto". Bitcoin came into use in 2009, when its open-source code was released. By June 2023 there were over 25,000 different cryptocurrencies with a market capitalisation of more than $1 billion. In recent years a number of cryptocurrency exchanges have been established. In 2021 Bitcoin was adopted as legal tender in El Salvador. The same year China made all cryptocurrency transactions illegal. The fact that ownership of bitcoin is completely anonymous has led to its use by criminals and several internationally-recognised terrorist groups. One reaction has been that its use has been banned in several countries. Others continue to seek ways to regulate its use so that it can continue to trade as a legitimate asset.

Stablecoins are cryptocurrencies whose value is pegged to another currency (e.g. USD), a commodity (e.g. price of gold), or a financial instrument. The objective is to provide an alternative to the high volatility of the value of most cryptocurrencies while maintaining other advantages of cryptocurrency.

12.2.2.1

Probably best known as the technology underlying cryptocurrency, blockchain can also be found in other areas of fintech, including providing the infrastructure for 'smart contracts'. These are digital contracts on a blockchain that automatically execute when specific conditions are met, using the logic of "if/when ... then ...". They are

[3]The functions of money are generally recognised as: (1) a generally acceptable medium of exchange, (2) a measure of value, and (3) a store of value.

recorded on the blockchain for transparency and security. Smart contracts are used in decentralized finance (DeFi), supply chain management, real estate, healthcare, insurance and gaming. Key benefits include speed, efficiency, accuracy, trust, transparency, security, and cost reduction.

Blockchain is a subset of distributed ledger technology (DLT) and is a system where replicated, shared, and synchronized digital data is geographically distributed across a wide range of sites, countries, or institutions. It employs cryptography—an encryption method—using a set of mathematical algorithms to create and verify a continuously growing data structure. Designed to operate without any central authority, Blockchain possesses its own process of authentication and authorisation. Cryptographic keys are used to identify, time stamp, and give access to the asset. The key component of blockchain technology is that once a transaction is verified it is added to the ledger in 'blocks'. Each block is linked cryptographically to its predecessor, forming a chain, hence Blockchain. Development of cryptocurrencies begins with computers performing calculations—'mining'—via trial and error to solve difficult mathematical problems verifying past transactions, which rewards the 'miner' with crypto. Successful miners obtain new cryptocurrency as a reward.

On the downside, Hebous and Vernon-Lin (2024) discovered that by 2027 crypto mining was likely to generate 450 million tons of CO_2 emissions, equal to 0.7 percent of global emissions, or 1.2 percent of the world total.

Historically, regulation of finance has tended to be reactive. It usually follows some crisis or other and is often more burdensome than later proves to have been completely necessary (i.e. overkill). Thus, during less critical times the regulation is often rowed back, leading to a repetitive cycle of regulation and deregulation. Finance is often the most innovative sector in an economy, as financial firms seek to exploit further profitable opportunities and also find ways to avoid regulation, which for all of its noble objectives places a financial cost on the financial system.

Because much fintech is quite new the ramifications remain uncertain, so that regulation which is proactive and designed to prevent crises is infeasible. However, some aspects of fintech are already covered by existing regulation. For example, in the USA, P2P loans are usually less costly than credit cards. However, P2P is usually unsecured (riskier), therefore subject to SEC regulation and also relevant state laws.

12.2.3 *Central Bank Digital Currencies (CBDCs)*

While most fintech development has occurred in the private sector, central banks are keen to be involved. Many central banks have been considering the provision of a **central bank digital currency** (CBDC). This is a digital currency issued by the central bank, a liability similar to issued coins and banknotes. Compared with crypto which is decentralised, CBDCs are issued by a single authority, the central bank. Thus, it is unlikely that CBDCs will use a DLT such as a blockchain.

The first major economy which has introduced a CBDC is China, with the *digital renminbi.* At the time of writing this is technically still in a public testing phase. Nine other countries have launched CBDCs. 38 countries and Hong Kong have introduced CBDC pilot programmes. 120 countries, including the UK and USA as well as the ECB are considering the introduction of a CBDC. However, in the USA several states have passed legislation banning state payments using CBDCs, citing concerns over privacy.

CBDCs can operate at both retail and wholesale levels. The former are primarily for everyday transactions by households and business, while the latter is for financial institutions. Wholesale CBDCs operate in a similar manner to central bank reserves.

CBDCs are subject to multiple criticisms, especially regarding privacy and the possibility that they might be used for coercion and control. CBDC implementation might impact the private sector, affecting bank balance sheets and private payment methods, as well as the transmission channels of monetary policy.

12.3 The limitations of finance and its future

The various tools of finance in this book play an important role in helping corporate decision-makers arrive at robust and trustworthy conclusions. However, as with any tools, the conclusions at which executives arrive are only as trustworthy as the manner in which the tools are used. For a tool to operate most effectively it has to be applied in the appropriate manner: it is absurd to use sandpaper to knock a nail into a wall! The proper use of financial tools in decision-making depends on a full understanding of what the tool can deliver and where its shortcomings lie. If decisions suggested by the use of financial tools were infallible, there would be no need for any human input; a computer programme could apply the relevant financial tools to the corporate and market data and make the decision. This has not yet been feasible nor trusted.

There are commentators who foresee the future of finance using AI without human input or oversight. It would be possible to run a business successfully using only computer-generated decisions. My own view is that while this might be the case, it will be a very long time before AI becomes *that* capable. People and companies should not become overly reliant on the tools of finance but use them and their output as one important element—guidance—for decision-making. Decisions should be made partly on the basis of the objective advice proffered by using the relevant financial tools combined with an element of judgement, which comes primarily from experience and is therefore subject to a degree of subjectivity. The promise of fintech is still just that: a promise. And ultimately, there is no reason why technology such as AI will be able to make better, more accurate predictions about the future.

It has been the aim of this book to try to bring the basics of finance to the reader in a focused and readable manner. I hope it has whetted your appetite for an exciting and ever-evolving field of both study and practice. Should you succeed in a career involving finance, hopefully this book will remain on your shelves as a useful reference.

Bibliography

Bachelier, L. (1900) "Théorie de la spéculation". *Annales Scientifiques de l'Ecole Normale Superieure*, III-17, 21–86. (English translation by A. J. Boness in P. H. Cootner (ed.) 1967. *The Random Character of Stock Market Prices.* Cambridge MA: MIT Press).

Berle, A. A. and Means, G. C. (1932) *The Modern Corporation and Private Property.* New York: Macmillan.

Bernoulli, D. (1738) "Exposition of a new theory on the measurement of risk". Translated by L. Sommer, *Econometrica* **22** January 1954 23–36.

Black, F. and Scholes, M. (1973) "The pricing of options and corporate liabilities". *Journal of Political Economy* **81**(3): May–June.

Blume, M., Irwin F. and Randolph W. (1980) *US survey: Impediments to Capital Formation.*

The Boston Globe (1967) "Fin-Tech New Source of Seed Money". (August 27: 116).

Bromwich, M. (1976) *The Economics of Capital Budgeting.* Harmondsworth, Middlesex: Penguin Books.

Coase, R. H. (1937) "The nature of the firm". *Economica* 386–405.

Clayton, G. (1962) "British financial intermediaries in theory and practice". *Economic Journal* **72**: December 869–886.

Clayton, G. and Osborn, W. T. (1965) *Insurance Company Investment: Principles and Policy.* London: Allen and Unwin.

Chen, N.-F., Richard R. and Stephen A. R. (1986) "Economic Forces and the Stock Market". *The Journal of Business* **59**(3).

Consumers International (2017) *Banking on the future: an exploration of FinTech and the consumer interest.* (July) www.consumersinternational.org/media/154710/banking-on-the-future-full-report.pdf (Last accessed November 1st 2024).

Cowles, A. (1933) "Can stock market forecasters forecast?" *Econometrica* **1**(3): July 309–324.

Cox, J., J. Ingersoll, Jnr. and Ross, S. (1981) "A re-examination of traditional hypotheses about the term structure of interest rates". *Journal of Finance* **36**(4): September.

Cox, J., J. Ingersoll, Jnr. and Ross, S. (1985) "A theory of the term structure of interest rates". *Econometrica* **53**(2): March.

Culbertson, J. (1957) "The term structure of interest rates". *Quarterly Journal of Economics* **71** November.

Dean, J. (1951) *Capital Budgeting.* New York: Columbia University Press.

Dixit, A. and Robert P. (1994) *Investment Under Uncertainty.* Princeton University Press.

The Economist. (various issues).

Fernández, P., de la Garza, D. G. and Lucía Fernández A. (2024) "Survey: Market Risk Premium and Risk-Free Rate used for 96 countries in 2024" (March 10, 2024). Available at SSRN: ssrn.com/abstract=4754347 or dx.doi.org/10.2139/ssrn.4754347.

The Financial Times. (various issues).

Fisher, I. (1930) *The Theory of Interest.* Macmillan.

Gaughan, P. A. (2018) *Mergers, Acquisitions, and Corporate Restructurings.* Wiley.

Gordon, M. J. (1959) "Dividends, earnings, and stock prices". *Review of Economics and Statistics* **41**: May.

Graham, J. and Harvey, C. (2001) "The Theory and Practice of Corporate Finance: Evidence from the Field". *Journal of Financial Economics* **60**: May/June.

Hicks, J. R. (1946) *Value and Capital,* second edition. London: Oxford University Press.

Hirshleifer, J. (1958) "On the theory of optimal investment decisions". *Journal of Political Economy* August.

IFRS (March 2018) Conceptual Framework for Financial Reporting. Available online at www.ifrs.org/content/dam/ifrs/publications/pdf-standards/english/2021/issued/part-a/conceptual-framework-for-financial-reporting.pdf (Last accessed June 20th 2024).

Hebous, S. and Nate V.-L. (2024) "Carbon Emissions from AI and Crypto Are Surging and Tax Policy Can Help." (IMF **15**, August) www.imf.org/en/Blogs/Articles/2024/08/15/carbon-emissions-from-ai-and-crypto-are-surging-and-tax-policy-can-help (Last accessed October 30th 2024).

Jensen, M. C. and Meckling, W. H. (1976) "Theory of the firm: managerial behavior, agency costs and ownership structure". *Journal of Financial Economics* **3**(4): October.

Jensen, M. C. (2010) "Value Maximization, Stakeholder Theory, and the Corporate Objective Function". *Journal of Applied Corporate* Finance (**22**)1, 32–42: March (https://doi.org/10.1111/j.1745-6622.2010.00259.x).

Kendall, M. (1953) "The analysis of economic time series. Part 1: Prices". *Journal of the Royal Statistical Society* **96**(1).

Keynes, J. M. (1921) *A Treatise on Probability*. London: Macmillan.

Keynes, J. M. (1936) *The General Theory of Employment, Interest and Money*. London: Macmillan.

Knight, F. H. (1921) *Risk, Uncertainty and Profit*. New York: Houghton Mifflin.

Kolb, R. W. (1985) *Understanding Futures Markets*. Scott Foresman.

Laidler, D. E. W. (1985) *The Demand for Money*, third edition. Harper & Row.

Lintner, J. (1965) "The valuation of risky assets and the selection of risky investments in stock portfolios and capital budgets". *Review of Economics and Statistics* **47**: February.

Lorie, J. H. and L. J. Savage (1955) "Three Problems in Rationing Capital". *Journal of Business*, October.

Malkiel, B. (1966) *The Term Structure of Interest Rates: Expectations and Behavior Patterns*. Princeton: Princeton University Press.

Malkiel, B. (various years) *A Random Walk Down Wall Street*. New York: Norton.

Markowitz. H. M. (1952) "Portfolio selection". *Journal of Finance* **7**: March.

Markowitz. H. M. (1959) *Portfolio Selection: Efficient Diversification of Investments*. New York: Wiley.

McCallum, J. S. (1975) "The Expected Holding Period Return, Uncertainty and The Term Structure of Interest Rates". *Journal of Finance* **30**(2), 307–323: May.

Michaelsen, J. B. (1963) "The Term Structure of Interest Rates: Comment". *Quarterly Journal of Economics* February 166–174.

Michaelsen, J. B. (1965) "The Term Structure of Interest Rates and Holding-Period Yields on Government Securities". *Journal of Finance* September.

Miller, M. H. (1977) "Debt and taxes". *Journal of Finance* **32**(2): May 261–275.

Modigliani, F. and Miller, M. H. (1958) "The cost of capital, corporation finance and the theory of investment". *American Economic Review* **48**(3): June 261–297.

Modigliani, F. and Miller, M. H. (1963) "Corporate income taxes and the cost of capital". *American Economic Review* **53** June: 433–443.

Modigliani, F. and Richard S. (1967) "Debt Management and the Term Structure of Interest Rates". *Journal of Political Economy* August: supplement.

Mossin, J. (1966) "Equilibrium in a capital asset market". *Econometrica* **34**(4): October.

Office for National Statistics (ONS) (2021) UK pension surveys - Office for National Statistics.

Roberts, H. (1959) "Stock market 'patterns' and financial analysis: methodological suggestions". *Journal of Finance* **14**(1): March 1–10.

Roberts, H. (1967) "Statistical versus clinical prediction of the stock market". Unpublished manuscript, CRSP. Chicago: University of Chicago.

Ross, S. A. (1976) "The arbitrage theory of capital asset pricing". *Journal of Economic Theory* **13**(3): December.

Roy, A. D. (1952) "Safety first and the holding of assets". *Econometrica* **20** July 431–449.

Ryan, T. M. (1973) "The demand for financial assets by the British life funds". *Oxford Bulletin of Economics and Statistics* **35**: February 61–67.

Ryan, T. M. (1978) *Theory of Portfolio Selection.* Macmillan.

Samuelson, P. A. (1970) "The fundamental approximation theorem of portfolio analysis in terms of means, variances and higher moments". *Review of Economic Studies* **37**(4): October 537–542.

Sharpe, W. (1964) "Capital asset prices: a theory of market equilibrium under conditions of risk". *Journal of Finance* **19**: September.

Silber, W. L. (1970) *Portfolio Behavior of Financial Institutions.* New York: Holt, Rinehart and Winston.

Taleb, N. N. (2001) *Fooled by Randomness: The Hidden Role of Chance in Life and in the Markets.* New York: Random House.

Taleb, N. N. (2007) *The Black Swan: The Impact of the Highly Improbable.* New York: Random House.

Thakor, A. V. (2020) "Fintech and banking: What do we know?" *Journal of Financial Intermediation* **41** (January).

Tobin, J. (1958) "Liquidity preference as behavior towards risk". *Review of Economic Studies* **25**: February.

World Economic Forum (April 17 2023) "Ranked: The largest bond markets in the world". Available online at www.weforum.org/agenda/2023/04/ranked-the-largest-bond-markets-in-the-world/#:~:text=Valued%20at%20over%20%2451%20trillion%2C%20the%20U.S.%20has%20the%20largest,16%25%20of%20the%20global%20total (Last accessed 20th July 2024).

Working, H. (1934) "A random difference series for use in the analysis of time series". *Journal of the American Statistical Association* **29** March.

Index

C

D

www.ingramcontent.com/pod-product-compliance
Lightning Source LLC
LaVergne TN
LVHW010334220926
848484LV00004BB/898